SYSTEMIC TREATMENT of INCEST

A Therapeutic Handbook

Brunner/Mazel Psychosocial Stress Series
Charles R. Figley, Ph.D., Series Editor

1. *Stress Disorders Among Vietnam Veterans,* Edited by Charles R. Figley, Ph.D.
2. *Stress and the Family Vol. 1: Coping with Normative Transitions,* Edited by Hamilton I. McCubbin, Ph.D., and Charles R. Figley, Ph.D.
3. *Stress and the Family Vol. 2: Coping with Catastrophe,* Edited by Charles R. Figley, Ph.D., and Hamilton I. McCubbin, Ph.D.
4. *Trauma and Its Wake Vol. 1: The Study and Treatment of Post-Traumatic Stress Disorder,* Edited by Charles R. Figley, Ph.D.
5. *Post-Traumatic Stress Disorder and the War Veteran Patient,* Edited by William E. Kelly, M.D.
6. *The Crime Victim's Book, Second Edition,* By Morton Bard, Ph.D., and Dawn Sangrey
7. *Stress and Coping in Time of War: Generalizations from the Israeli Experience,* Edited by Norman A. Milgram, Ph.D.
8. *Trauma and Its Wake Vol. 2: Traumatic Stress Theory, Research, and Intervention,* Edited by Charles R. Figley, Ph.D.
9. *Stress and Addiction,* Edited by Edward Gottheil, M.D., Ph.D., Keith A. Druley, Ph.D., Steven Pashko, Ph.D., and Stephen P. Weinstein, Ph.D.
10. *Vietnam: A Casebook,* By Jacob D. Lindy, M.D., in collaboration with Bonnie L. Green, Ph.D., Mary C. Grace, M.Ed., M.S., John A. MacLeod, M.D., and Louis Spitz, M.D.
11. *Post-Traumatic Therapy and Victims of Violence,* Edited by Frank M. Ochberg, M.D.
12. *Mental Health Response to Mass Emergencies: Theory and Practice,* Edited by Mary Lystad, Ph.D.
13. *Treating Stress in Families,* Edited by Charles R. Figley, Ph.D.
14. *Trauma, Transformation, and Healing: An Integrative Approach to Theory, Research, and Post-Traumatic Therapy,* by John P. Wilson, Ph.D.

BRUNNER/MAZEL PSYCHOSOCIAL STRESS SERIES No. 15

SYSTEMIC TREATMENT of INCEST

A Therapeutic Handbook

By

Terry S. Trepper, Ph.D.
and
Mary Jo Barrett, M.S.W.

Routledge
Taylor & Francis Group
New York London

First published 1989 by Brunner-Routledge

Published by Routledge
711 Third Avenue
New York, NY 10017

Published in Great Britian
Routledge
2 Park Square
Milton Park, Abingdon
Oxfordshire OX14 4RN

First issued in paperback 2014

Routledge is an imprint of the Taylor and Francis Group, an informa business

Library of Congress Cataloging-in-Publication Data

Trepper, Terry S.
Systemic treatment of incest : a therapeutic handbook / by Terry S. Trepper and Mary Jo Barrett.
p. cm.—(Brunner/Mazel psychosocial stress series ; no. 15)
Bibliography: p.
Includes index.
ISBN 0-87630-560-5
1. Incest—Treatment. 2. Family psychotherapy. I. Barrett, Mary Jo. II. Title. III. Series.
RC560.I53T73 1989
616.85'83—dc20 89-9739
CIP

ISBN 13: 978-0-87630-560-7 (hbk)
ISBN 13: 978-1-138-00468-9 (pbk)

To our families

Editorial Note

Although I have worked with all kinds of traumatized people and families, for me the most distressing group of victims to treat are those who were sexually abused as children. Among the people these children depended upon for love, protection, and nurturance were those who took advantage of them—who played upon their powerlessness and vulnerability.

The entertainment and news media are exposing the horror and tragedy of these victims. And there are many books now that report on or theorize about how and why these children are abused. A small number of these books describe treatment programs for the victimized children and others for the offending family member. Few books, however, describe a *family* treatment approach.

And until now, no book has provided a comprehensive perspective on both understanding and treating these incestuous abusing families as a unit of treatment, as a client family. *Systemic Treatment of Incest: A Therapeutic Handbook* is the first book that provides a step-by-step guide to actually *ameliorating* the abuse and enabling the family to remain together or reunite as a result of treatment.

It is the authors' intention to prepare and encourage clinicians to provide at least some appropriate crisis intervention for the family or families involved. And if a referral is to be made, the clinician can make informed judgments about who should treat what, when, and under what circumstances.

Thus, it is with considerable pleasure that the Editorial Board of the Series and I welcome this, the fifteenth volume, to the Brunner/Mazel Psychosocial Stress Series on such a vital topic. The Series was established many years ago to develop and publish books that in some way make a significant contribution to the understanding and management of the psychosocial stress reaction paradigm. These books are designed to advance the work of clinicians, researchers, and other professionals involved in the varied aspects of human services which confront issues of psychosocial stress reactions.

The Series is among the few which are "refereed." The quality and significance of the Series is guided by a nationally and internationally respected group of scholars who compose the Editorial Board. The Board must review and approve each book that is to be published in the Series. Like the readership, the Board represents the fields of general medicine, pediatrics, psychiatry, nursing, psychology, sociology, social work, family therapy, political science, and anthropology.

Books in the Series focus on the stress associated with a wide variety of psychosocial stressors. Collectively, the books and chapters in the series have focused on the immediate and long-term psychosocial consequences of extraordinary stressors such as war, divorce, parenting, separation, racism, social isolation, acute illness, drug addiction, death, natural disasters, rape, incest, and other kinds of crime victimization, sudden unemployment, job stress, and other issues that focus on the conceptualization and treatment of psychosocial stress generally, and particularly traumatic stress.

Collectively, the authors of this seminal book, Terry S. Trepper and Mary Jo Barrett, have worked with abusing families for over a quarter century in various capacities. I take considerable delight in having introduced them and urged them to form what has become such an excellent writing team. Their first effort resulted in the highly acclaimed book and *Journal of Psychotherapy and the Family* special issue, *Treating Incest: A Multiple Systems Perspective*.

Terry S. Trepper is the Director of the Family Studies Center and Associate Professor of Psychology at Purdue University (Calumet). He was also formerly Director of the Human Sexuality Program and is currently Coordinating Consultant to the Southlake Center Family Studies Program. He also has a private practice in Chicago. He has served as guest editor for a special issue by the *Journal of Sex Education and Therapy*. Dr. Trepper has presented scholarly papers at the annual conferences of all of the major national mental health associations and has developed a family treatment program for incest that is currently being used in a number of sites nationally. He will begin his first term as Founding Editor of the *Journal of Family Psychotherapy* in 1990.

Mary Jo Barrett is Director of the Midwest Family Resource Associates (Chicago), which has one of the largest case loads of incest families in the country. She is a member of the adjunct faculty of the Institute for Juvenile Research, University of Illinois, Chicago and field instructor for both the University of Illinois and the University of Chicago. She has presented numerous professional workshops on family abuse, including child sexual abuse, nationally and internationally. She has many years of experience with treating incest as a practitioner, clinical supervisor, and administrator.

This book represents these authors' years of experience with these families and a genuine commitment to solving an extremely complex and difficult problem. They forgo "cause and effects" of incest offered by other books and provide a comprehensive manual for *treating* the family system.

The central theme of the volume, according to Trepper and Barrett, is that effective treatment of incest requires a systemic approach in what they call their Multiple Systems framework. In this approach, they emphasize understanding, confronting, and changing family patterns. Such an approach views incestuous activity as the *product* of a problematic family system, rather than the cause. Moreover, this approach sees *all* family members as sharing in both the development and maintenance of the problem. At the same time, the authors are sensitive to individual, personality/behavioral dynamics of the family members, though the unit of treatment is the family system.

Thus, a *multiple systems* perspective monitors and modifies *all* systems involved, including the larger ecosystems (e.g., environmental or community conditions), as well as the family and its members. This approach is in stark contrast to the prevailing approaches which view incest as primarily the result of *individual factors* associated with the perpetrator or victim. The purpose of the volume, then, is to provide practitioners with the state-of-the-art approaches to assessing and treating incestuous families from a *multiple* systems perspective.

Early in their book, they note that many of their colleagues wish, as I once did, to avoid working with incest abusing families. They have found that working with these families is extremely enjoyable and rewarding, that the treatment objectives are quite clear, and that the Multiple Systems model works; as a result, they have effected extraordinary progress and change. Finally, while *hating sexual abuse,* they have come to appreciate their client families and what these families have taught them (and us): "While we teach them how not to abuse, they teach us that families can be in need, yet strong; can sometimes stumble, yet be resilient; and can be afraid and yet courageous."

After reading this book, I have changed my views of the treatability of incest and incest abusing families, and, as a result, no longer refer these families to colleagues. I am sure that this volume will have a similar kind of impact on my colleagues and readers of the Series.

Together with *Systemic Treatment of Incest,* the books in this Series form a new orientation for thinking about human behavior under extraordinary conditions. They provide an integrated set of source books for scholars and practitioners interested in how and why some individuals and social systems thrive under stressful situations, while others do not. Certainly this important book by Trepper and Barrett will help us to understand and appreciate the power of the family to both traumatize and heal and the extraordinary impact of their Multiple Systems approach. I would enjoy hearing readers' reactions to this book and others in the Series and, of course, suggestions for other books.

Charles R. Figley, Ph.D.
Series Editor
Florida State University
Tallahassee, Florida

Contents

Preface

Of all the problems facing society, incest is one of the most enigmatic. It is considered *the* sexual taboo, bringing its violators the wrath of the populace, and yet we are becoming aware that incest is frequently part of childhood and adolescent experiences of a great many individuals. One can barely pick up a newspaper or magazine without seeing a story about incestuous abuse, yet in most abusing families incest is shrouded in silence and secrecy. In fact, many children have grown up doubting their own reality-testing ability because their early disclosures about incestuous abuse were ignored by the adults around them.

Also enigmatic is the divisiveness among many workers in the area of incestuous abuse. When incest was considered a one-in-a-million occurrence, the few people working in the field had little disagreement as to the causes, effects, and treatments. With increased attention, a variety of "interest groups" entered the scene, each claiming to be the *only* true protectors of abused children, and even accusing other workers of subtly contributing to the abuse (e.g., Armstrong, 1987). It has become apparent that much of the infighting has less to do with sexual abuse but instead is a reflection of long-standing battles between old political rivals. So we have, for example, child-protection groups fighting family rights groups, and feminist therapists fighting family therapists (Larson & Maddock, 1984)—and all under the banner of "stopping the abuse." Ironically, these political factions appear to act like the very families they are trying to help.

To increase the confusion, there is even a debate as to the seriousness of the incest experience itself. Some have suggested that while the problem of sexual abuse is problematic, it may not be the epidemic suggested by the popular press. Further, our intense desire to protect child victims may actually be "backlashing," by causing panic, mistrust, and even setting children against adults (Tucker, 1985). And there are even those who question the most honored underlying assumption, namely, that intrafamily child sexual abuse is even *abuse* at all. Those writers suggest that the real problem is society's sexual repression which inhibits our ability to express affection, even in the family (e.g., Williams & Money, 1980).

Enter the arena the therapist. He or she is being called upon in increasing numbers to muddle through the enigma to provide help to families and individuals torn apart by incestuous abuse—the therapist who listens to a mother pour out her heart, feeling anger, guilt, confusion; who hears an offending father say he indeed had sex with his daughter, but "It didn't cause her any harm"; or who watches the 10-year-old daughter cry and say that her daddy did it, but she still loves him and doesn't want him to go to jail because it was her fault. This therapist, who is human, and who maybe has children, and who maybe was sexually abused him- or herself. . . this therapist faces all the confusion and fear and anger experienced by us all concerning the enigma of incest, and at the same time is expected to "cure" the family. It is for this therapist that the book is written, and to this therapist we hope to provide some help.

PURPOSE OF THE BOOK

While there have been many excellent books dealing with the causes and effects of incest representing a variety of orientations, there have been few dealing specifically with *treatment*. Many works have included "treatment" of incest in the title, but relegated therapy to only one or two chapters, usually at the end, and then often have not provided detailed enough information for therapists to use effectively.

This book is different. While we will provide some essential background information on incest families, the primary focus is *treatment*. As such, this may be considered a "treatment manual," whose main purpose is to present a teachable, theoretically consistent, and effective treatment program. Recent research suggests that while an increasing number of clinicians are working with incest cases, most feel undertrained (Dietz & Craft, 1980). This is further evidenced by the increased number of workshops around the country providing training for therapists working with incest. Our goal is to provide enough information so that experienced clinicians will feel comfortable working with these highly complex families.

At the onset it should be made clear that we believe incest to be "treatable." This means that as a result of therapy incestuous abuse of children in a family can be halted and in many cases can be accomplished without the disuniting of the family. Further, we believe that the severe psychosocial stress that is both the result of and a contributor to the incest can be ameliorated through intensive treatment. While this seems to be a reasonable position for us to take, having effectively treated hundreds of incest families over the course of 10 years, we recognize that many feel that therapy is a way of excusing the crime of incest and that therapists are (unknowingly) contributing to that societal excuse (Armstrong, 1987; Brickman, 1984). While we are sensitive to that view, we clearly do not share it.

ORGANIZATION OF THE BOOK

As mentioned, this book is conceived as a treatment manual with the primary audience being therapists who work with incestuously abusing families. The book's organization is designed to provide therapists with enough information to develop their own treatment program, yet provide the flexibility to accommodate their own individual style and orientation.

Our attempt is to make this book as readable as possible. To this end, we have elected to keep the "scholarly" aspects to a minimum, not because we feel research is unimportant, but because our main task is to provide essential information on the "how-tos" of intervention. We therefore have chosen to summarize areas of research rather than describe them, and have also kept down the number of citations to the bare minimum. Finally, we have decided to have more and shorter chapters to allow the therapist to "pick and choose" material as needed rather than necessarily read the entire book sequentially, although the latter would certainly yield the most to the interested therapist.

DEFINITIONS AND TERMINOLOGY

It seems it would be easy to define incestuous abuse. It is one of those concepts that everyone appears to recognize without further qualification. And yet the inability to accurately and consistently define incestuous abuse, and all its variant terms, has led to severe problems by: (1) making it difficult to generalize the results of empirical studies; (2) creating havoc for the social-legal system; and (3) preventing consistent communication among therapists working in the field.

There are a number of specific questions that emerge when trying to define incestuous abuse. First: What behaviors constitute sexual abuse? It certainly would include intercourse, oral sex, and fondling, but what, for example, constitutes a "sexually abusive" kiss? Would showing one's child a sexually explicit photo or film constitute sexual abuse or merely bad judgment? And in the collection of data, are these experiences analyzed continuously (intercourse is scored more "severe" than "kissing") or discretely (all experiences are counted as one incident)?

A second important question is: What constitutes "incestuous" or "intrafamilial?" Operational definitions in the literature usually include children having sex with parents, stepparents, siblings, grandparents, and uncles or aunts. But is sexual abuse by a grandfather who lives across town more "intrafamilial" than by a trusted friend of the family, or by a babysitter to whom the child feels very close? Many have argued, in fact, that sexual abuse should not be dichotomized into intra and extrafamily abuse at all, but instead should be considered along the child sexual abuse continuum (e.g., Conte, 1982; Finkelhor, 1984; Frude, 1982).

A third question that plagues the easy defining of incestuous abuse is: What constitutes "abuse"? or its subset: Can there be *non*abusive incest? Most would agree that consensual sex play among siblings is not abusive. And further, although possibly raising some concern, many would not consider consensual sex among similar-aged siblings or relatives to be incestuous *abuse*. But how wide an age gap must there be before even consensual sex is considered abusive? And an even more ominous question: Can sex between a parent and child ever be "consensual" at all? And if it can be, is it still "abuse"?

These questions must be answered by the therapist working with incest cases, if for no other reason than to provide a philosophical frame for treating the families. We will offer the definitional guidelines we use in our programs, with the understanding that ultimately the therapist must decide for him- or herself.

Definition of Incestuous Abuse

We have expanded Russell's (1984) definition of incestuous abuse to include:

1. Any sexual contact, defined as:
   a. *Touching*, with the intention to sexually arouse the child, or to provide sexual arousal for the offending adult relative;
   b. *Kissing*, in a prolonged manner, or by one whose purpose is similar to *touching* (see above);
   c. *Fondling* of genitals or other parts of the body in a sexual manner;

d. *Overt sexual contact,* such as oral-genital contact, manual stimulation of genitals, or intercourse.

OR

2. Any behavior that is intended to stimulate the child sexually, or to stimulate sexually the offending adult relative through the use of the child. This might include showing the child erotic materials, photographing the child in a sexual manner, or "talking dirty" to the child.
3. To be considered *incestuous,* these contacts or behaviors would be initiated by an:
   a. Adult relative, including a stepfamily member, with the understanding that the degree of impact is increased the closer the relationship is to the child.

   OR

   b. Adolescent or child relative (including step-) who is more than a few years older than the child, or at least in a different childhood "generation" (e.g., a 14-year-old and a 12-year-old would not be considered in the same childhood generation, whereas a 15-year-old and a 17-year-old might). However, even if they can be considered "cohorts," the sex acts must be consensual or they would be considered incestuous abuse.

As can be seen, parent–child incest, the primary focus of this book, is *always* considered "abusive" using this definition. We clearly take the position, along with Finkelhor (1979), that sex between adults and children is always wrong by any social or moral analysis because it can never be truly consensual. That is, children should not be put in the position to engage in behavior that they do not fully understand, behavior that can have such powerful ramifications for them and their families. For an adult to put a child in such a position is exploitive and thus abusive.

Alternative Terms Used in this Book

In therapy, we encourage the families we are treating to use accurate terms for the incestuous abuse, no matter how disquieting, rather than "softer" euphemisms. In this book we will use terms like "incestuous abuse," "incest," "molestation," and "intrafamily child sexual abuse" interchangeably to provide some variety for the reader, with the understanding that what is meant is "incestuous abuse."

The program described, although designed primarily for father–daughter (and stepfather–stepdaughter) incestuous abuse, has been used extensively with other incestuous relationships (e.g., mother–son, father–son, uncle–child and/or sibling), and even with nonrelative-but-incestuous relationships (e.g., the trusted family friend who was, in all essence, a family member). In this book, however, we refer almost exclusively to the *father* and to the *daughter* when describing the incestuous relationship. It should be understood that this is done merely for economy of words, and that *father* can be substituted by *stepfather, grandfather mother*, or *entrusted caregiver*. Where a distinction is necessary, of course, it will be made clear exactly what relationship applies.

LIMITATIONS OF THE BOOK

Although a great deal of material relating to child sexual abuse will be covered, there are certain limitations that must be made. First, our focus is primarily father-daughter since this is by far the most commonly presented in therapy. We will outline the different issues and treatment strategies needed for treating extrafamilial child sexual abuse in Chapter 16.

Second, except where it specifically relates to the sexual abuse, the book will *not* attempt to deal with other forms of abuse such as physical abuse or neglect. People working with incest families often overestimate the amount of physical abuse associated with incest, assuming it occurs in over 80% of incestuous relationships (Dietz & Craft, 1980). In fact incestuous abuse does not usually involve much physical violence (Russell, 1986), and only about 10% of incestuous fathers even consistently use strong discipline (Julian & Mohr, 1979). This is not to suggest that we consider physical abuse an unimportant problem; in fact, we feel it is important enough to warrant a separate consideration.

Third, what is presented here is the idealized version of an effective incest treatment program. There will be many families for whom this program or its components would not be appropriate. Also, problems can arise at each stage or substage of therapy that will need clinical intervention not described in the book. With all of the possible combinations and permutations of individuals, families, agencies, and therapists, it is impossible to address every conceivable problem. However, the basic framework and many, if not most, of the interventions will be applicable to the great majority of cases. The experienced therapist will have to ultimately rely on his or her clinical judgment and skill to solve more difficult problems that are not addressed in this book.

Finally, although we have found this program to be extremely useful in our clinical work, it should definitely not be viewed as a panacea in the treatment of incestuous abuse. There are many ways to help incestuous families: many types of therapy, many community services available, many "systems" who do an excellent job in stopping intrafamily sexual abuse. What we offer can be used as an entire package, or elements can be taken to complement other intervention programs. What we hope to do is to challenge the therapist to expand his or her thinking about therapy for incest.

A PERSONAL NOTE

The two authors have worked with incestuously abusing families for a combined total of over 25 years. Neither has gone one week during this period where someone has not asked, "How can you work with these families? Aren't they the most difficult, frustrating, and nonrewarding cases imaginable?" The answers vary, depending upon how successful our last therapy sessions were. However, the fact remains, no matter how surprising: we *like* to work with incest families. There are a couple of reasons why.

First, because the problems are so great, the objectives become quite clear. Where sometimes more typical clinical problems have more nebulous and perhaps even Utopian goals (such as "happiness" or "personal growth"), the goal with an incest family is certain: stop the sexual abuse and change the individual and family patterns so that it will be next to impossible to occur again.

Second, we feel very positive about our treatment program. We have used a variation of the program for so many years that we now can predict with a certain degree of confidence that a family or person successfully completing therapy will not abuse its members anymore. Although a large scale, longitudinal evaluation of the effectiveness of the program is currently in progress, we do have preliminary data that support our positive view.

We recently completed a random survey of 30 families who had completed the program during the past two years. With a combination of telephone and written interviews, all of the previously abused children reported no further attempts at abuse; 90% of them reported that they felt safe or very safe with their previously abusing parent, whether or not he lived in the home; 90% of the families were satisfied or extremely satisfied with their therapy; and 90% of the couples who had completed treatment without divorce had remained together at follow-up, although approximately 30–40% of the parents separate or divorce either directly prior to entering treatment or during the early part of Stage I of therapy. The most gratifying information, which was provided by our two state child protective services (CPS) agencies, was that our treatment programs throughout the 10 years of operation had less than a 1% recidivism rate; that is, less than 1% of our "matriculated" families reentered the CPS system as a result of child abuse.

A third reason we like to work with incest families is that the reward is so great. Through the course of the two years of a family's treatment we see them travel from their lowest depths to their highest highs. Sometimes it feels like we have taken our clients from birth through adulthood.

A final reason, and perhaps the most intangible, is that while we *hate* sexual abuse, we truly *love* our families. While we teach them how not to abuse, they teach us that families can be in need, yet strong; can sometimes stumble, yet be resilient; and can be afraid and yet courageous.

T.S.T.
M.J.B.

Acknowledgments

Writing a book is a bit like doing therapy. It is both frustrating and exhilarating; it goes smoothly and then reaches an impasse; it seems like it will never end and then is finished all too soon. And like therapy, writing a book is about *people*. More than theories, more than paradigms, more than interventions. People. And so, here is our heartfelt thank you to some of the important people who really *are* this book.

The senior staff at Midwest Family Resource in Chicago—Vicki Halverson, Susan Hoke, Cece Sykes, and Mack Winn—have offered both important ideas and assistance throughout this project. Dr. Irving Borstein, the founder of Midwest, has continually provided guidance and support. A special thanks must also go to the directors at Southlake Center for Mental Health, in Merrillville, IN, who continue to have faith in the treatment program throughout the years. Also, thanks goes to Dr. Ellen Traicoff for her contributions to the development of the "Apology Session" (Chapter 9).

We would also like to acknowledge our appreciation to the staff and students at the Family Studies Center, Department of Behavioral Sciences, at Purdue University Calumet. These sturdy folks provided two years' worth of library searching and data entry, and only have glazed eyes to show for it. We want to particularly thank Laura Eich, Linda Mika, and Larry Gorski. And at Purdue, West Lafayette, a special thanks to Fred Piercy for some wonderful sentences that were well worth stealing.

To our therapists, both at Midwest and Southlake, we want to offer both our thanks, our envy, and our condolences. To work with incestuous families 52 weeks a year requires all three. You all *are* the program.

Finally, to our spouses and children, we can only say what we told you after the last book. We *promise* this really will be the last one.

SYSTEMIC TREATMENT of INCEST

A Therapeutic Handbook

1

Introduction

INCESTUOUS ABUSE AS PSYCHOSOCIAL STRESS

It is self-evident that ongoing incestuous abuse is both a psychosocial stressor and a result of psychosocial stress. Few family problems cause as much disruption and negative consequences for all as intrafamily child sexual abuse. While sex can be one of the closest ways people bond with one another, within a family it can result in chaos. Parent–child sexuality is one of the only universal taboos among world cultures, indicating that there is something inherent in the family relationship which can be devastated by the sexual crossing of generational boundaries.

The Extent of the Problem

It has proven most difficult to accurately estimate the incidence (the number of incestuous cases that have occurred over a period of time) and prevalence (the number of people who have been victims during their lives) of incestuous abuse. Estimates have risen from one child in a million during the 1950s (Weinberg, 1955) to one in three in the 1980s (Herman & Hirschman, 1981). There are many reasons why it is difficult to obtain accurate estimates. These include difficulties in defining incestuous abuse; the problems inherent in obtaining accurate information from clinical samples in retrospective studies; and the potential nonrepresentativeness of samples of families who have come to the attention of the authorities.

In general, we can summarize the extent of the problem as follows:

1. Sibling incest is probably the most common form of incestuous activity, although it is not always abusive (see definitions below) (Finkelhor, 1980b; Kempe & Kempe, 1984).
2. Father–daughter and stepfather–stepdaughter incest accounts for three-fourths of all *reported* cases of incestuous abuse (Kempe & Kempe, 1984), although only between 1% and 5% of the general population of women were incestuously abused by their fathers (Finkelhor, 1980a; Russell, 1986).
3. Sexual abuse is five times more likely in reconstituted families (Finkelhor, 1980a), and 17% of adult women raised by a stepfather in their first 14 years of life are sexually abused by him before the age of 14 (Russell, 1986).
4. Although it is less common, father-son, mother-son, and mother-daughter incest are being reported in increasing numbers (Chasnoff et al., 1986; Dixon, Arnold, & Calestro, 1978).
5. Some suggest that the large increases in reports of intrafamily child sexual abuse may be more a perception resulting from increased media attention (Bullough, 1985); however, recent evidence suggests that the incidence of incestuous abuse may have more than quadrupled since the turn of the century (Russell, 1986).

Although there is much diversity in estimates of the incidence and prevalence, and some disagreement whether there are more actual cases or not, what is clear is that incestuous abuse is not an *un*common occurrence and is, in fact, a large part of a great many families' life experience. Therapists should not be among those who view incestuous abuse as a rare and relatively unimportant phenomenon.

Effect on Individuals and Families

Most clinicians justify therapy for incest victims and families based on the assumption that incest leads to long-term psychological and family problems. While this contention is intuitive, the empirical evidence is not overwhelming (Constantine, 1981; Henderson, 1983). There have unfortunately only been a handful of studies attempting to examine the consequences of incest, and many of these have serious methodological flaws (cf. Scott & Stone, 1986).

What we do know about the effects of incestuous abuse on individuals and families can be summarized as follows:

1. *Severe psychopathology for victims.* Although somewhat counterintuitive, most incest victims are not severely psychologically impaired in adulthood (Gagnon, 1965; Meiselman, 1978; Owens, 1984; Tsai, Summers, & Edgar, 1979). This does not mean that many women's lives are not devastated by the experience; only that the assumption that severe psychopathology will be present in an adult "survivor" cannot be made without further assessment. Not surprisingly, studies using clinical samples are more likely to find psychological problems than those using nonclinical samples.
2. *Negative perception of the experience.* Most adult women incest "survivors" report the experience being negative and traumatic (Herman, Russell, & Trocki, 1986; Russell, 1986), and only a tiny fraction report the experience being positive (Russell, 1986).
3. *Common long-term effects.* The most common negative long-term effect for women is a response-inhibiting sexual dysfunction (Becker et al., 1984). Other commonly cited effects include low self-esteem, a tendency to use denial as a defense mechanism, and difficulty developing close interpersonal relationships, especially with men (Owens, 1984). Of course, individual clinical manifestations may be far more serious, including borderline personality disorder and psychosis (Barnard & Hirsch, 1985).
4. *Factors relating to the severity of long-term effects.* The more "sexual" the abuse, the more physical abuse associated with it, and the closer the relationship (i.e., if the offender is the father versus an uncle) all correlate with increased likelihood of long-term negative consequences (Russell, 1986). These negative effects can be mediated by their emotional and cognitive responses at the time of the incident (Tsai, Summers, & Edgar, 1979) or, ironically, by the presence of a supportive family during this period (Fromuth, 1986).
5. *Effects on the rest of the family.* Although thorough empirical studies on the long-term effects of incest on the family have not been done, clinical experience has shown that incestuous families suffer inexplicable pain and suffering as a result of the incest and/or its discovery. Nonoffending mothers may feel guilt, shame, anger, and mistrust; nonabused siblings feel shame, anger, fear of the offending parent, and can even display jeal-

ous feelings for the "special" relationship that has developed between the offending parent and the victim. The family system as a whole displays secretiveness, denial, a withdrawing into itself, increased coercion among its members to "keep the secret," and individual members often begin to display behavioral symptoms such as acting out and substance abuse.

Effects on the Therapist

A not well-documented but important concern is the stress experienced by most therapists working with incestuous families. Although therapy is a stressful business in general, "abuse therapists" experience problems specific to this field which, if unaddressed, can lead to rapid "burnout."

Training. A common complaint among therapists working with incest families is their lack of formal training to deal with the complexities of incest (Dietz & Craft, 1980). In our view, a successful incest therapist is one who feels comfortable dealing with incestuous families; is well trained in individual and family therapy theory and techniques; has special training in human sexuality and treatment of sexual disorders; has had formal coursework in family abuse and violence; and, of course, has had training and supervision specifically in the treatment of incestuous abuse. While these would seem minimum requirements for any other "specialty" area, they are almost utopian expectations for incest treatment today. However, without such training, therapists are certain to become quickly overwhelmed and frustrated.

Support of agencies. Although there are a few specialized incest treatment programs around the country (e.g., Giaretto, 1982), most services are provided by therapists within agency settings. The problems inherent in mental health service delivery, such as relatively low pay, large case loads, unrealistic administrative requirements, and so forth, are exacerbated when treating incestuous families. We have known agencies where over 30 abuse cases were seen in a week by individual therapists; where individual case files and notes for every member had to be taken after each *family* session; where the many extra hours spent in contact with welfare, court, and school personnel for each case were *not* counted toward the therapist's work load; and even an agency where the therapist was not permitted to continue treatment beyond 12 sessions under any circumstances, even if the cessation of continued abuse could not be guaranteed!

Values of the therapist. Few areas are as emotion-laden as incest and incestuous abuse. The most *powerful* of the sexual taboos has been broken: incest and having sex with children (and in the case of father-son, uncle-nephew, etc., the homosexuality taboo). Therapists, being human, are subject to the same strong emotional reaction to the breaking of these taboos as other people; however, therapists are expected to go beyond these feelings and in an unbiased way "treat" people they may despise. Unless therapists can come to terms with their own values associated with incestuous abuse, they may be unable to effectively treat incest families; worse yet, they may unconsciously "abuse" the clients by acting out their own unresolved hostilities (Trepper & Traicoff, 1983). We would suggest that part of the training for abuse therapists be a formal values-clarification process dealing with feelings about sexual abuse and family sexuality.

Therapists who were abused. Although an underresearched area, it is well known by those of us working in the field that a good many "abuse therapists" grew up in incestuous families and were the victims of sexual abuse. Those therapists who have experienced such abuse and successfully worked it through can provide a deep and empathic feeling for these families, have much to offer from their own experience, and can make some of the finest therapists. At the same time, those who have *not* worked through their own abuse or do not acknowledge the "interface issues" with the families may render themselves ineffective. Because of the potentially high number of therapists for which this may apply, we think it is essential for programs treating incestuous families to carefully screen therapists for those who were abused and may want to be abuse therapists to resolve their own family experiences. Therapy for the therapist may be an appropriate alternative.

Resistant families. Resistance to therapy, while an extremely common occurrence, still provides therapists with a great deal of stress. Incestuous families are notoriously resistant for a variety of reasons. And although the first stage of our treatment program deals specifically with managing such resistance, therapists who are particularly susceptible to stress associated with resistance may wish to reexamine their desire to work with abusing families.

BELIEF SYSTEMS

One of the first tasks we ask of our families is to consider their belief system surrounding sexual abuse. We contend that our underlying belief systems contribute to our behavior, if not in a one-to-one relationship then at least concomitantly. For example, we discuss with families how a belief system that tolerates the subjugation of women and children is an important contributing factor to sexual abuse. In training our therapists to work with incest families, we also ask them to consider *their* belief systems about incest families.

Thus one of the first tasks for therapists reading this book is to evaluate their belief systems, values, and feelings about incest families. To do this will help identify those values and attitudes that may impede effective therapy, allowing the therapist to obtain additional training and supervision, or to make the decision not to treat incest families at all.

To help the therapist accomplish this self-evaluation, we will describe 10 commonly held beliefs about incest and incest therapy. These beliefs, although not all-encompassing, are examples of widely held views. Next, we will present the therapeutic ramifications of each of these beliefs. Finally, because we feel it is essential that the reader knows the values underlying *our* treatment model, we will present our view of each belief and how it impacts our therapy with incest families.

Ten Commonly Held Beliefs

There are regional and cultural predispositions to incest. A common belief exists that certain regions of the country and subcultural groups are more prone to incest than others. For example, many have heard the jokes about Appalachian families. Inherent in these jokes is the acceptance of the stereotype that Southeastern mountain families are more prone to incest than the rest of us. We have also heard the same said for blacks, hispanics, the poor, rural families, and so on. Unfortunately, at this time we do not have adequate or reliable reporting systems available to accurately gauge if there are indeed these predispositions. For example, it is well known that *reported* child abuse is a mostly lower-class phenomenon; however, many therapists agree this is as much an artifact of the social service and mental health delivery systems as it is a reflection of truth (Finkelhor, 1984). Given the fact that all states in the country report increasing numbers of abuse cases from both rural and urban, poor and rich, black and white, it appears that the existence of a great incest haven is totally illusory.

Many therapists inadvertently accept the subcultural stereotypes of incest families. This leads to surprise, and sometimes disgust, when families present who do not fit into these categories. We have heard of a therapist who told a "pillar-of-the-community family" that had been referred because of incestuous abuse that she "could expect *that* from the families from ______________ (a local community of transplanted Southern families) but not from here!" Of course, this type of stereotyping is clinically inappropriate and may ultimately impede her ability to work with incest families.

We feel there may be societal, community, and even larger cultural influences on families vis-à-vis their attitudes toward sexual abuse that may increase their vulnerability to incest, but these must be understood for each individual family and community. Of course, being from a community which is more tolerant of incest does not mean the family from that community accepts those values. And certainly, there is no evidence that being from a specific *region* of the United States makes a family more incestuous than any others.

2. *Parents who have sex with their children are more emotionally disturbed than most people.* This is the therapeutic variation of the popular view that incestuous parents are evil, deranged, morally decadent, and so on. As will be discussed in Chapter 6, it is not at all a given that incestuous parents are more *diagnosably* disordered than other parents of families who present for outpatient counseling (Meiselman, 1978). It is rare, for example, to find offending parents to be psychotic or to exhibit any other serious psychopathology. In fact, therapists new to working with incest families are consistently surprised at the apparent "normalcy" of the individuals involved. Still, some argue that the incestuous behavior itself is *ipso facto* evidence of psychological disturbance, and that if DSM-III-R (APA, 1987) does not have incestuous behavior as a diagnosis, future revisions certainly should.

We have found that, although most offending parents do not easily fit into DSM diagnostic categories, some important intrapsychic and emotional patterns exist for many of the fathers. To assume them to be "crazy" is not particularly useful; however, to individually assess them on a wide range of possible intrapsychic and interpersonal dimensions is essential. At the same time, we remain cognizant that sometimes diagnosis is just the clinical way of chastizing. "He's sick" is not really very different from "He's evil." We prefer to understand the whole, complete individual and the complex of feelings, behaviors, attitudes, and social interactions he displays under varying circumstances. A diagnosis of "He's sick!" is easier, but ultimately not useful clinically.

3. *Most incest perpetrators were themselves victims.* It is widely held that abused children, both physically and sexually, are likely to themselves

become abusing parents. It turns out that this is simply not true. The best estimate made so far is that there is an approximately 30% intergenerational transmission rate for abuse (Kaufman & Zigler, 1987). This means that approximately two-thirds of abused children will *not* be expected to abuse their children. Further, there appear to be important mediating factors that can reduce the likelihood of the intergenerational abuse, such as family love and support, the family's ability to reduce stress, and an awareness of their own potential for abuse (Kaufman & Zigler, 1987).

An important ramification of acceptance of this myth is that therapists will view the daughter as an almost inevitable abuser in the future (or, a variation we have heard, she will certainly *marry* an abuser). Another result of adherence to this belief is that therapists may not really ever believe the parents when they insist they have never been abused, leading to an initial mistrust between therapist and parents that may not quickly dissolve.

Our view is that abuse can be cyclical, or at least the *style* that made the family vulnerable is cyclical. Although an abusing father may not have been sexually abused himself, he may have grown up in a family that was rigid, viewed men and women as unequal, taught that men receive affection through sex, and so forth. We have found that most abusing fathers, although not always sexually abused, were emotionally traumatized, leaving them dysfunctional in their adult relationships. In any event, what is important therapeutically is how the abusing parent has cognitively organized his family-of-origin experiences, and then how he can relinquish those experiences and feelings that have contributed to the abuse of his daughter.

4. *The mother always knows about the sex between the child and father.* Many therapists believe that a mother, even though she may state that she was never aware that her husband and daughter were incestuously involved, *must* have known at some level. Some point to the mothers who were themselves victims as children, and yet deny being aware of this fact. At the other end of this continuum are those therapists who categorically accept the mother's insistence that she did not know and that she should not be "indicted" along with the offending father, who is ultimately culpable.

There are serious ramifications to both views. The therapist who believes "they all really know, deep down inside" may be unconsciously *blaming* the mother for behavior that ultimately is the responsibility of the offending parent. This view may even represent a subtle misogynist therapeutic bias. The therapist who totally exonerates the mother from *any* responsibility, however, may be naively assuming that family members do not interact with one another, that whatever goes on in a family does *not* affect everyone else, and that the father is not only responsible for the abuse, but is also the sole *cause*.

We believe that whether the mother knows about the abuse is not necessarily the only question. Even when they most vociferously deny awareness of the sexual abuse, most mothers report that they knew "something was wrong at home." We assess those family elements that may have happened in the family that prevented the mother from going the next step and discovering that sexual abuse was occurring. For example, we are interested to know if there were serious communication problems between the mother and daughter that prevented the latter from disclosing the abuse, and/or in what ways did the abusing parent manipulate the family so that the mother-daughter relationship was impaired. And, of course, it is important for us to know if the mother *was* informed by the daughter but did not respond effectively.

5. *Father-son incest is very rare.* Father-son incestuous abuse *is* fairly uncommon, so much so that no epidemiological data have been reported in the literature; only clinical descriptions are presented. Some have argued, however, that father-son incest is an underreported problem and that there are many more families affected by it than is evidenced by the statistics (Dixon et al., 1978).

There are two common ways therapists deal with the low reported numbers of father-son incest. The first is to confuse its *uncommonness* with its *impossibility*. A therapist may simply not think to ask the boys in a sexually abusing family whether they were victimized, because it simply did not cross the therapist's mind. The other is to assume that all incestuous fathers *must* be capable of and interested in abusing *all* the children in the family. Both of these positions can lead to incorrect clinical judgments.

We believe that although more rare, father-son incest is a possibility that must be assessed along with all other forms of abuse in the family. We also are aware that although father-son sexual abuse is unusual, the sexual abuse of boys by other adult family members and trusted friends is fairly common (Finkelhor, 1984). It can be assumed that a family that has had difficulty protecting its female children from *intrafamilial* sexual abuse might also have trouble protecting its male children from *extrafamilial* sexual abuse.

6. *Substance or alcohol abuse is a primary cause of incest.* This is one of the most widely held beliefs regarding incestuous families, by both therapists and nontherapists alike. There is evidence supporting this notion; primarily, the data that indicate that the majority of all incestuous episodes occur under the influence of alcohol, and up to 50% of the incest fathers are clinically diagnosable alcoholics (Virkkunen, 1974; Meiselman, 1978).

The error, in our view, is made in accepting alcohol or substance abuse as the *cause* of incest. The vast majority of alcoholics do not sexually abuse their daughters, nor do most of the population who periodically become inebriated. We prefer to view alcohol use and abuse as a *precipitating event* that may elicit an incestuous episode in an already vulnerable family (see Chapter 2). We believe it is necessary for the abusing father to stop drinking, but we do not believe that this is sufficient.

7. *Children are often voluntary participants in incestuous activities.* One of the more controversial issues surrounding the treatment of incest families is whether or not the daughter was a voluntary participant in the incestuous activities. Therapists present a range of beliefs concerning this unprovable notion: from the view that children can be "seductive" and sexually engaging with their fathers, or at least sometimes enjoy these activities, to the belief that all incestuous activity is rape, and the daughter is never even tacitly involved in the sexual activities with her father. Certainly, the retrospective studies of Russell (1986) and Herman, Russell, and Trocki (1986) suggest that most adults who were incestuously involved with their fathers were *not* voluntary participants. However, family therapists working with incestuous families continually report more involvement beyond passive acceptance of a rape by many daughters.

Our view lies somewhere in between these two positions. We have never known of a daughter to *initiate* sex with her father, nor do we believe that, left to their own devices, these daughters would choose for incest activities to continue. At the same time, we understand that incest occurs within the framework of an ongoing, intimate, and complex set of relationships within the family, and that sometimes the daughter's role of "victim" within these relationships contributes to her continued abuse.

We accept that children are sexual beings and that they are capable of feeling sexual pleasure. And although they are often confused by the feelings that are stimulated by sex with their fathers, part of that confusion comes from the fact that they may have felt sexual arousal. Again, neither of these points should be construed as suggesting that the daughters are to *blame* for the incestuous activity, but that we as therapists must be able to accept some "unacceptable" notions about the nature of intimate family relationships and childhood sexuality to fully understand the dynamics of incest.

8. Daughters will have severe emotional problems as a result of incestuous experiences. The belief that incest will lead to severe emotional problems has been the cornerstone of all therapy for incest. Most therapists believe this without hesitation, and probably justify some of their more intrusive therapeutic measures on it. The research on the long-term effects of child sexual abuse has been quite mixed, however, with some finding minimal psychological problems in adulthood (e.g., Gagnon, 1965; Tsai, Summers, & Edgar, 1979) and others showing clear effects that impair some aspect of psychological or social functioning (e.g., Finkelhor, 1984; Herman & Hirschman, 1981; Meiselman, 1978).

In addition to the obvious view that some adult women who were sexually abused will suffer long-term psychological problems and some will not, we believe that the incest and the concomitant family problems will be a part of the victim's life in some way forever. For example, although it does not have to be the organizing factor in her life, it will most likely be incorporated in her world view. This might involve how she experiences relationships, men, and families, and may presuppose a family structure with her husband and children that may include abuse. However, when we work with an adult woman who has been incestuously abused, we *never* assume that she is psychologically "damaged," that she hates her father, or any other victimizing assumptions. We try to treat her with dignity and to help *her* determine the impact the abuse has had.

9. The most effective treatment for incestuous fathers is intensive individual psychotherapy. The belief that intensive individual therapy for incest fathers should be encouraged is probably the clinical version of "throw the bum in jail." In a tolerant and rehabilitative society such as ours, there is a tendency to believe that therapy is preferential to incarceration, even for the most noxious problems such as incest. And if a little therapy helps most small problems, then a great deal of (or intensive) therapy must be best for the "big" problems.

Although we are aware of no studies comparing individual therapy with other modes, our belief, based on the traditionally high recidivism for incest fathers having undergone individual therapy alone, is that the most effective treatment is a combination of family, individual, and group therapies. As will be stated throughout the book, our view is that incest is the result of many causal factors acting in consort with one another. To treat one without the others would prove as ineffective as treating a heart attack by only reducing cholesterol, while not altering other important factors, such as smoking, stress, and weight.

10. Incest families are difficult to treat. This is a widely held view, accepted, interestingly enough, more by therapists who have *not* worked with incest families than those who have. Incest families, as will be shown, do usually present severe family dysfunction, are often in states of crisis, and are often extremely resistant. However, we have found them to be more challenging than frightening, more interesting clinically than mundane, and more treatable than untreatable. Many of the therapists in our program have commented that they prefer to work with abusing families than with other families because the problems that need to be corrected are so apparent, the sequences of behavior displayed by the family so dysfunctional, and the ultimate change that occurs as a result of therapy so dramatic.

HOW CHANGE OCCURS

Just as it is essential for therapists reading this book to understand their own beliefs regarding how change occurs prior to attempting to effect change in clients, we feel it is important for readers to know *our* beliefs regarding how change occurs prior to accepting our program of therapy. We will briefly outline how we view the origin of problems, how change occurs, and how this view has affected our treatment of incestuously abusing families.

We have been unabashedly influenced by the systems view of problem development, problem maintenance, and problem solution, and have applied that to our work with individuals and families. We believe that individual feelings, experiences, and behaviors are in constant interaction with those of other individuals in the system (be it family, work, community, etc.); at the same time, the system itself interacts with and influences its individual members' feelings, experiences, and behaviors. Most problematic symptoms, according to this view, are the result of dysfunctional feelings, behaviors, and interactions within individuals and among family members. Consequently, change will occur when these dysfunctional interactions are interrupted and new sequences of behaviors replace them.

The Multiple Systems model, described in detail in the next chapter, grew out of this systemic view of problem formation and solution. This orientation allows us to focus on the individual offending parent's contribution to the incestuous abuse as well as examining the influences from the larger societal systems, the dysfunctional interactions among family members, the families of origin and their influences on patterns of abuse, along with many other factors contributing to a family's vulnerability to incest. This orientation also permits us to intervene at many levels of the systems involved, and also to provide help to family members not directly involved with the abuse, but certainly who are affected by it.

2

The Multiple Systems Model

It is surprising that so many therapists treat incest families without an organizing framework for the cause and maintenance of intrafamilial sexual abuse. Recently, there have been increased suggestions from those working in the field for the building of etiological theories for incestuous abuse (e.g., Conte, 1986; deYoung, 1982; Finkelhor, 1984; Tierney & Corwin, 1983). This interest has developed because of both the expanded research on sexual abuse and the recognition that effective treatment programs must be based upon a cogent framework.

There are a number of reasons why therapists should have a conceptual model when providing treatment for any problem, especially incestuous abuse. First, an etiological model helps therapists to clarify their assumptions and values surrounding a problem and its therapy (Stuart, 1980). This is particularly important when dealing with an emotion-laden problem like incest, where at times values can override judgment (Trepper & Traicoff, 1983, 1985). Second, etiological models provide the basis for the assessment and treatment schema that will be used. For example, a program which as its etiological model assumes incestuous abuse to be the result of sexual and personality problems in the offender will likely focus almost exclusively on assessing and treating the "sexual pathology" of the father. Third, etiological models allow for ease in communication among therapists who use a similar model. Conversely, therapists adhering to *different* etiological views of incest can barely communicate with one another since each views the other as inept, uninformed, or unethical.

CAUSAL MODELS FOR INCESTUOUS ABUSE

The development of causal models for incestuous abuse is following the same historical path as have causal models for other clinical problems.

The first step in this process is that a problem is described by those working with it most often. These clinicians usually make some etiological assumptions based upon their own theoretical orientation. Next, those working with the same problem but from a different therapeutic orientation add to the literature by explaining the problem from their school's perspective. About this time comes a proliferation of case studies and clinical examples to support each school's etiological contribution. Next comes the emergence of treatment *programs* based upon these various orientations, which in turn begin to collect descriptive data on clients with the problem and some rudimentary data on the effectiveness of the program. Finally come experimental clinical studies comparing one program with another, and hopefully with this increased control comes the ability to answer the important question: What treatment program is best for what client-type under what circumstances (Jacobson, Follette, & Revenstorf, 1984)?

Theoretical deliberation about the causes of and treatments for incest have followed this process fairly closely. The literature has gone from primarily clinical analyses and causal speculations (e.g., Bender & Blau, 1937; Marcuse, 1923; Summit & Kryso, 1978; Weinberg, 1955; Zimrin, 1984) to program treatment descriptions based upon specific counseling orientations (e.g., Barrett, Sykes, & Byrnes, 1986; Giaretto, 1982). We are still basically at this program-refining stage. Perhaps we will soon be ready to begin empirical studies to examine particular etiological factors (such as the groundbreaking study by Parker & Parker, 1986), and those to compare the effectiveness of various treatment programs that treat incestuous abuse. We are currently in the process of just such an endeavor, with a longitudinal study of incestuously abusing families who have participated in our treatment program.

Although most clinicians and researchers in the field are anxious for more empirical research on the causes of incest, there are a number of factors that have inhibited such studies. First, as previously discussed, the field has just now entered the stage during which such research could realistically be accomplished. Second, there are still serious enough definitional problems as to hamper comparative etiological investigations. For example, a major question has not been effectively answered: Are *intra*family and *extra*-family child sexual abuse based on the same causal phenomena, or are they based upon completely different etiological vari-

not particularly successful in terms of its own goals: that is, to remove the father while shoring up the victim and the mother. The family often wishes to remain together. The father, if not jailed, often returns home without the knowledge of the therapist or the courts. If he is jailed, he usually receives no treatment and returns home eventually to a family system that is fundamentally the same as when he left.

3. Isolating the daughter from her father may subtly contribute to her continued victimization by communicating to her that she is incompetent or unable to effect change on her own. This may hold true for the mother as well.

Family Systems Model

The family systems model for explaining and treating incestuous abuse grew out of the family therapy movement of the 1960s and 1970s. Since many of the therapists who were called upon to treat incestuous families were family therapists, it is not unreasonable that they would apply their orientation to this problem as well. This model views incestuous activity as the *product* of a problematic family system rather than as the cause, and sees all family members as sharing in the cause and maintenance of the incest. To this end, all family members are both perpetrators and victims of the abuse (Alexander, 1985; Kennedy & Cormier, 1969; Magal & Winnik, 1968; Machotka, Pittman, & Flomenhaft, 1967; Straus, 1973).

The therapy that ensues from this approach is, of course, family therapy, which has been increasing in popularity as a treatment modality for incestuous abuse since the 1970s (deChesnay, 1985). There are both benefits and problems emanating from this model as well (from Larson & Maddock, 1984):

Benefits

1. The family model addresses and impacts a larger field than the individually oriented therapies, which arise from the perpetrator-victim approach. This allows the therapist to assess not just individual pathology but also the *interactions* of the individuals.
2. It is seen as a preventative model as well as an ameliorative one; that is, the restructuring of families prevents future generations of the family from being abused or abusing.
3. It minimizes the emphasis on shame and punishment, since each family member is viewed as having a part in the problem.

4. It is less traumatic for the children in the family; they are not forced to turn their parents in, nor is there an attempt to disunite the family.
5. It is more likely to result in the family remaining together, with all of the concomitant emotional and economic benefits.
6. It supports the "uninvolved" family members who have certainly been affected by the discovery of the abuse, the separation of members from the family, and the involvement of social service agencies with their family.
7. It promotes the integration of new behavioral patterns *in vivo,* leading to longer-term, more meaningful change.

Problems

1. It may lead to a child being left in an unsafe home.
2. It may lead to the unacceptable message that all family members share an equal responsibility for the abuse, thus getting the father "off the hook."
3. It may not focus sufficiently on serious underlying psychopathology of the father.
4. It may not provide enough support for the child victim, who may appear outwardly unimpaired but in reality may be suffering greatly.
5. It may reinforce the traditional sex roles which contributed to the abuse to begin with. For example, there is a tendency to "blame mothers" and "idealize fathers" in family therapy (Bograd, 1984).
6. It ignores the larger societal context which permitted incestuous abuse to occur.

The Ecosystemic Model

Ecosystemic models for understanding the causes and maintenance of incestuous abuse have been suggested recently by a number of writers (e.g., Dixon & Jenkins, 1981; Tierney & Corwin, 1983). Briefly, an ecosystemic model understands a disorder not from the "inside out," but from the "outside in." These models look at the larger socioenvironmental context when attempting to explain emotional and family-related problems, and also how the family interacts back with its environment (Figley, 1983). These models have so far tended to be primarily theoretical in nature, and have not led to specific treatment programs, although many therapists remain aware throughout treatment of the social and environmental influences upon family problems.

Multiple Systems Model

Some writers have suggested that multiple factors probably contribute to physical abuse in the family (e.g., Garbirano, 1977; Gelles, 1980; Straus, 1980). The Multiple Systems Model is an attempt to integrate the more salient features of each of the above three models to understand the origin and maintenance of incestuous abuse. Certainly, each of the other etiological models has its benefits and problems, and it seems counterproductive to ignore the important contributions of each. This model suggests that there are *many* systems that impact individuals with regard to incestuous behavior: cultural systems, family-of-origin systems, family systems, and individual psychological systems. Each of these contribute to incestuous abuse, and each of these must be assessed and intervened in to stop incestuous abuse.

Even though multiple systems is somewhat of a compromise position, there are some important philosophical and pragmatic differences between this perspective and either the perpetrator-victim or family systems models (see Table 2.1). In general, Multiple Systems attempts to understand the *interaction* among the various external, family, and internal systems rather than to focus attention solely upon one. The therapy which follows from the Multiple Systems Model will invariably include the whole family (if possible), but will also work intensively with individual family members (especially the offending father), the parents' families of origin, and even outside friends, work acquaintances, and extended family. The underlying theme of this model is that the therapist must not treat just one "system" (such as the offender only), but instead must intervene upon *all* systems which contribute to the abuse.

Vulnerability to Incest

At the center of the Multiple Systems Model is an assessment scheme called the *Vulnerability to Incest* model. This framework is based upon the general vulnerability (Gottschalk, 1983; Zubin & Spring, 1977) or diathesis-stress (Rosenthal, 1971) models common in the field of abnormal psychology. These suggest that assessment of a clinical disorder should not attempt to isolate the one underlying cause of the problem. Instead, it should identify how *vulnerable* a person or system is to the problem, based on the presence or absence of many possible contributing factors. What is assessed, then, is the likelihood of *expression* of the disorder when presented with a precipitating situation.

The Multiple Systems Model operates, then, on the following basic

TABLE 2.1
Perpetrator-Victim, Family Systems, and Multiple Systems Approaches
(After Larson & Maddock, 1984)

Perpetrator-Victim	*Family Systems*	*Multiple Systems*
Children are vulnerable; need protecting	Children are resilient, don't necessarily pick up pathologies	Most children are resilient, but some show masked symptoms that need to be assessed
Incest is rape, a crime, power-oriented, and should always be punished	Incest is a form of family pathology representing a misbalancing in the family and should be thus treated	Incest may be rape or power-oriented, but may also be an act of love; if not punished, there should be consequences
The pathology of the perpetrator is the critical issue, and should be labeled as sick	Pathology of the family is critical and should be labeled dysfunctional	All factors contributing to the family's vulnerability to incest are critical
Punishment makes it clear who is responsible, to alleviate the guilt of the victim	Punishment increases the shame of the perpetrator and exacerbates the problems of the family; victim feels guilty and gets too much power	Punishment may be a useful strategy to demonstrate consequences to a resistant family; alternate strategies to demonstrate responsibility without contributing to the problem may be more appropriate
Incest is always traumatic for the child, and thus treatment is always indicated	Incest is sometimes traumatic, but not always; need to assess the child and family in order to see if something is needed	Incest is invariably traumatic for the family as a result of the discovery and subsequent intrusion by social services; therapists must be concerned also with that trauma, work to reduce it along with the incest
Because children are basically vulnerable, they need to be treated individually or with peers but never with parents because that could increase the trauma	Treatment must include the entire family, since all may have contributed to the family problem underlying the abuse	Although the family is the cornerstone of treatment, individual sessions used to both assess individual needs and strengthen self-esteem and empowerment
Someone, preferably the perpetrator, should always leave home when the incest is discovered; father should be separated from daughters	Leaving home is not necessary, can upset the homeostasis and be more traumatic on the family, and put undue emotional and economic hardship on the mother	Leaving home should occur when the safety of the child cannot be ensured, and as a strategy to encourage change; can be father, daughter, both, or neither

(continued)

TABLE 2.1 *(continued)*

Perpetrator-Victim	*Family Systems*	*Multiple Systems*
Children should confront parents directly and be taught how to report the abuse if it were to happen again	Professionals should do the confronting since this gives children an inordinate amount of power in the family system and will have negative consequences for the child, such as grandiosity	Confronting need not be done at all; if it is, both parents and child should have their confrontation time; preferably an Apology Session to allow parents to apologize for the current status of the family
Incest is *the* problem, and treating the incest so it does not happen again is most important	Incest is a symptom of family pathology, not the problem itself, and treatment should focus primarily on restructuring the family	Incest must not recur but is seen as the product of a number of factors, including individual, family, and social, all of which must be changed so the abuse is never likley to occur again, and will not continue into another generation
Stress court evaluation for both the perpetrator and the victim; treatment for each, must keep them separate	Stress family evaluations	Do integrated assessment of individuals, family systems, and social systems
Mother is a victim, too, as a result of the father's abuse	All family members are both perpetrators and victims	The notion of perpetrator *and* victim is not useful in creating change; must think in terms of all possible contributions to the problem, on a case-by-case basis, then develop strategies to reduce factors.

assumption: *There is no one cause of incestuous abuse. Instead, all families are endowed with a degree of vulnerability based upon environmental, family, individual, and family-of-origin factors, which may express as incest if a precipitating event occurs and the family's coping skills are inadequate* (Trepper & Barrett, 1986; see Figure 2.1).

This model is clinically and theoretically derived, although there are a number of studies ongoing at this writing designed to test and refine it. It has been found to be extremely useful in clinical assessment and as the basis of treatment planning (for a complete discussion of each factor and its clinical assessment, see Chapter 6).

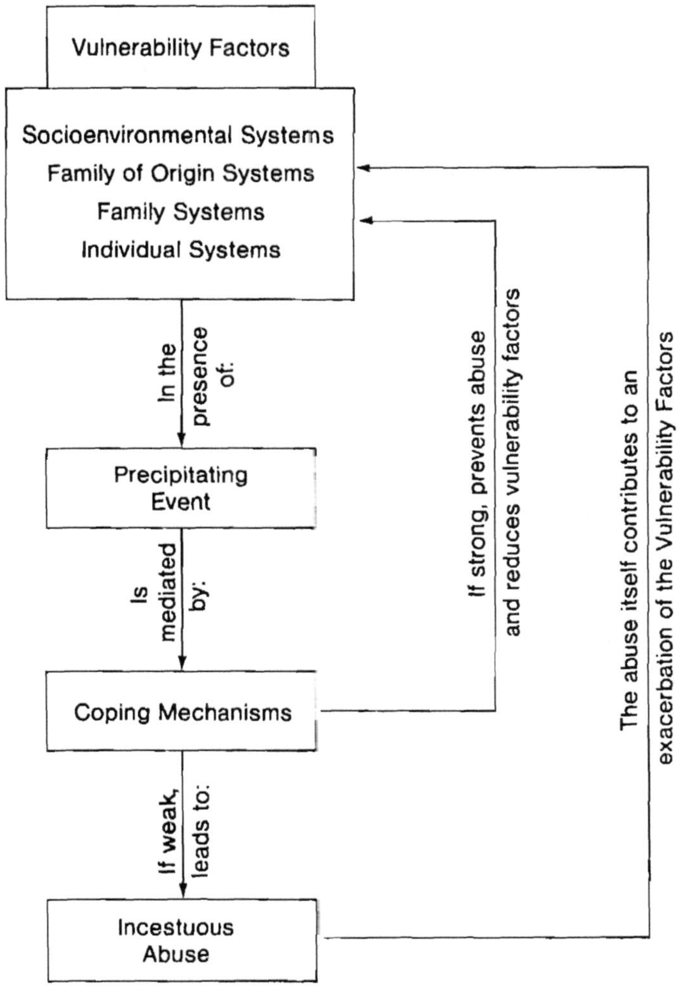

Figure 2.1. Vulnerability to Incest model.

Vulnerability Factors

There are four major vulnerability factor areas that therapists assess. These are: (1) *socioenvironmental* factors; (2) *family-of-origin* factors; (3) *individual psychological* factors; and (4) *family systems* factors.

Socioenvironmental factors. The culture and society in which we live contribute greatly to our "world view"; that is, the way in which we develop our values, organize our lives, and express specific behaviors under specific conditions. In understanding incestuous abuse, we must also understand the cultural framework surrounding male-female relationships, the messages provided about abuse and sexuality, the types and amount of chronic stressors and social isolation, and the interaction between the family and these environmental influences. There have been a number of socioenvironmental dimensions hypothesized as contributing to a family's vulnerability to incest. These socioenvironmental influences include the family's: (a) acceptance of male supremacy and power; (b) adherence to the differential manner in which men and women traditionally display affection; (c) living in a community that tacitly accepts incest or other forms of child abuse; (d) social isolation; and (e) chronic stress.

Family-of-origin factors. Recent reviews have countered the time-worn belief that abusing parents were usually abused children themselves (Kaufman & Zigler, 1987). However, few would doubt the influence the family of origin plays in the development of marital and parental *style*. That is, people learn from their parents how to act with their spouses, and how to parent their own children (Bandura, 1977). And recent findings have suggested that child sexual abusers *perceived* being maltreated as children to a significantly greater extent than nonabusers (Langevin & Lang, 1985). The Multiple Systems Model takes into account the abusing parent's families of origin, both in terms of what was taught about marriage and childrearing, and any influence that the family of origin may still have on the family of procreation.

Family systems factors. Although some have argued that *intra*family child sexual abuse is not as distinct from *extra*family child sexual abuse as family systems therapists would wish us to believe (Conte, 1986; Finkelhor, 1984), the Multiple Systems Model suggests that the family itself represents another integral system involved in the origin, maintenance, and ultimately amelioration of incest (Trepper & Barrett, 1986). The family systems factors assumed to contribute to a family's vulnerability to incest include: (a) the family's abusive style; that is, What is the underlying *intent* of sexual abuse in the family? Is the incestuous abuse reflective of an affection exchange, erotic-exchange, aggression-exchange, or a rage process (Larson & Maddock, 1986)? (b) the structure of the family; that is, How does the family organize its interactions with regard its hierarchy, rules, roles, and the cohesion of its members? and (c) the communication style of the family, such as its use of secrecy and double-binding communication, and its inability to respond to affective communication.

Individual personality/psychopathology factors. The Multiple System Model views individual personality and psychopathology as a "system" unto itself. These individual characteristics and/or disorders contribute to a family's vulnerability to incest, particularly when certain of these characteristics in one person interact in a certain way with those of another. For example, the dominant style of an incestuous father will contribute more significantly to the family's vulnerability *if* his daughter has a passive-dependent personality style. On the other hand, a pre-incestuous live-in boyfriend who has impulse-control difficulties and fantasies of sex with young girls might not abuse his paramour's daughter if the *mother's* personality style is self-assured, assertive, and vigilantly protective of her children. In other words, the Multiple Systems Model examines not only the individual characteristics contributing to a family's vulnerability to incest, but also the interactions among the family members' personalities.

Summary of vulnerability factors. A family increases its vulnerability to incest when more of the vulnerability conditions listed above are present; the more of these conditions, the more vulnerable. In the most extreme case (and most of the families who present for treatment are extreme cases), one example of a highly vulnerable family might be the family:

1. that is relatively isolated from others;
2. that lives in a community which tolerates the male domination of women and children, at least tacitly;
3. that adheres to rigid sex roles;
4. that sexualizes much of their routine interactions;
5. that displays extreme rigidity with regard to change, a high value to strict adherence to rules, and yet is extremely enmeshed with regard to their emotional bondedness;
6. where secrecy in communication is tolerated and encouraged;
7. where the father has poor impulse control, has a sense of total entitlement concerning his children, and has a sexual fantasy of total sexual power and possession;
8. where the mother has a passive-dependent personality style, and where she has a greater felt-need for personal protection and sustenance than for protection of her children;

9. where the daughter has a great need for affection, has a conflictual relationship with her mother and close emotional alignment with her father, and is psychologically estranged from her other siblings; and
10. where the father was emotionally abused and neglected during his childhood, and the mother was sexually abused and/or emotionally neglected in her childhood.

Precipitating Events and Coping Mechanisms

Even the most vulnerable family may not express itself incestuously, according to the Multiple Systems Model. For an incestuous episode to occur, not only must the family have a high degree of vulnerability, but there also must be a *precipitating event* which will trigger the abuse. Although most precipitating events are idiosyncratic, they can include an alcohol or drug binge by the father, an acute situational stressor such as loss of a job, or a unique opportunity factor such as the mother entering the hospital for an extended stay.

An incestuous episode still may not express itself in a vulnerable family, even in the presence of a precipitating event, if the family has adequate *coping mechanisms*. These refer to the myriad of strategies individuals and families use to prevent psychosocial stress from resulting in dysfunctional behavior (Trepper, 1989), and can include the effective use of social networks, a strong religious belief system, and the use of therapy and self-help groups (Gaudin & Pollane, 1983).

However, if the highly vulnerable family described above also had strong precipitating events present and lacked effective coping strategies, it would very likely be incestuous, according to the Multiple Systems Model. It is sad yet interesting that so many families display the vast numbers of dimensions needed for incestuous abuse to occur. It is likely that these dimensions are not independent from one another, but interact systematically to increase the likelihood of one occurring based upon the presence of another (see Figure 2.1).

CONCLUSIONS

The Multiple Systems Model has a number of advantages over the perpetrator-victim and family systems models. First, although it is more complex, that very complexity increases its clinical utility. It takes far more effort to understand, assess, and intervene using this framework, but there is a powerful payoff in that the therapist has so many more clinical options open. Second, it forces the therapist to assess a greater field and thus allows for processing more varied information. Third, the Multiple Systems Model encourages treatment where it is needed, not where it is assumed to be. Some fathers may need intensive individual counseling for pedophile fantasies and behaviors, but others may not. When no *a priori* assumptions are made, time is not wasted on unnecessary interventions.

A fourth advantage the Multiple Systems Model has over the other causal models is that this model has practical meaning for the family in terms of the eternal question: "What made this happen to us?" Rather than tacitly responding, "Because Dad is crazy," or "Because Mom isn't a good mother," or the horrific, "Because daughter is seductive" (none of which is ever fully accepted by a family anyway), the Vulnerability to Incest framework can be presented to the family as the "cause." In our experience, the family can usually fully understand and appreciate the complexity of incestuous behavior.

Finally, the Multiple Systems Model, being somewhat of a compromise position, is "palatable" to those from differing clinical-political orientations. This model of assessment and treatment has been embraced by clinicians from both child-advocacy and family systems backgrounds. Its acceptability allows its adoption in a variety of clinical settings. Most important, the Multiple Systems Model has worked successfully for our program as the underlying framework for over 10 years, permitting us to help thousands of families cease the previously unending patterns of incestuous abuse.

SECTION I

3

Introduction to Stage I: Creating a Context for Change

The first stage of our therapy program, which lasts approximately four to six months, is conceptualized by its title, "Creating a Context for Change." Many family therapists (e.g., Anderson & Stewart, 1983) have suggested that for change to be elicited, a context must first be established that encourages such change. This context must be positive, must create an expectation for change, and must recognize the difficulty in producing such change. Many programs that treat incest appear to the families to operate within a context of *punishment*. We, however, have found that a punishment context usually results in increased resistance on the part of the family, which leads to an increase in a punitive therapeutic posture, which leads to more resistance, and so on.

Incest families typically feel at their lowest when treatment begins. The "crisis" of discovery has not subsided, and the family as a whole feels ashamed, angry, and frightened. Stage I therapy attempts to: (1) create the context that change is possible and expected; (2) acknowledge that change is difficult and that there will be setbacks during therapy; (3) introduce flexibility into the family system so that the members can change; and (4) make it clear that although the therapist *hates* incestuous abuse, he or she does not hate any member of the abusing family; that is, they are all respected and cared for as people. This last point is particularly important given the negative way incestuously abusing families often feel about themselves and each other.

GOALS OF STAGE I THERAPY

There are a number of specific goals the therapist hopes to accomplish during this first stage of therapy. First, the problem must be fully defined for the family members. When they enter therapy, the "problem" to them is the intrusion into their lives by caseworkers and therapists; or that the abused daughter "squealed" on Dad and got the family into trouble; or that Dad is an alcoholic and needs help. By the end of Stage I, *the* problem has been clearly defined as a *sexual abuse* problem, and the other issues are put in the perspective of "contributing factors."

The second goal of Stage I therapy is to create "workable realities" for the family (Minuchin, 1981). People often see problems, particularly severe ones such as incestuous abuse, as insurmountable, caused by demons and devils lurking within. An important goal of Stage I is for the therapist to invoke an image of the problem that makes its amelioration seem *possible*. For example, if the father sees himself as a sick abuser (an image that may have been supported by his friends and family), he may feel hopeless to change. However, if the therapist can create the reality that "only part of you is an abuser, while there are other parts which are loving, caring, and appropriately paternal," then the goal becomes that these latter parts and a "functional self" will always be in control. The father now has an attainable framework from which to begin serious change.

The third goal of Stage I therapy is to manage the resistance that is inevitably present, especially during the early months of treatment. Some of the reasons that incestuously abusing families are resistant will be discussed briefly below.

RESISTANCE TO THERAPY BY INCEST FAMILIES

One of the most important contributions from the family therapy field has been the reevaluation of *resistance* to psychotherapy. Originally, resistance was seen as a *symptom*, as a proof of inherent psychopathology. Family therapy has redefined resistance to therapy as a *normal* process—that instead of indicating pathology, resistance is actually a sign of health. And although continued and unaddressed resistance can ultimately lead to failures in therapy, interventions can be directed that utilize the strength behind the resistance to effect positive family change (cf. Anderson & Stewart, 1983).

It is curious that while most family therapists realistically appraise and successfully intervene with resistance in *other* clinical family problems, many cannot accept the resistance displayed by incestuously abusing families. Some therapists see resistance as an "affront" to the help that they offer. We have even observed in some therapists a "How can he be resistant after what he's done?" attitude. This sentiment usually reflects a normal response to a situation therapists find abhorrent. However, it is critical that therapists "resist" this tendency, and understand and manage resistance to therapy by incestuously abusing families in the same manner they do other clinical populations.

Reasons for Resistance

In addition to those reasons typical of all families in therapy, incestuously abusing families have some reasons to resist that are unique to their situation. These include the following:

1. *Extreme crisis.* Incest families almost always enter therapy during an extreme crisis phase in their lives. This crisis usually leads to a "retrenchment" for the family as a whole. The family can become extremely self-protective and build barriers to communication around itself, making easy access for the therapist difficult.
2. *Fear of litigation.* Criminal and/or civil actions against the offending parent are a very real possibility, and resistance to complete "openness and honesty" with the therapist may not be perceived as prudent. It is not uncommon for the victims and nonoffending family members also to fear criminal action against the father, and they may resist full disclosure to protect him (see Chapter 7).
3. *Embarrassment.* The family, particularly the nonoffending members, may feel extreme embarrassment at being labeled an "incest family." In some families this leads to a protective denial and resistance to complete disclosure.
4. *Uncertainty of the role of the therapist.* Families are not certain at the beginning "whose side the therapist is on." They may have had harsh treatment from caseworkers, police, and court, and are not certain whether the therapist will continue in what they perceive as hostile intent. Also, they may have had what they believed were unsatisfactory results when they cooperated with other agencies (someone being removed from the home, criminal charges being filed, etc.). This leads to a cautious if not

defensive posture on the part of many families in subsequent dealings with other "helpers."

5. *Family dysfunction*. Specific family problems which may have contributed to the incest may also contribute to resistance to therapy. These problems include secrecy, denial, enmeshment, poor communication, and rigidity.

STAGE I TREATMENT MODALITIES

One of the advantages of the Multiple Systems Model for treating incest families is that the therapist has a great deal of flexibility. And the greatest flexibility comes when deciding with which system or subsystem to work. The therapist can and should have separate sessions with the family, the marital subsystem, the children, and the individual family members. There are a number of "decision rules" that can be used by the therapist to help decide which therapeutic modality to use during Stage I. These are only a few of the possible combinations and rules for them:

1. If the therapist feels "stuck" (i.e., the family's resistance is not being lessened but the therapist's resistance to the family is *increasing*), then it is useful to switch modes. For example, if the family cannot get beyond their conflictual façade during sessions, the therapist might only see individuals for a few sessions. This change often gives a new perspective to the therapist and allows for more creative interventions.
2. The therapist needs to see as many people in the family *together* as possible to fully assess their vulnerability factors. Therefore, although individual sessions are essential during Stage I, whole family and subsystem sessions are also critical.
3. If either parent is denying the facts about the abuse, the abused child and that parent should not be in the same room for therapy sessions. The rest of the family (minus the denying parent) can and should meet as a whole, however.
4. Simply because family conflicts are present is no reason to avoid having family sessions. For example, in the instance where the siblings are angry at the abused sister for "forcing" their father out of the house, it will be very important to have the siblings and daughter together so that everyone's feelings can be discussed and hopefully resolved.

5. If the mother admits to the facts of the abuse while the father denies, the therapist can use marital sessions to encourage his admission of the facts and acceptance of the responsibility.
6. If the father continues to deny, the therapist should have individual sessions with the father, and family sessions for the rest. Again, it is important not to put the daughter in the position of having to defend her disclosure or, worse yet, to feel forced to recant it.

It is very important for the therapist to "read the system" when deciding whom to see for a session. Two possible problems emerge which influence such a decision, both of which can lead to problems. A therapist might inadvertently avoid working with a subsystem that needs attention because another is easier to work with. For example, every time the couple is together for a session they become conflictual with each other and confronting to the therapist; however, when seen individually, both are engaging, and even fun for the therapist. In this case, could one blame a therapist for having fewer marital and more individual therapy sessions, even though the opposite is probably indicated? On the other hand, a therapist might respond to the continual crisis of one subsystem and ignore another. A therapist might find that he or she is working exclusively with the marital dyad because the couple are in constant turmoil, and avoiding having sessions with the children, who appear to be doing just fine but in reality might be harboring emotional problems in a less obvious way than their parents.

Family Sessions

There are many purposes for entire-family sessions during Stage I of therapy. The first is to assess the interactions among family members. Since the family structure, abusive style, and communication patterns are all important vulnerability factors, it is self-evident that sessions in which everyone is present are necessary. Second, the therapist creates a language for the family surrounding the abuse itself. The family is given a word, such as "incest" or "molestation," rather than the euphemisms common among abusing families. Third, the therapist can teach the family systemic thinking, since systemic change is an important goal of the program. Fourth, the therapist can test how flexible the system is to change, and to the intimacy and intensity necessary to produce change.

A final purpose of entire-family therapy sessions during Stage I is to begin to prevent the abused daughter from becoming a lifelong "victim." Through family sessions during Stage I, the child is encouraged to be assertive, and the father is encouraged to take responsibility for the sexual abuse. This combination allows both of them to begin a new relationship that approximates father and daughter relationships in nonabusing families. This can best be accomplished during entire-family sessions because the others can provide help, reassurance, and love during these sometimes difficult encounters. Another reason is to model this "new" relationship between father and daughter for the rest of the family, particularly other siblings, who can see that they never need be lifelong victims, but can indeed be effectively assertive when necessary.

Marital Sessions

One excellent use of marital sessions is to help reduce the denial inevitably present in one or both of the parents. In essence, one partner is used to "work on" the other. For example, if the father is denying facts, the mother can be encouraged to take a stand which supports the facts and her daughter, while showing her husband that she can do so and still love and support him in other ways. Also, the father may be introduced to the concept of his abuse of power in the marriage. When denial is not the major issue, marital sessions are used to reinforce the parents as the "executive subsystem" from which the family operates. Quite often in incestuous families the marriage does not provide nurturance and support and the partners feel isolated or estranged from one another. Stage I marital sessions allow for assessment of this possibility and for the creation of the context for change in the marriage to begin to meet these fundamental needs of both partners.

Sibling Sessions

Often forgotten during the early "crisis" stages of incest therapy, the children as a subsystem are often in need of attention by the therapist. During Stage I the therapist assesses what each knows and does not know about the incest; if the siblings do not fully understand, the therapist may explain it to them, especially if the parents are unable or unwilling to do so. The therapist also focuses on the anger the siblings may have for the father, the mother, or the abused child herself. It is not uncommon, for example, for the siblings to blame their sister for their family being separated. The therapist must always be alert to denial on the part of the children, and should confront that denial directly during this stage of therapy.

The nonabused siblings often suffer from a type of "survivor guilt." Another important purpose in having sibling therapy sessions is to help them process their own guilt and remorse. They also may suffer from anxiety, particularly from two sources. First, they may have felt distressed while wondering, "Will I be the next to be abused?" Second, if they had known about the abuse while it was occurring but could do nothing about it, they may have felt anxious about maintaining the secret.

Individual Sessions

As in the marital sessions, one of the most important purposes of individual sessions is to address the denial more directly than is possible in subsystem or whole family therapy. Individual sessions also permit assessment of areas that are difficult to assess with other family members present. For example, the sexual fantasies of the father can usually only be evaluated individually. As another example, issues regarding the father's misuse of "power" can often only be addressed in his individual sessions, because to do so with the rest of the family present would reduce his power! It is difficult for many people to display their vulnerabilities to those closest to them. During this assessment period it is essential to allow "private time" so the individuals can express these feelings completely and without fear of "systemic reprisal." And even though this is a family-oriented treatment program, it is important for individuals to feel that their integrity is supported. Having individual sessions during Stage I reaffirms this.

COMPONENTS OF STAGE I THERAPY

There are a number of components addressed during Stage I of therapy. These include creating a therapeutic environment conducive to treating incestuous families, intervening upon resistance to therapy, and developing specific interventions which provide for the expectation of change (see Table 3.1). Although many of these will be explored more fully in the following chapters (see Pretreatment Planning [4]; First Clinical Sessions [5]; Clinical Assessment [6]; Denial [7]; Structural Session [8]; and Apology Session [9]), some specific interventions to meet these goals include the following:

TABLE 3.1
Stage 1 Interventions and Specialized Sessions

Intervention	*Purpose*
— Interaction with outside systems	— Assure these systems will work with the therapist to effect change
— Joining the family	— Reduce resistance, allow for more accurate assessment
— No-Violence contract	— Clarify the seriousness with which violence will be taken, formalize consequences
— Creating a workable reality	— Encourage family to see themselves as changeable; create a sense of hope
— Pretreatment planning and first clinical sessions	— Provide clarity, structure, appropriate boundaries among various "systems"
— Clinical assessment	— Evaluate the family's vulnerability to incest, common precipitating events, and coping mechanisms
— Therapeutic contract	— Set realistic goals for family
— Challenging and confronting denial	— Reduce the four types of denial: fact, awareness, responsibility, and impact
— Structural session	— Provide an explanation for the incest in a language the family can understand
— Negative consequences of change	— Restrain change to paradoxically elicit it
— Clarifying responsibility	— Make certain the family understands that ultimate responsibility for incest lies with the father
— Enactments	— Problems are demonstrated rather than talked about, allowing for greater input by the therapist
— Positive connoting/reframing	— Reduce resistance and denial; create a more positive therapeutic environment
— Apology session	— Clarify responsibility; express hope, which acts as a milestone, whose passing permits the entrance to Stage II

Larger-system structural interventions. An important element of Stage I is to utilize the "other systems" involved with the families, such as protective services, legal, probation, school, and so forth. These systems can powerfully impact the therapy program, and it is an essential goal of Stage I to make that impact a positive one. Therapists should regard their interactions with these other systems as part of the program and should design ways to "intervene" effectively with these other systems (see Chapter 4).

The design of the program itself. Although seemingly tautological, the design of the incest treatment program itself contributes to the Stage I goal of "Creating a Context for Change." For example, the decision to focus on entire *family* treatment not only reflects an important philosophical underpinning, but also reduces resistance, creates a positive context for change, and allows for more flexibility in interventions. The program is designed to communicate therapeutic competence, to provide a format that has proven successful to others, and to create a therapeutic structure that can serve as a model for strengthening the family's *own* structure (see Chapter 4).

Joining the family. The concept of *joining,* first described by Minuchin (1974), implies acceptance of and accommodation to the family, their style, and their values. Of course, with incestuously abusing families this must be done carefully, without accidentally joining those factors contributing to the abuse. However, the basic joining techniques which leave a family with the feeling that their therapist understands and likes them are kept intact and used therapeutically (see Chapter 5).

No-Violence contract. A No-Violence contract is made with the family to emphasize the seriousness with which the therapist will take any violent acts within the family during the course of treatment. Also, the signing of a contract is a ritual which accentuates the consequences that will ensue if an act of violence should take place. Finally, the contract itself implies that family members have *control* of their actions. The victim also signs a contract for protection. An example of a No-Violence contract is provided in Figure 3.1.

Creating a workable reality. It is very important that incest families can see themselves as *changeable.* That is, in the midst of crisis, confusion, and fear, they must be given "an out." This out is provided by the therapist in the form of: (1) positive expectations regarding the outcome of therapy; and (2) a new way of looking at their own family that seems reasonable and possible. This "upbeat" approach may seem inappropriate to those who see the purpose of incest therapy as primarily punitive. However, we feel it is essential to Stage I to ultimately effect meaningful change (see Chapter 5).

Pretreatment planning and first clinical sessions. The context for change is created immediately upon referral of the case. The success of the case is often dependent upon how well the therapist works with the other

I ________________ agree not to inflict any damage physically or sexually on any person, particularly in my family, or on myself. This includes no hitting, kicking, biting, throwing objects, scratching, or excessive yelling or name calling. I will not destroy any property of mine or of anyone else.

When I feel as though I may become violent I will (to be filled in by client with appropriate strategies determined in therapy session)

____

____

____

I also agree on the method which my spouse has chosen as a way to protect her/himself in the case where I threaten violence by action or word. Her/his actions of protection will not cause me to threaten or be further violent.

If I become violent at any time, defined by the conditions above, I then agree to do one or more of the following:

____

____

____

____

(examples might be to pay restitution, to call the police, to move out, to be hospitalized)

I am signing this of my own free will.

Signature ________________________

Date ________________________

Witnesses ________________________

____

Figure 3.1. No-Violence Contract.

agencies involved with the family, how clearly defined everyone's roles are, and how understandably the program is explained to the family. Therapists who do not carefully weave each "system" into the therapeutic process often pay for it later with highly resistant families (see Chapters 4 and 5).

Clinical assessment. During Stage I the therapist and family enter into a formal "assessment contract," during which time all elements of the family are evaluated for their vulnerability to incest, the precipitating factors present before incestuous episodes, and the family's coping skills. After the assessment, the therapist reports her findings to the family, and then discusses with them whether or not she feels she can help them. The family members also decide whether they wish to continue in the program, given what will need to be done to reduce their vulnerability (see Chapter 6).

Therapeutic contract. If the family agrees to stay in therapy, a session is set aside to develop a therapeutic contract. This is begun by asking the family for the one thing they wish *not* to change in their family (de Shazer, 1985). This approach begins the contract process positively and acknowledges that the family recognizes there are things about the family that they would rather not change. After that, each member states his or her own goals for therapy and the goals that "outside systems" would have for them (e.g., for mother to be able to protect her daughter from further abuse). Any goals the therapist may have are also incorporated. The family then contracts with the therapist for four or five sessions, after which time everyone reevaluates the progress that has been made. This process of recontracting should occur throughout therapy, as it gives the family an important element of control in their counseling.

Denial. During Stage I, one of the most important elements that must be addressed is denial. The four types—denial of facts, denial of awareness, denial of responsibility, and denial of impact—are all assessed and challenged by the therapist. To restrict the denial of facts is considered essential for Stage I to be complete; the other three should also be reduced. A series of direct and indirect interventions are used to achieve this important goal (see Chapter 7).

Structural session. The structural session formally begins to answer the common question, "How did this happen to us?" by providing a framework for the abuse in a language the family can understand. The therapist didactically presents family diagrams which illustrate family "structures" commonly exhibited by sexually abusing families. Through the use of visual metaphor, the family and therapist have a common basis for discussing the changes that will be necessary for the family not to be incestuous again (see Chapter 8).

Negative consequences of change. Sessions are held when all members have the opportunity to explore the question: "What will be the negative consequences of your family changing?" Each of the goals that have been set down in the therapeutic contract are questioned with regard to their negative consequences. For example, one negative consequence of the incestuous activity between the father and daughter might be that the daughter will get less "special favors" than she had when her father felt compelled to purchase her silence. And while most family members insist that whatever negative consequences might be present are totally outweighed by the positive consequences, the therapist should still somberly predict that these negative consequences must be understood and respected. This intervention, which can be used throughout treatment, allows the therapist to "restrain change," which paradoxically can result in the family demanding change even faster.

In the following illustration the therapist explores the negative consequences of a change of parenting styles:

Therapist: You know, if you two became closer and began to parent more effectively and as a unit, I could see how that change would affect a lot of people, and not all positively.

Father: I don't see what you mean. How could it not be positive for everyone involved?

Therapist (to Father): Well, let's look at you, for example. What would change for you that might not be positive? You'd have to be at home more, right?

Mother: Yeah, no more stopping off at the bar on your way home from work. You might need to call me from work sometimes during the day so I can ask your opinion on some matter with the kids.

Therapist: Exactly, I see you understand what I mean, Jean.

Father: I think I get it.

Therapist: What else can you come up with, Lou?

Father: Well, that's a biggy right there, being around more. Let's see, I'd have to control my temper because Jean doesn't like to hit the kids. We always disagree on that one. I guess we'd have to spend a lot more time talking about these things . . . not that that would be bad, but it would be different, and we could end up fighting and making matters worse.

Therapist: You got it. Now do you see why sometimes people would rather stay the same than risk changing? It's safer. How about you, Jean, any ideas?

Mother: I suppose we could find out we could never agree, then we'd have to decide what to do. You know . . .

Therapist: I wonder if you think that that will be the negative consequence of therapy all together—that through this process you'll find out that you two can't get it together on most things, and that you'll end up divorced.

Mother: I think about it all the time. I wonder if we shouldn't have been already.

(Later in the session the therapist asks Jean about her family's involvement in the crisis.)

Therapist: How about your mother, Jean, when you and Lou can't handle the kids, or are in one of your fights . . . or even right now, where is Jackie (the victim) placed?

Mother: At my mom's.

Therapist: So what happens if you start parenting well together and stop having all these crises, and Lou stops abusing your kids? What will your mother do for a job?

Mother: I guess she will be unemployed (*laughs*).

Therapist: Sounds like it. So you can understand that even though she wants the best for you, she might not be in such a hurry for you to take over your own life. What will she do with hers?

Mother: Good question. She spends most of her time running all of her adult children's lives. Geez, I never thought of all this before.

Therapist: Part of this will have to be finding your mother another way to be involved in your life that doesn't hurt you or make you feel incompetent. And Lou, your friends stand something to lose, too, if you start working with your wife and parenting more.

Father: Like you said, I'd probably be hanging out with them a whole lot less.

Therapist: And you can be sure that they will try to talk you out of going home or into going with them and to forget the family. They will want the "old Lou" back and fight hard for him. Jean, you are not used to fighting hard or fighting clean . . . it isn't going to be easy. And Lou, you don't usually act worth fighting for. You two have an awful lot of "negative consequences." I think we can agree with all of these that you can't jump into any of this too fast.

Father: I don't understand, we are coming here to change and now you are telling us to stay the same (*laughs*) . . . make up your mind, lady!

Therapist: I am telling you both, with all the risks, that you are the ones who have to make up your minds.

Responsibility. Our program makes a clear distinction between *cause* and *responsibility,* and while we see the causes of incest to be many (see

Chapter 2), we see the ultimate responsibility for the abuse lying with the offending parent. In addition to making that assumption clear throughout Stage I, we make direct and indirect interventions which focus the responsibility of the abuse on the father, while beginning to extricate the victim and mother from those feelings of responsibility that they may harbor. It should be understood that many families do not fully accept during Stage I of treatment the notion that the father was ultimately responsible; it is usually well into Stage II before this is internalized by family members.

Enactments. Unlike most individually oriented therapists, who by the practical limitations imposed by one-to-one counseling must talk *about* a problem with the client, family therapists have the luxury of encouraging clients to *do* the problem behaviors right in the session. With *enactments* (Minuchin & Fishman, 1981), a therapist encourages the family to actually demonstrate the patterns of behavior that have proven dysfunctional, then suggests alternatives to adjust their interactions to more effective patterns. Although a more common intervention in Stage II of therapy, enactments can be useful during Stage I to help the family and therapist begin to identify those patterns contributing to the family's problems.

An enactment is quite simple to begin. The therapist simply redirects a discussion back to the family and tells them to talk to each other rather than to the therapist. The therapist may also encourage the family to "Do what you do at home," and may even advise individuals to say things that may lead to a conflict.

For example, in this particular session the family has discussed how the mother and her daughter seem to fight continuously, and how the mother "shuts her daughter out" if the daughter does not agree with what she says. The mother sees the daughter as a big mouth, smart alec, and disrespectful kid. The daughter views the mother as rigid, punitive, and cold. Through the enactment the therapist looks for recurring dysfunctional communication patterns that take place between the mother and her daughter. The therapist also looks for an opportunity to build a workable reality from which to effect change.

Therapist: I know what I am about to ask you to do is going to be very difficult because it appears that you two don't like talking to each other. But I really want to see how the problem happens. Joan, can you tell your daughter what behaviors you see as disrespectful?

Mother: She is constantly telling me what I don't do right and how I should change what I'm doing. She tells me how to raise the other kids.

Therapist: Talk with her, I know it is tempting to tell me.

Mother: She's heard it all before.

Therapist: I know, but just try so I can see how it happens.

Mother: I am sick and tired of you thinking you always know more than me. You don't. I'm not sure what you know. I can handle my family myself. I don't need your help with my kids or with my husband.

Daughter: If you can handle everything so well, how come the family is falling apart? Anyway, make up your mind, either you want my help or you don't.

Mother: What do you mean?

Daughter: You're always telling me to do everything for you. I feel like I am the mother and then when I start being the mother you get mad.

Therapist: Sounds confusing.

Daughter: Damn right it is.

Mother: Can't a mother get some help from her oldest child?

Daughter: Yeah, but then don't kick me in the face for it!

Mother: Don't kick me in the teeth for asking!

Therapist: (*after a long pause*) Believe it or not this is helpful. (*Both look at the therapist puzzled.*) I understand a lot of things just from the past five minutes. First of all, you both have the same goal—trying to give the family what is best. You both care a lot about the well-being of the family, and you both want to be good at providing the strength, guidance, and love. I know you don't believe me but from where I sit it's obvious that you both have the best of intentions. It's also obvious that you are competing for the title of mother.

Daughter: I don't want the stupid title of "mother," she can have it, but she'd better stop demanding things from me.

Mother: There she goes again with that smart mouth, telling me what I should and shouldn't do.

Therapist: Hold it. You two are going to have to figure out a way to do this thing together. You agree that you both want what is best for the family? (*Both nod their heads.*) And you certainly both agree that you will have to figure out another way to do this because what you are doing now is not working. It seems to only stir up more problems and bad feelings. (*Again, they both agree without hesitation.*) I believe I can help you do this if you will try to find a little patience for each other and give me some time to help you find a new style. Will you try to find new ways of being together with my help? I can't help but think you both want the other one off your back.

Mother: I can give it a try. I sure would like this family more peaceful.

Therapist: Trying is great. I can't ask for more . . . because I know if you try, something good will happen. How about you Sally?

Daughter: Sure I'll try, but I can't believe that she'll do anything different. I've been trying to get her to change for years.

Therapist: Boy, you sound like a mother there. Just agree and then we'll see what we can do.

Positive connoting/reframing. Positive connoting, or reframing, is the process by which the meaning or intention of something is changed by changing its context (Watzlawick, Weakland, & Fisch, 1974). For most clinical problems, therapists are usually quite adept at positively connoting and reframing clients' feelings and actions. Many therapists, however, are unwilling to use this intervention with incestuously abusing families, particularly the abusing fathers, for fear of sounding too accepting of the incest behavior. That is unfortunate. The selective but continued use of this intervention can be particularly useful in reducing the resistance and denial of the family, in more effectively joining the family, and in creating a positive, workable environment in which to do therapy. This intervention should begin during the first session and continue throughout the course of counseling.

Although the incestuous abuse itself should never be positively connoted, family members' motives, feelings, and nonsexual actions can be reframed by the therapist. Some examples of positive connotations that can be used include:

1. The incestuous abuse may indicate that your family loved each other too much, and so we'll have to find another way for you all to show your love.
2. Your secrecy was a way to keep your family close to each other.
3. The pain of your own childhood has closed you off from your feelings, and you have become abusive as a way—although a confused way—to get your needs and feelings met.
4. You didn't tell about having sex with your dad as a way of protecting your family.
5. You, as the mother, had limited choices when you discovered the abuse, and that's why it was so difficult to disclose it to anyone.

As can be seen, these positive connotations may fit more closely with the family's reality and also allow the therapist to view the family in a more positive, less punishing light.

The Apology Session. The Apology Session is a ritualized intervention which acts to demarcate Stage I from Stage II of the treatment program. This intervention allows family members to express their sadness, remorse, and anger about the incest, and to express their hopes about their future as a family. During this intervention, the abusing father apologizes publicly to the entire family for the facts of the abuse, and verbally takes responsibility for it. The nonabusing mother apologizes for her part in the abuse; for example, she might apologize for not encouraging the type of relationship with her daughter which would have allowed the girl to tell her when the abuse actually was occurring. The children's responses to the apology are solicited, and then the family talks about what lies ahead for them. Finally, the therapist congratulates them all for successfully completing Stage I of therapy, and previews for them the trials and joys they can expect during the next stage of their program (see Chapter 9).

4

Pretreatment Planning

Experience has shown that, for a number of reasons, it is essential for the therapist working with incest families to engage in a fair amount of pretreatment planning that is not required when treating other family disorders. These reasons include the severity of the problem itself, the number of outside agencies and persons typically involved, and the likelihood that the therapist will have to testify in a civil or criminal action. Another important reason for pretreatment planning is that there is often resistance to treatment that emerges from seemingly unlikely places; that is, from the agency in which the therapist works, and from the outside agencies with which the therapist will collaborate (Anderson & Stewart, 1983). Like therapeutic resistance, these resistances are best confronted prior to their occurrence.

Pretreatment planning refers to the activities that are involved before meeting with the family for the first time. Such activities include: the work done within the therapist's own agency to facilitate effective treatment; the relationships that are made with other agencies' personnel assigned to the case; and the initial assessment of and hypotheses about the family itself.

The therapist has certain goals that should be attained during the pretreatment phase. These are to: (1) become familiar with the details of the case and attempt to understand what the family is experiencing; (2) formulate some hypotheses about the family's vulnerability factors and possible reactions to treatment; (3) understand clearly what will be expected of him or her as the therapist; that is, is he or she expected to provide something that he cannot provide? (4) develop relationships with the other professionals assigned to the case with whom the therapist will be working intimately; (5) clarify the roles of each agency and professional and ensure the ongoing clarity of those roles.

To achieve these goals, we feel that there must be a certain program structure within the agency and that strong relationships will need to exist between that program and the outside agencies assigned to the case. Without these minimal considerations, the likelihood of resistance from within and without are increased greatly, worsening the prognosis for the family in therapy.

STRUCTURE WITHIN THE AGENCY

Most incest treatment programs reside within an agency setting. This could be a community mental health center, hospital, educational institution, private counseling service, or church-sponsored family counseling center. It is more rare to find private practitioners providing extensive family therapy for incest, since it usually requires a great amount of extra time and resources that are often unavailable to those working alone.

Using a "Program" Model

Most working in the field suggest a "program" approach to treating incest (e.g., Giaretto, 1982; James & Nasjileti, 1983; Justice & Justice, 1979; Kempe & Kempe, 1984; Mayer, 1983), rather than the less planned approach that experienced therapists use in treating not-as-difficult cases. A program approach means that the therapist subscribes to a specific etiological paradigm, uses a fairly standard assessment strategy, and follows a generally prescribed treatment protocol. Of course, even with a program approach, therapists should adapt therapy to the needs of the individual family.

There are obvious benefits to using a program approach, including facility in training new therapists, the ability to evaluate the program consistently (and alter as needed), and to allow for common communication and comparison among therapists working in the program. There is another, more strategic reason to use a program approach. The family entering a therapy *program* has the sense that this is a more formalized and thus serious clinical experience than might be otherwise felt when simply "in counseling." The term *program* carries with it an atmosphere of experience, continuity, and professionalism that can be quite important when dealing with potentially resistant or more seriously dysfunctional clients.

Team Approach

Just as it is clinically useful to employ a program approach, it is equally useful to employ a *team* approach within the agency. Treating incest families carries with it a certain challenge that other cases do not. To prevent therapist burnout, to allow for creative treatment planning, and to encourage a sense of camaraderie which can help dissipate the massive frustrations common for incest therapists, it is recommended that an "incest team" be formed within the agency.

Ideally membership on this team should be voluntary and should be made up of experienced family therapists. It should also have a clear team leader or supervisor who is experienced in the family treatment of incest and, of course, for whom the team has respect. The staff needs to have a sense that they are working with others in a supportive context.

The team should be somewhat independent from the rest of the agency, with policies and procedures that make sense for the type of work it will be doing. We do not think it is wise for members of the team to treat incest cases only; that could be overpowering.

Finally, team members should have somewhat smaller caseloads, since working with large numbers of abusing families can become overwhelming. At the very least, the agency should have a mechanism for applying to the therapist's workload utilization credit for nondirect service relating to the case, such as meetings with protective service workers and phone calls to attorneys.

Training and Supervision

Because of the severity of incestuous abuse and the special needs of therapists providing services, the agency should supply training and supervision experiences for the team members. This can include providing time off and registration fees for local workshops and conferences on the treatment of incestuous abuse, or bringing in professionals who are experts in the field. Although there is an expense associated with such training and supervision, it is essential if the program and team are to be able to provide these difficult clinical services in an ethical and competent manner.

Strategies for Implementing

If an agency has a commitment to treating incest families, either by mandate or interest, it should not be terribly difficult to develop a program, form a team, and begin to see families. Incest families are usually not considered the most desirable clients in many agencies, and those who show an interest in treating them will certainly not be discouraged. More difficult will be to obtain support from the agency in reducing caseloads of team members, in receiving special training, and in relaxing some of the agency procedures that may impede treatment.

There are a number of ways to gain intra-agency support for the program. An important first step is to make the team a distinct unit within the agency. This can be accomplished through informal discussions with other staff members and formal presentations on incest treatment by the team to the agency as a whole. Another way is to demonstrate to the agency's administration the benefits of providing these extras, especially in terms of retaining therapists and reducing the likelihood of malpractice litigation resulting from inexperienced therapists dealing with potentially volatile cases. Finally, support will be ensured if the program can bring in its own funding, which is often available from local and state departments of public welfare to ongoing child abuse treatment programs.

RELATIONSHIPS WITH OUTSIDE SYSTEMS

One aspect of treating abusing families that is different from treating other families is that it is a certainty that the therapist will have to work with professionals from other agencies and institutions. Because intrafamily child sexual abuse is illegal in all jurisdictions, the local police, district or city attorney, and criminal court can all be involved. And because a child's safety and welfare are at risk, the local child protective service, juvenile court, and an attorney *ad litem* will likely be assigned to the case. And because of the severity or notoriety of many abuse cases, the local school district, private attorneys, and even news organizations may have an impact on the therapist's work with the family. For the therapist to assume there will be the private, independent, and confidential relationship that is a given in most counseling activities is erroneous and naive.

Potential Problems when Working with Outside Systems

Although each professional assigned to the case is ultimately working for the ongoing and future protection of the abused child, the formal role of each is different and sometimes even adversarial. For example, the clinician should understand that his or her role as family therapist, which may include a goal of keeping the family united, may be in conflict with the district attorney, whose goal may be to prosecute the offending father. This is not a personal affront to the therapist, nor a rejection of the therapist's "values." It is simply the *role* of a district attorney to prosecute and convict those who violate the law.

Problems often emerge based on *informal* roles and relationships, as well as from a misunderstanding or insensitivity to the work in which the other professional engages. We have known therapists who see child protection workers as the "enemy," who never want to reunite families or believe that therapy can make lasting changes. And we have known an equal number of child protection workers who view therapists as the "enemy," who are naive in their belief of the offending parent who promises never to do it again, and who are willing to risk the protection of a child to justify their own philosophical orientation. Of course, both of these positions are inaccurate. More significantly, however, these stereotypes lead to dissidence between two professionals who should be acting as colleagues on the same "team" instead of mirroring the conflictual styles of the abusing families.

Essentials for Working with Outside Systems

It is critical that therapists do whatever is needed to prevent unnecessary antagonism with case workers, lawyers, police, and the rest. Moreover, if the therapists properly plan it, they can turn potential resistance into support for their treatment plan.

The key to achieving this is to *make the other professionals from outside institutions a part of the treatment team*. Most of these workers will be flattered to be included and will prize the opportunity to do "intervention." For example, protective services workers, who often have large case loads and often feel ineffective in helping families, usually appreciate being included in the treatment planning and implementation and enjoy seeing the changes that occur as a result of therapy.

The simplest way to include the other professionals is to schedule regular team meetings with them. These meetings should be treatment focused, and the "outside" members should be made to feel like insiders. Although these outside professionals are a working part of the team, it is still the therapist's responsibility to organize the overall treatment strategies, including how to effectively "use" these new team members. The therapist might arrange a meeting in the following manner:

Therapist: I was hoping that you would help me in organizing a meeting to gather all the professionals together who are involved in the Jones's case. The idea of another meeting makes me ill, too, but the idea of four hostile phone calls and subsequent meetings sounds even worse to me. I would like for all of us to get together to avoid future problems on the case and certainly avoid misunderstandings. I want us to get clear on each other's roles and for you to know a little about the treatment. I also would love to hear any information you have that might be helpful to the treatment. I also need to know what you are expecting of me in order for me to be helpful to you. All I need from you now are some dates, times, and places, and I can set up the meeting and someone will get back to you.

To effectively work with outside systems, the therapist will have to do the following during the pretreatment sessions:

Define the roles of each agency involved. Nothing can lead to a therapy failure more quickly than a family "triangulating" the therapist and one of the outside agencies, usually protective services. This means the family may, in a nonconscious but isomorphic fashion, interfere with the defined roles of each. For example, a family member may call the therapist and say, "My caseworker says its totally up to you when my child can come home."

The following is a list of questions that might be helpful in defining the different roles of the professionals involved in the case:

1. How often will the caseworker visit the family?
2. Who needs to be at the different court appearances? Do the reports need to be verbal or written?
3. Who is going to communicate with the foster parents about their role?
4. Who is going to facilitate services for the family (i.e., public aid, job placement, and medical services)?
5. How will the different family visits be orchestrated and who is responsible for supervising these visits?

6. What have the different professionals told the family about therapy?
7. How often does this group want to have communication with one another and in what form?

Understand their belief systems. Just as it is important to assess the belief system of a family in therapy, it is equally important to assess the belief systems of the other professionals and agencies working on the case. What do they believe is the "cause" of incestuous abuse? Are fathers "always at fault" or are daughters "usually seductive"? How is reunification of the family viewed? Should mothers be counseled toward eventual divorce, since "incest fathers can never change," or should the goal always be reunification because the "sanctity of the family is always paramount"? And how is the therapist viewed? As "naive and always taking the side of the family"? Or as a "colleague"?

An accurate interpretation of the other workers' belief systems will allow the therapist to develop a strategy for working with them. For example, if the caseworker has the following belief constellation: (a) fathers are always at fault; (b) mothers should be encouraged to divorce their abusing husbands; and (c) therapists are bleeding hearts who always get suckered into believing the father will change; then the therapist will have to "intervene" with the caseworker. The therapist might ask what the caseworker will need to feel comfortable that these beliefs are not accurate and will not materialize. The therapist might also supply the caseworker with information that will refute these beliefs. Or, more strategically, the therapist might encourage the caseworker to keep a log of all his or her concerns regarding the case, and to call the therapist with these concerns on a weekly basis.

The following is an excerpt from a pretreatment planning meeting where a therapist is sharing her belief system with a group of professionals involved with a case:

Therapist: (*to group*) I want to let you know a little about how I see the problem of incest. I hope it will be helpful for you in understanding what clients are talking about when they discuss their therapy, as well as understanding some of the techniques utilized in our treatment program. I also think if we know a little bit about each other and how we each see the problem of incest in general, it might prevent any future problems or misrepresentations. I know we will differ and I think that is fine. Hopefully, we can model for the family how to "agree to disagree" and how to do it constructively and respectfully. Like in incest families, when you don't do it exactly as the family expects, you can be totally abandoned. I guess I just shared one of my beliefs right there.

Clarify their working hypotheses for this family. Most professionals, despite their overall belief systems concerning incestuous abuse, develop specific hypotheses for each family regarding the causes of, maintenance of, and ways to stop the incest. It is the therapist's responsibility during this pretreatment period to understand these hypotheses and to augment them with his own. This is done so that what will evolve is a treatment plan accepted by all, and not subject to the sabotage possible when "teammates" quietly disagree with each other.

The skill of the therapist, of course, is to obtain this conceptual agreement among everyone without forcing one view on anyone. To do this, the therapist may have to go "indirect"; that is, use a more strategic approach with the other professional. This is not dissimilar to a therapist gaining support from a family for an unpopular or counterintuitive intervention by using an intervention that is not explained fully to the family.

There are many indirect techniques a therapist might use. The therapist might try "the illusion of alternatives," where only two options are presented—one unsatisfactory to everyone, the other option the one the therapist would like to see used; playing "one down," in which the therapist, claiming to have tried everything he or she knows, then asks the caseworker for a suggestion, which usually will be the idea the therapist had and the caseworker resisted in the first place; or getting the other professional to play "good guy, bad guy" (Anderson & Stewart, 1983), where the therapist takes the "good guy" position and asks the caseworker if he or she would "mind" taking the other side, the "bad guy" position, for therapeutic purposes only. The following excerpt is an example of an initial phone call with a department of social service worker.

Therapist: (*to caseworker*) Tell me what you know about the Jones's and how you see the family having gotten themselves into this. I really do want your opinion. You are the professional who knows the most about them at this point. I'd be interested in your view of each family member and how they fit into the problem, and what you think they do to maintain their difficulties. Do you know how they're feeling about therapy? What type of crisis has the discovery led to? Have they "shut off" from the outside world, or are they in enough pain that they want help?

After the therapist has heard the caseworker's views but is aware that the two do not share the same conceptual framework, she says:

Therapist: Your information is terrifically helpful. Many of the things you said I might not have seen in that light. It is probably good that you and I come from different perspectives as well as different work contexts. It will be really helpful later on in therapy, or if the family is resistant for a prolonged period of time, for us to split our roles, with you taking the "hard guy" position based on your agency's role and me taking the "good guy" role. What I mean by this is I can keep them motivated and connected to me based on the fact that I can help them through the bureaucratic mess, and you can push them to stay "with the program."

Clarify their expectations for the therapist. The therapist sometimes finds him- or herself in the unpleasant situation of being expected to do things that are "not in the job description." This may include being a formal or informal investigator for protective services and the courts, making the final decisions as to when the child can be returned home, or being asked to make visitation or even custody decisions. The therapist may also be expected to provide transportation for families in treatment and to make arrangements with schools, foster parents, and employers for time off for family counseling. We believe these are usually inappropriate expectations for a therapist, but they can often informally creep into place. The therapist should clarify the expectations for and among each of the professionals working with the family, and also: articulate the realistic goals of therapy; set timetables for visitation and eventual reunification; plan procedures for reporting the family's progress in therapy.

The following questions must be answered for the clinician to clearly understand his or her role beyond that of "therapist."

1. Is the investigation over, or is the therapist still expected to investigate the incest?
2. Is the therapist expected to testify in court, and whose side is he or she expected to be on?
3. Will the therapist be responsible for the decision regarding reunification of the family?
4. Is the therapist expected to do any transporting of children or family members?
5. What role in the coordination of services is the therapist supposed to have?

6. What does each professional in the case expect can and will occur as a result of therapy? What do they think change will look like for this family?
7. How informed do people want to be of the therapeutic process and the meeting of or failure to meet therapeutic goals?

Obtain court documents and orders for the family. Although the therapist does not usually work for the court, therapy is often court-ordered, and court-mandated decisions for the family will often impinge upon the success of therapy. It is therefore quite important for the therapist to understand fully the court orders and expectations right from the beginning. These documents can usually be obtained through the caseworker, but often there is an attorney *ad litem* representing the children who may be monitoring the success of treatment. Another reason for the therapist to be aware of the specifics of the court orders is that sometimes the court will "forget" about a case that is in treatment, believing that the therapist will be effectively monitoring the family. The therapist has a powerful therapeutic "motivator" in the court order, and this should not be ignored. Many a resistant family has been "helped along" by the reminder that a court order exists and that the therapist will have to exercise his or her responsibility if the family is uncooperative.

The answers to the following questions regarding the court will need to be answered for therapy to begin:

1. What is the court involvement in the case? Is it being presented in juvenile court, family court, criminal court, or all three?
2. Is there going to be a trial? Has there been a trial? And, if so, what kind of trial—with a judge or a jury?
3. If there are criminal charges, who filed them?
4. Is there any pertinent information from the court proceedings that would be helpful (e.g., in one case the offender had a gun in the court room and threatened the bailiff)?
5. Did the offender serve any time in jail, or is he currently incarcerated?
6. What information is there about the judge on the case and his or her previous record with child sexual abuse cases?
7. Is therapy mandated in the court order?

Assess the level of commitment to solving problems which may arise. The other professionals working with the therapist on an incestuous abuse case are as busy, if not busier, than the therapist. (We know of case workers, for example, who have ongoing case loads of over 200 families!) And like all professionals, some manage their time better than others. The therapist should assess how able, interested, or committed the other person is to working with the therapist to solve the various problems that will arise during the course of treatment. The possible range is from extreme interest and involvement on the "team" to benign neglect. Many caseworkers, for example, will appear extremely committed to working with the therapist, attending team meetings, providing current reports, and so on; however, when it comes down to it, they are rarely available. Once the level of involvement of each outside worker is understood, the therapist can make realistic decisions about how to effectively utilize each outside person on their "treatment team."

Therapist: I feel like we really accomplished a lot by talking with each other. I feel much better about us working together and much less alone with respect to this case. I see how this hour is going to save us a great deal of time in the future. How do you think we should keep this communication going?

Attorney: You aren't talking about another meeting?

Therapist: Not necessarily. I just don't want any of us to run into any surprises. One thing we did on another case I was working on was that we all got releases and that we mailed each other information that we might be writing up for other purposes. So, for example, my quarterly reports could go to all of you. Certainly before any court dates I think we all need to talk. I hope I am preventing extra work, not creating it.

LIVING ARRANGEMENTS OF FAMILY MEMBERS

A common practice upon the discovery of intrafamily child sexual abuse is the separation of the abused child from her abusing parent. One of the important pretreatment tasks is to decide the short- and long-term living arrangements of family members. Although these decisions are usually made by the court and protective services, the therapist usually has an influence on that decision and therefore should have an opinion about these living arrangements.

Father Removed from the Home

This is the most common arrangement in many areas of the country. Its appeal is obvious. The father is the offender, so he should be the one who should suffer the most by a change of residence. In this arrangement, he will have the "burden of proof" that he has sufficient amount of change in order for him to return home. Also, if there is any community embarrassment resulting from a change in domicile, he should be the family member to experience it.

There are negative factors associated with the removal of the father from the home. Some families will allow him to return and then lie to the therapist and caseworker about it. Of equal concern is the father who returns home against the will of the family, but threatens them in some way if they reveal the fact; this, of course, puts the abused daughter at even greater risk and maintains the father's abusive role in the family. Finally, there is often an increased financial burden placed on the family if the father, who is often the sole provider, must now pay for a second dwelling. This is a significant concern since many abusing families who come to the attention of social service agencies have significant financial problems.

Child Removed from the Home

Many jurisdictions around the country remove the abused child, and sometimes other children in the family, rather than force the father to leave. It is hoped that by doing this the problems associated with removal of the offending father can be alleviated. Unfortunately, there are also serious problems associated with the removal of the child.

First and foremost, although there are many fine foster placements, it is not unheard of for foster homes to be abusing homes as well (Pagelow, 1984). To move a child from one abusing home to another should be unthinkable, but it does unfortunately occur. There are also nonabusive traumas to a child by removing her from her own home, including separation from her family, adjustment to the adults in the new home, and sometimes being placed in a new school and community (Turbett, 1979). Of equal concern is the subtle message given the child that somehow the abuse was her fault, a message that cannot help but be communicated when it is she who is plucked from her home and placed in that of a stranger.

Both Father and Child Removed from the Home

In rare cases, the decision is made to remove both father and child(ren) from their home. This is done in cases where there has been severe abuse, the father and mother deny the facts of the abuse, and the mother is deemed unable to protect her child or the other children from further abuse. The same negatives apply to this condition as to each of the ones above, except that protection of the child from the offending father is virtually guaranteed in this case.

Remove No One from the Home

Increasingly, jurisdictions are experimenting with the option of not removing anybody from the home. One of the main reasons for this option, other than to reduce the negatives associated with each of the other options, is that foster placement is more expensive than intensive family therapy; moreover, it is becoming increasingly more difficult to find adequate foster placements (Pagelow, 1984). Keeping the family intact could be considered if each of the following conditions exist: if the facts are admitted by all; if the mother is seen as able to protect the child if further abuse were to occur; if the abuse was of less intensity and/or of short duration; if it is felt that there is virtually no possibility that sexual abuse will occur again; if there is no alcohol or substance abuse; if there are no suicidal threats or ideation by any of the family members; if the family is committed to therapy and the therapist feels she can effectively monitor the family; and most important, if the child feels safe in her home.

Reuniting a Family

In cases where the family has been separated for a time but has been progressing through therapy successfully, the decision will need to be made when they can reunite. Our program is somewhat different than most in that it encourages the reuniting of families as early as possible. While we do not wish to put the child in any danger of further sexual or emotional abuse, we do try to get the families living together if that is what they wish, both as individuals as well as a group.

This is done for several reasons. First, we are cognizant of the terrible emotional, systemic, and financial strain placed on a family and its members when they are separated from one another. We do not wish the "cure" to be worse than the "disease." Second, since most of our goals are systemic ones, the family can best "practice" the changes made as a result of therapy *as* a family. Third, for most families, reuniting is a reward and, like all reinforcers, must be administered when the desired behavior is exhibited. If families are indeed making major changes in their patterns of behavior that made them vulnerable to incestuous abuse, they should be "rewarded" with reunification. Finally, if the family wishes to reunite, they will, in spite of what therapists and caseworkers think, especially if the family perceives the length of time spent apart to be unfair. It is far better to use reunification as a "carrot" than to threaten the "stick" if the family members get back together too soon.

Certain decision rules are used by therapists to form a judgment on whether a family can be reunited. Each of the following conditions should be met in therapy before the family is reunified:

1. The child verbalizes in individual sessions on a number of occasions that she feels safe from further abuse in her home.
2. The child has and can implement a safety plan. For example, she will tell *both* her mother and grandmother immediately if she feels threatened or is abused again.
3. This safety plan can be verified by the therapist.
4. The factors contributing to the family's vulnerability to incest are understood and accepted by the family.
5. A major change in the precipitating factors has occurred; for example, if alcohol use by the offending father was a precipitant, he no longer drinks.
6. There is no denial of the facts of the abuse by any member of the family.
7. There is a lessening in the other types of denial: awareness, responsibility, and impact.
8. Mother is seen as able to protect her children from further abuse.
9. The incestuous abuse is no longer a secret in the family, and important extended family members also are aware of its occurrence.

The therapist should make certain that the family understands that reunification does not have to be permanent. Many families who have been reunited later make the decision to separate. The family should, as much as possible, be encouraged to make their own decisions, to feel safe, and to maintain their dignity.

5

The First Clinical Sessions

The first clinical sessions with the family are actually an outgrowth of the pretreatment planning that has already occurred. If the therapist has the cooperation of the other agencies involved with the case, has an understanding of the details surrounding the abuse, and has some initial working hypotheses about the family's dynamics, then the first clinical sessions will merely be a continuation of "treatment." It is only when the therapist has failed to obtain these important prerequisites that the first sessions will seem formidable and awkward.

GOALS OF THE FIRST CLINICAL SESSIONS

There are four goals of the initial clinical sessions. These are somewhat interrelated and the attainment of one goal may lead to the attainment of another. These are: to begin to *join* with the family; to *obtain information* about the immediate needs of the individual and family system; to *provide information* to the family about the program; and to understand and manage the *crisis surrounding the discovery* of the incestuous abuse.

Joining

The notion of *joining* in family therapy was first described by Minuchin (1974), but has undoubtedly been understood and practiced by therapists since the beginnings of psychotherapy. Any family, with or without problems, will be suspicious and resistant to an outsider who attempts to change them. This is a normal and functional response. A therapist must become a *part* of the system before attempting to change the system. Family therapists use basic interpersonal counseling skills, such as to remain empathetic, to provide unconditional positive regard, to mirror self-disclosure, and to communicate acceptance and caring for the family.

Besides the application of basic counseling skills, family therapists join a family through a process of accommodating to the family system (Anderson & Stewart, 1983). This means that the therapist quickly assesses the hierarchy, the general rules, and the communication style of the family, and then adapts to their style rather than to immediately intervene and change it. For example, if the members of the family defer to the abusing father, who answers for everyone and interrupts when another is talking, it would be very tempting for the therapist to try and change this pattern immediately. However, the therapist's goal is first to join; therefore, the therapist may ask the father *more* questions and might even defer to the father in the same manner as the rest of the family. This will not be permanent; in fact, the therapist most likely will make this dysfunctional communication sequence a focus of an early intervention. If the therapist were to challenge the system too quickly, however, the family would not understand nor tolerate it, leading to more resistance and additional time in treatment.

Joining may be very easy for therapists when working with most family problems, but many find it difficult to join with incestuously abusing families. There is a tendency on the part of some therapists to challenge the family too quickly or, even worse, to forget their basic interpersonal counseling skills. If this should occur frequently, the therapist may wish to examine his own values surrounding incestuous abuse and reevaluate whether he wishes to work with incest families at all. Joining is the basic intervention necessary to working with any family, incest families included. If a therapist finds himself unable to be empathetic and provide positive regard to all, and to accommodate to the family's style as a way of accessing their system, the case will undoubtedly end in failure.

Obtaining Initial Information

During the first clinical sessions a therapist must obtain enough information to quickly answer a number of questions. These include: (1) Is anyone in the family at risk for further abuse? (2) Is anyone in need of psychiatric hospitalization, at risk for suicide, or potentially dangerous in any way to others? (3) Who can or should be seen together during these first clinical sessions? (4) How did the discovery of the abuse occur, and what have been the consequences? and (5) Who might display the most resistance to therapy?

The answers to these questions can usually be obtained through direct questioning of the family and family members. This is not a formal assessment of the family's vulnerability to incest; instead this might be seen as a thorough "intake" and assessment of their current status. The therapist will also have most of these data from the pretreatment planning sessions, and should work with the protective services worker to obtain additional information regarding the safety of the child and the specifics surrounding the discovery.

Providing the Family with Information

Another important function of the first clinical interviews is to provide the family with answers to their questions about the treatment program. Rather than give vague answers to questions like: How long therapy will last? ("As long as it is necessary") or What will happen in therapy? ("Whatever is needed for you to change"), the therapist should instead be clear and honest about what the program entails. Of course, there are many unknowns at this point in time, but there is nothing wrong with the therapist saying:

Therapist: Most of our families are in therapy for about 18 months to two years, and therapy usually entails a period of assessment, where we all learn why sexual abuse has happened in your family. After that will be the "meat and potatoes" of therapy, where you all will be expected to change some of the things that contributed to the abuse. Finally, if all goes well and you have made these changes, we will start to have fewer and fewer sessions, until we will just get together once in a while for a "checkup."

The family should also be provided with specific information concerning the roles of protective services, the court, and, of course, the therapist. The therapist can take this opportunity to clarify that he or she may be asked to go to court, and although one important role is to be the family's advocate when it is warranted, he or she may also be painfully truthful. The therapist might say:

Therapist: You, of course, would not ever want me to lie to you, and I will never lie to the court or protective services either. The credibility that I have established by being truthful at all times, even if it may "hurt" a family for the short run, may help you someday when I make a recommendation in your favor.

The Crisis of Discovery

The final goal of the first sessions is to understand and manage the crisis surrounding the discovery of the abuse. The therapist, during the pre-treatment planning sessions, usually has a fundamental understanding of how the discovery was made. What needs to be clarified is what *impact* the discovery has had on the family and how it will affect treatment.

It should be recognized that the *discovery* of the incest, and the incredible family upheaval that usually follows, often has a more profound impact than the abuse itself (Burgess, Holmstrom, & Mocausland, 1977; Tyler & Brassard, 1984). Discovery usually leads to shame in their community, the intrusion into their lives by a myriad of "helpers" who often treat the family with disdain, and a partial splitting up of the family (with all of the emotional and economic ramifications that follow). And while the incestuous abuse *indirectly* affects everyone in the family, the crisis of discovery affects each family member *directly*.

The therapist should first examine who was involved with the discovery. The most frequent source of the initial report is the child victim herself (Vander Mey & Neff, 1984). But who she told, under what conditions, and with what consequences is quite important to understand. The therapist should ask:

1. *Whom did she tell?* There are many first sources, such as the mother or other family member, an extended family member, a school counselor, or a friend. It is also possible that she did not disclose the abuse herself, but instead it was discovered by someone else.
2. *Why did she pick the person she told?* For example, if she chose to disclose to a school counselor, that may suggest she will be receptive to supportive counseling. If she told a friend, whom she swore to secrecy but who told *her* mother anyway, this may indicate a fear of reprisal or a secretive style, both of which may impede the development of a therapeutic relationship.
3. *Did she try to tell others, but was rebuffed?* The most essential concern is whether she told her mother on one or more occa-

sions, but was ignored or even punished when she did. This certainly would suggest the mother may have difficulty protecting the child from further abuse in the short run, which would probably lead to a decision to place the child in another home rather than removing the father. Occasionally, an incestuously abused child will have told another family member or friend, but her disclosure was ignored. This could suggest that the child has a history of lying, or that these others have a personal interest in protecting the status quo.

4. *Did the child plan her disclosure, or did it happen spontaneously?* If the daughter planned her revelation, this may indicate that she will be able to follow through on protection plans offered later in therapy. At the same time, a spontaneous disclosure could mean the child reached a breaking point, but also that she could recant it when the full impact of the disclosure is realized.
5.. *What are the implications of the revelation being made to an extended family member?* It could be argued that anybody to whom the child has entrusted the disclosure has *ipso factor* become a member of that system. However, when the child has chosen to tell an extended family member, such as a grandmother or aunt, the therapist must discern if this person was merely the most convenient person, or if this person has an integral part in the family's dysfunction. An extremely common situation, for example, is for the grandmother and mother to have had a long-standing conflictual relationship; this may have included arguments over the mother's choice of husband, and a questioning of her competence as a mother. When the sexual abuse is discovered, the grandmother reports it, takes the child in her home, and is often one of the most resistant family members to therapeutic intervention. In this case, the discovery and report should be understood as an isomorph of the larger systemic dysfunction.
6. *What caused the daughter to disclose the abuse when she did?* Assuming that the child wished the incest to stop from the beginning, it is important for the therapist to know what precipitated the revelation *now*. For example, to disclose because the father for the first time attempted sexual intercourse after primarily fondling his daughter is quite different from disclosing because he refused her a previously promised favor. The first example suggests a daughter who has reached her limit when the abuse took a turn that she could no longer endure; this indicates her ability to take action to meet her needs when necessary. The second

example suggests the father and daughter may have entered into a *quid pro quo*, exchanging sex for a heightened position in the family.

7. *What were the daughter's expectations regarding her disclosure and were they realized?* A daughter may have a very clear idea about what the ramifications of telling will be, or may have none at all. This depends first of all on the age of the child; obviously, the younger the child, the less she will anticipate the reactions of others. The daughter may also have believed the school counselor or the friend's mother when she was told that nothing bad would happen if the abused girl just told the truth. How did she respond, then, when based upon her disclosure, she was placed in a foster home, or her father was put in jail?
8. *What was the reaction when she made the disclosure?* Therapists working with incest families are always unhappily surprised when, rather than observing comforting and consolation of the abused child after the discovery, instead she is ostracized by the family. The child may not even be believed by all members of the family. There are many reasons this can occur. For example, the chlid and mother may have a serious ongoing conflict, or the mother may herself have been abused by the father and be afraid to support her daughter for fear of retribution. Whatever the case, it is always important for the therapist to discern if the child is being blamed for the abuse during these first sessions. This is to help the therapist decide if the child can be protected from further abuse, and to help the therapist begin to understand the complex dynamics operating in the family.
9. *What is the current status based on the discovery?* The obvious information which must be gathered is whether someone is in jail and for how long, whether the family has separated or is intending to, and where the children are living and under what conditions. A very important concern is whether *nothing* happened after the disclosure, despite the hopes of the daughter. For example, did the daughter expect that her father would be forced to leave the home, but a judge decides while the family is in therapy that the living arrangements should remain the same? And are the family systemic patterns that directed the discovery still operating (e.g., Is the daughter now living with the grandmother who made the disclosure, who has the history of long-term conflict with *her* daughter, and now refuses to let her abused granddaughter participate in family therapy)?

STRUCTURE OF THE FIRST CLINICAL SESSIONS

The management of the crisis of discovery is not unlike other family crisis intervention. The therapist should keep in mind, again, that the crisis of disclosure may be more relevant to the family than the fact that sexual abuse has occurred. The family will probably focus on practical fears and concerns, such as the living arrangements, financial obligations, and the possibility of incarceration.

The therapist must resist the temptation to move too quickly in response to a family in crisis, with multiple problems, and who is demanding an immediate fix. Instead, the message should be, "We have a lot of work to do, but we also have a lot of time; we will move one step at a time." This can be comforting to the family, but can also be frustrating. Outlining the course of treatment, with examples of other sexually abusing families who have successfully completed the program, may be helpful.

Who Should Be Seen During the First Clinical Sessions?

With the information provided during the intake process and the pretreatment planning, the therapist can be fairly certain about who should be seen for the very first session. Although ideally the entire family should be present, this is rarely possible for a variety of reasons. There are two cardinal rules which can help guide the decision, however. The first is that *a child should never be placed in the same room with a parent who is denying the facts about the abuse.* If there is any indication that this is the case, the parents should be seen without the children until more information is provided. And if there is any doubt, the second rule is *to always err on the conservative (child-protecting) side.* There will be plenty of time to see the entire family; it does not have to begin with the first session.

The therapist may have several "first sessions" to make certain everyone in the family is seen from the start. Many of the same questions will have to be asked, and the therapist will have to obtain a composite picture of the system from its component parts.

The Other Siblings

It is quite common for the parents in incestuously abusing families to insist that the other children, particularly the younger ones, do not know about the sexual abuse and wish to keep it that way. This is understandable. The abuse is both an embarrassment and potentially frightening for the other children, and if they can be protected from that pain, isn't that best?

The therapist should not attempt to force the other children to attend the first session if the parents feel strongly about it. This, after all, is the *joining* phase. The parents should be told, however, that it is the philosophy of the program that all family members must *eventually* be told, for a number of reasons.

First, the other children most often *do* know about the sexual abuse, or at least that something is seriously wrong between the offending parent and the abused child. Because children tend to "catastrophize" family problems, and because of their limited understanding of sexuality, it is likely that what they *think* happened between their father and sister is actually more extreme than what actually occurred.

Second, usually someone has been removed from the home by the state; to tell the other siblings that "Daddy and Jenny are not getting along right now, so Jenny moved into this other family's house" usually will not work with inquisitive and intelligent children. The children will continue to receive the message, "If we do not get along, or we don't do what we are told, we will be abandoned by being sent away." In most incest families, there has been a history of deceit; to continue to lie under the guise of "therapy" may communicate a contradictory message to the family and not offer the respect to the other children that they deserve.

Third, younger children particularly have a tendency to personalize crises. It is quite common for young children to believe they did something wrong to cause Daddy to leave. It is far less cruel to tell them the truth than to risk their misunderstanding and personalizing of the family's crisis.

Fourth, this is a *family* treatment program, which has as its basis many family-related activities. If everyone in the family did not know the details of the abuse, these activities would be awkward. Also, while the other siblings are not in any way responsible for the abuse, they are part of the interactional processes that may have contributed to the family's vulnerability to incest.

Finally, it is essential to know if the abuse has occurred with any of the other siblings, and the only way to know is to ask. A goal of the program is to prevent future abuse, not just of the previously abused child, but of all of the other children; and not just for now, but for when *they* are parents. For the interventions necessary for this to occur all family members must be part of the therapy.

CASE EXAMPLE

To illustrate some of the components of the first clinical sessions, let us consider the following case example.

Background information. The family was referred by the state social services department to the agency for family therapy. The father admitted to allegations of fondling, attempted oral sex, and attempted intercourse. At the time of the first clinical session the father had been incarcerated for three months, and only the mother had been permitted to visit him in jail. The mother had originally brought criminal charges against the father, but then dropped them and told her daughter not to testify in court.

The daughter had initially disclosed the abuse to the maternal grandmother. The grandmother called the local child abuse hotline, but did not tell her daughter (the mother of the child) that the abuse had happened or that she reported it. The mother found out about the abuse when the state investigators arrived at the family home.

There was juvenile court involvement, and therapy was mandated for the entire family. The father would not be able to participate in therapy until he was out of prison, except for that which he received there.

The daughter was placed in foster care because of acting-out behaviors and because of the mother's decision to drop the criminal court proceedings. It was believed that the mother may have difficulty providing protection for the child, or that she herself may possibly abuse the child.

At the time of the referral, the father was 37, the mother was 36, and the daughter was 14. There was also a 10-year-old daughter and a six-year-old son. At the time of the first session it was unknown what the other siblings knew about the sexual abuse.

The mother was always distraught during her many interviews with protective services and the state's attorney, and everyone described her as highly resistant and uncooperative. The caseworker felt the mother was cold and distant with the victim and nonprotective. The worker could not get the younger two children, who remained at home with the mother, to talk with her. They appeared to be traumatized by the breaking up of the family. After meeting the family and engaging in brief social amenities, the therapist begins informing the family about the program.

Therapist: Let me tell you a little bit about the program. This is a program that specializes in sexual abuse. We have helped a lot of families,

families that I am sure are like yours in many ways. What has happened in your family is tragic, but things can change and we will help you make these changes. Right now, it probably seems that you'll never feel good or be a family again . . . but you can. It'll take a lot of hard work and a long time, but it can happen. I don't expect you to trust me or believe me. You have no reason to; you don't know me yet. But hopefully you believe things can change . . . I do.

So today I will be telling you about our program. I'll tell you a little about myself and then you can tell me a little about who you are and what has been happening to you with respect to this crisis in your family.

First let me give you a pamphlet describing our program. (*After the family has looked over the written material*) To be accepted into our program you must agree to participate in individual, family, and group therapy. We will meet together for four weeks. In that time I will get a chance to meet with all of you individually as well as together. You will have a chance to decide if you want to work with me, and I can decide if it seems like a good match for me, too. It's important for us to be able to get along. This is going to be a long, involved relationship and if we don't get along we had better find out from the beginning. At the end of four sessions we will decide where to go from here.

Another guideline for admittance to the program is that you must attend therapy regularly. We have many families who feel capable of change and want to be in the program. So if you miss a lot of sessions, we will take it as an indication that you don't want to be with us. I would prefer that you tell me rather than just not show up.

The session continued with the therapist explaining the program in as much detail as possible and allowing ample time for questions. When it appeared that the program was understood by the family members, the therapist then began to assess the family's view of the discovery of abuse.

Therapist: (*to Mother*) You seem really angry about this whole mess. I don't blame you; it is terribly painful and disruptive to a family, and you have no idea how and if it will ever end. It must feel like a terrible nightmare with no way to wake up.

Mother: You'd be angry, too, if you were treated the way we were treated. Everyone says they want to help us and all they do is hurt us time and time again.

Therapist: And now I am saying that I want to help you. I guess it makes it pretty hard to believe. How has everyone hurt you?

Mother: Where should I start? My mother said she wanted to help, so she doesn't tell me what she's doing and I find out by having state investigators show up at my door. Then she says she will help by taking my kids because I decided to stay with my husband and help him get help. It really doesn't mean a damn thing to have someone say, 'I'll help you, I'll take your kids.' Do you know what that feels like?

Therapist: It must feel like she's saying you are not a very good mother and that she can take better care of your kids.

Mother: Yeah, like there's something really wrong with me because I want to stay with my husband. Then the police say to my children, "Tell us what happened to you. We won't let anything happen to you or your daddy. He won't get hurt if you tell us everything. We will take care of you, we are your friends." Then my kids tell them everything and my husband goes to jail.

Therapist: Did you feel like anyone was taking care of you?

Mother: The state's attorney told me he thought my husband was an animal and didn't belong on the streets, and if I dropped the charges he didn't think I was much better than him.

Therapist; You probably aren't much more optimistic about our relationship.

Mother: Let's put it this way . . . I don't expect anything to be much better. You probably can't hurt me much more than I already am.

Therapist: All I know is that I don't want to hurt you. Sometimes I don't know what hurts and what doesn't. Can we make an agreement?

Mother: It depends on what that is.

Therapist: You need to let me know what hurts, as soon as you realize it's hurting. We are different people and you have to help me get to know you. Can we make an agreement that you will let me know when you are hurting, particularly if I inflicted the pain. I can handle the anger. As a matter of fact I want to hear about the anger, even if it's at me. But you have to let me know. What do you think?

Later on in the session the therapist returns the focus to the mother-grandmother relationship:

Therapist: I think it's going to be important to bring your mother into the sessions early on in the treatment. She seems to be very involved and certainly has opinions on this family's situation.

Mother: She definitely has opinions and I don't like any of them.

Therapist: Exactly, and that's why I think we have to get her in here. She isn't going to go away. She has your children in her home. She is very involved and you keep feeling worse. I want to help you get back in charge of your family. And in my experience the more we ignore her the louder she has to get in order to get our attention, and it seems her loudness makes you feel bad. The way to get a handle on these situations is to confront it.

Mother: You don't know my mother.

Therapist: You are right, I don't know your mother. But I know mine and a lot of others, and I know what it is like to be a daughter. And how hard it is to convince a mother who tends to love too much that you are an adult who wants to learn to take care of yourself and protect your family yourself. I can help you do that but not without her here.

Mother: I don't know, we'll just yell at each other the whole time until I give in.

Therapist: Yelling doesn't bother me. We aren't going to have her the next time, in fact not for a while. But I think it has to be sooner rather than later. You and I will prepare for the joint sessions so that you feel strong enough to handle it.

As seen from these brief excerpts, the first clinical sessions cover many content areas, thus providing the client and therapist with a sense of one another.

6

Clinical Assessment

CLINICAL ASSESSMENT IN MULTIPLE SYSTEMS THERAPY

Clinical assessment in multiple systems therapy is a complex process, which integrates traditional individual-psychological with systemic evaluation techniques. Whereas individual psychological assessment has become fairly standardized in approach among practitioners, family assessment is a new field with little in the way of standard practice. One reason for this is that most family therapy models are less based on pathotypes than traditional individual models. This results in few standardized constructs upon which to assess. Family assessment is usually based on the assessor's orientation and is thought of more as an adjunct to intervention than a clinical end unto itself.

Some commonalities among all schools do exist in family assessment. First, the process of assessment is ongoing and dynamic. Family assessment is rarely done by a clinician from outside the treatment program, who only has a few hours with the family. Instead, the family's primary therapist evaluates and refines his or her hypotheses during the course of therapy. Second, family assessment has rarely included the use of tests. This has not been because of lack of interest by clinicians, but because of the lack of standardized constructs and the lack of psychometrically sound tests to measure those constructs that have been defined. This is beginning to change as more and more research is beginning to provide the field with useful tests of family functioning.

A third commonality among family therapy schools is that their assessment usually involves the whole family. Having access to the entire family has allowed clinicians to be less inferential about their hypotheses, even when assessing an individual. For example, psychologists usually must infer from projective tests about an individual's relationship with her mother; the family therapist can *watch* that relationship. A fourth commonality is that most family assessment is based not on a desire to pinpoint pathology, but on an understanding of the interactional nature of the system. As such, family assessment is usually based on problem solving.

Clinical assessment in our program is based on this family therapy assessment tradition, combined with the essential elements of standard psychological assessment. As such, our assessment consists of the following components:

1. *Assessment is ongoing and dynamic.* Although we have a formal assessment period, we never stop reevaluating our families' systems.
2. *We utilize current, psychometrically sound family assessment devices.* Although we hope that better tests of family structure and function continue to be developed, we want to increase the reliability of our assessment by combining our own clinical judgment with objective measures.
3. *We include the entire family in our assessment.* This includes extended family and even members not easily accessible because of incarceration or placement outside the home.
4. *The purpose of the assessment is to solve problems, not to pathologize.* We try never to forget that the purpose of clinical assessment is to help design interventions to stop the abuse, not merely to label any member of the family or the system as a whole.

THE FUNCTION OF CLINICAL ASSESSMENT

The purpose of assessment in our program is to determine which factors contribute to the origin and maintenance of the incestuous abuse: that is, what factors contribute to a family's vulnerability to incest; what precipitating events occur which may trigger the vulnerable family to behave incestuously; and what coping mechanisms are lacking that might have prevented incestuous episodes.

This is no small task, given the complexity and interactional nature of these factors. To accomplish this, we use a variety of assessment strategies common among family psychologists, including interview techniques, paper-and-pencil family systems measures, and formal psychological testing. Given the seriousness of the problem, the interweaving of so many etiological variables, and the need for accurate information to secure a sound treatment plan, we believe that this extensive assessment is essential.

There are four main goals in the assessment program. First, we are interested in discovering any serious psychopathology in any member which may need immediate disposition. For example, it is essential that depression on the part of the victim be detected so that a suicide attempt can be averted. Second, we distinguish which factors contributed to the family's vulnerability to incest, and which are continuing to maintain the incestuous abuse. At the same time, we attempt to discard variables common to some families but not applicable to this particular family so that we do not "program" our treatment. Third, we attempt to assess the precipitating events which were present that precede and elicit an incestuous episode. Fourth, we assess what coping skills are lacking to the family which, if present, might deter abusive episodes.

TIME FRAME OF ASSESSMENT IN THE PROGRAM

The assessment of the multiple systems that contribute to the family's vulnerability to incest is one of the most important components of our program. This process includes both the ongoing and informal hypothesis-testing that family therapists typically employ during the course of treatment, and structured assessment using a variety of objective instruments interpreted by a family psychologist (see Table 6.1). The formal evaluation period begins after the first clinical session (see Chapter 5) and generally lasts between four and six weeks. During this time the therapist conducts "evaluation sessions" with the various individuals and subsystems, as well as the entire family, and the structured testing is administered by an evaluation team.

The assessment is completed when the therapist feels fairly confident that he or she understands what were the primary factors contributing to the family's vulnerability to incest. There is then a formal "report session" with the family to discuss in general terms what the therapist feels are the most important problems needing to be addressed.

It is during the report session that the therapist announces to the family

TABLE 6.1
Tests Commonly Used in Assessment

Test	*Purpose*
FILE (Olson et al., 1982)	Measures presence of chronic stress
F-Copes (Olson et al., 1982)	Measures family's coping mechanisms and strengths
Family Satisfaction (Olson et al., 1982)	Measures overall family satisfaction
FACES-III (Olson, Portner, & Lavee, 1985)	Measures a variety of family structural variables and the magnitude of dysfunction using the circumplex model
Clinical Rating Scale (Olson & Killorin, 1985)	A therapist-rated version of FACES-III
Minnesota Multiphasic Personality Inventory (MMPI)	Measures individual personality characteristics and pathology
Thematic Apperception Test (TAT)	A projective measure of personality and perception of self within the family
DSFI (Derogatis & Melisaratos, 1979)	Measures many components of an individual's sexuality
Purdue Sexual History Form	A guide for sexual history taking.

whether they can indeed be accepted into the program. In the 10 years we have been treating incest we have never totally refused to treat a family (although some offending fathers have been deemed untreatable for a variety of reasons). The purpose of the "acceptance-to-the-program" ritual is to solidify the seriousness of the program, to make the family feel that they are indeed receiving something "special," and to remind them implicitly that we do have the freedom to dismiss them from therapy if they do not comply. This latter threat, positively connoted by congratulating them for being "accepted into the program," has proven powerful. It is especially powerful for the majority of families who are under the watchful eye of child protective services and the court.

ASSESSMENT USING THE VULNERABILITY MODEL

As previously discussed, the assessment schema is based upon the Vulnerability to Incest framework. This states that all families are endowed with a certain degree of vulnerability to incestuous abuse, and this vulnerability reflects the presence and magnitude of specific variables which fall under the categories: (1) *socioenvironmental* factors; 2) *Family-of-origin* factors; 3) *family systems* factors; and 4) *individual psychological* factors. Whether a vulnerable family will indeed behave incestuously, however, is dependent upon the presence of precipitating situations, and further mitigated by the absence of effective coping mechanisms.

To aid in the assessment process, the therapist uses a Vulnerability Sheet, shown in Figure 6.1. The therapist can continuously jot down hypotheses concerning specific vulnerabilities the family possesses for each factor on the left side of the sheet, and then make note of ways to obtain support for these hypotheses on the right side of the sheet (see Figure 6.2). Besides forcing the therapist to think in terms of vulnerability variables, this worksheet can then be used to generate intervention strategies.

SOCIOENVIRONMENTAL FACTORS

The socioenvironmental system that we assess includes contributing themes from the culture as a whole, which provides the framework through which we all operate, and the subculture or community in which the family lives. Some examples of socioenvironmental factors follow:

Acceptance of "Male Supremacy"

Many feminist writers have pointed to the fact that the vast majority of incestuous abuse occurs *by* men *to* girls, and argue that the overriding causal variable is society's basic imbalance of power between the sexes (Breines & Gordon, 1983; Brickman, 1984). This view suggests that through society's support of male dominance both politically and sexually, a natural outgrowth is the acceptance of male sexual abuse or, more perniciously, not even defining this behavior as abusive at all. And male dominance is so ingrained in us all, argue these theorists, that even the victims see it as the accepted and even desirable norm.

Although not all families accept male dominance as a given, families that do have increased vulnerability to incestuous abuse. In some families, for example, the father may cognitively accept having sex with his daughter as his "right," and his daughter may also accept the behavior as tolerable because "Daddy said it was OK." As an abusing father reported, "I always taught her that what daddy said was the law, so when I told her to do this with me she just did it."

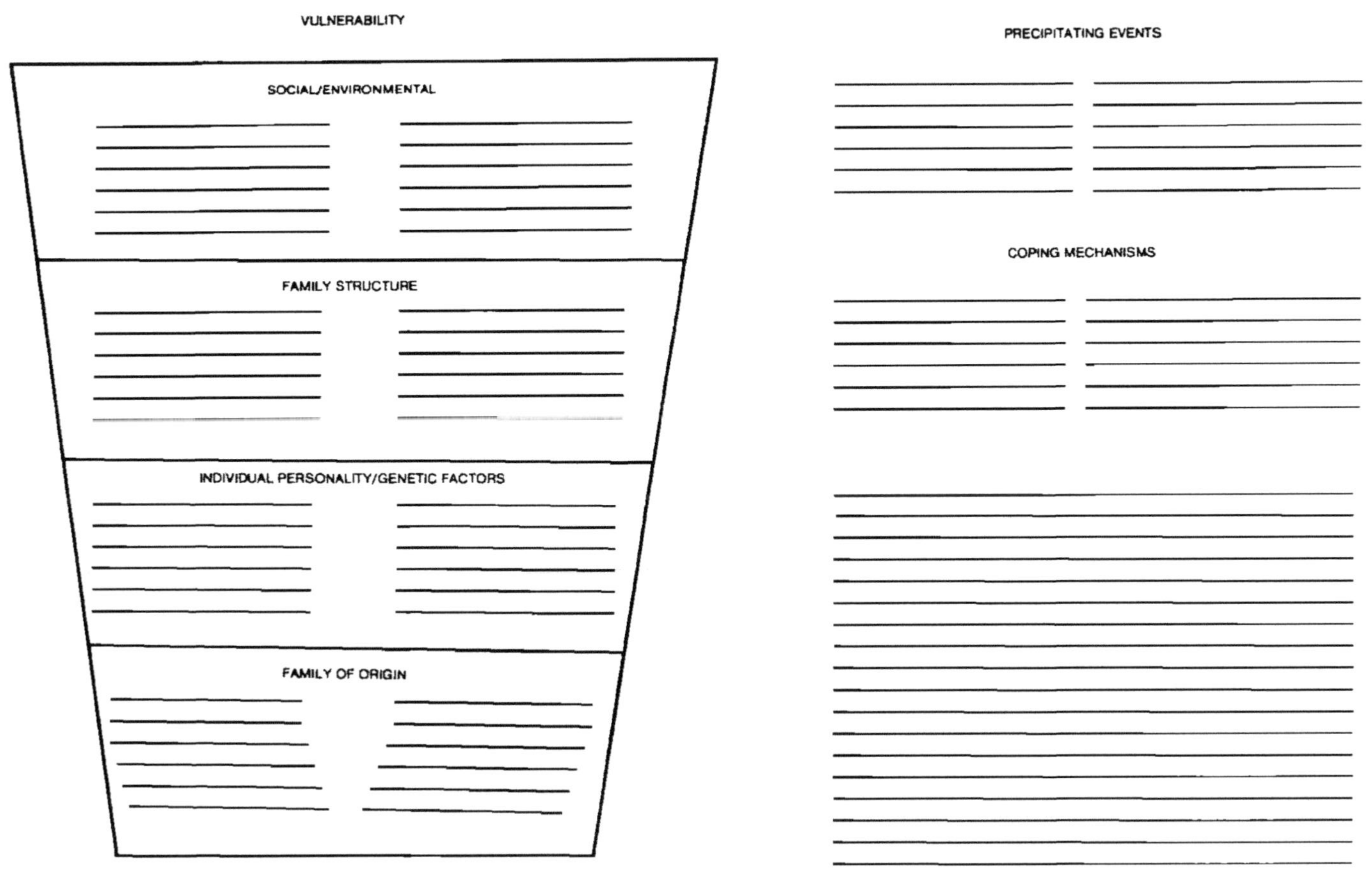

Figure 6.1. Vulnerability sheet.

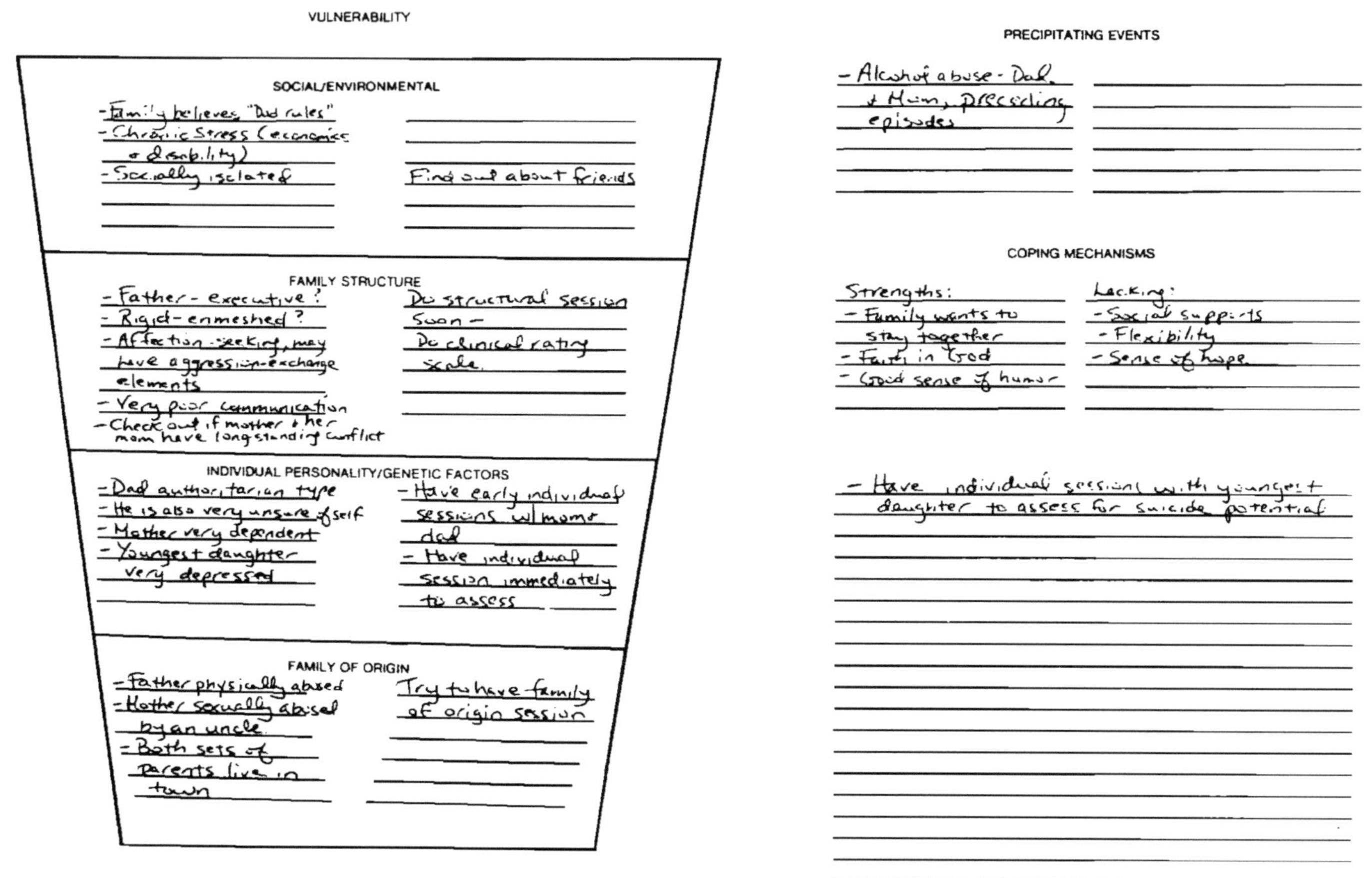

Figure 6.2. Vulnerability sheet with therapist's notes.

Adherence to the Differential Manner in Which Men and Women Traditionally Display Affection

It is apparent that boys and girls are socialized differently about sexuality and relationships, although this is changing to some extent. Teenage boys are taught, albeit indirectly, that sex is the primary way girls show affection to them. The notion, "If she loves me she will sleep with me," is not an uncommon one, reinforced by the verbalized if not exaggerated exploits of other male friends. Teenage girls, on the other hand, are usually taught that affection can and should be expressed in ways other than sexually, with the notion, "If he loves me he *won't* try to have sex with me," being prevalent. This differential view of sex and affection often continues into adulthood, and may be one explanation why men are more likely to sexualize their relationships with their children than are women.

Objects of Sexual Attraction

Another related socioenvironmental variable is that the type of person many men are taught to be sexually attracted to is shorter, younger, and more demure than themselves, and with less power (Finkelhor, 1984). This is certainly not the only type that all men are attracted to, but it is a culturally common "ideal," which unfortunately corresponds to the appearance and stature of a child. Although the type of sex partner who is attractive to the offending parent is an individual matter of preference, this choice can also be viewed as a socioenvironmental factor because of the prevalence in our culture of seeing the diminutive girl/woman as a desirable sex partner.

Differences in Relationships with Children

A recent study (Parker & Parker, 1986) showed that one of the primary predictive variables in all forms of child abuse is the degree of nurturing a parent provides for the child when he or she is very young. This may offer yet another reason why women are less likely to sexually abuse their children. That is, they are more likely to have provided the majority of early child care and nurturance. This may also explain why stepfathers are five times more likely than natural fathers to sexually abuse their children (Finkelhor, 1980a), since they were not present during the child's earliest years.

Tolerance to Incest in the Family's Community

Although it is difficult to believe with our current public outrage over incestuous abuse, there is a reasonable amount of societal "support" for incest. Some very popular "adult" magazines publish fantasy letters (supposedly written by those involved, but most likely written by professional writers of erotica) around incestuous themes. One booklet, "Family Letters," has chapters on "Father-Daughter," "Mother-Son," "Grandparents," "Uncles and Aunts," and "The Whole Family" (Piccolo Publications, 1987). Another example of this is the popularity of the "adult" movie series "Taboo." These videos, now easily accessible at neighborhood video stores, are a five-part series where family sex is the theme, and everyone in the family at one time or another has sex with each other. Family sex is never displayed as abusive, and even if someone resists, as in many erotic films, within a minute or two the resistance turns to ecstasy.

People viewing these materials obtain a sense of cultural support for certain notions that may make incestuous abuse tolerable: that incest is common, that it is never abusive, that even if there is resistance the other person "really wants it." Of more concern is that these books and videos are so very popular (obviously there is a "Taboo V" because of the success of "Taboo I–IV"). This popularity indicates the extent of the incestuous fantasy. Unfortunately, this very popularity may communicate the message that society finds incest acceptable.

Pornography is not the only context in which community support for incest occurs. Some social networks (in local bars, for example) may tacitly approve of sexually abusive behavior by reinforcing discussions of sexual exploits. An individual in that network, already vulnerable to incest, may interpret these discussions as support for his fantasies.

Social Isolation

Besides adhering to cultural values that tolerate various aspects of incest, a family can be vulnerable to incest because the members are isolated from the outside environment. When this occurs, the family does not fall under the scrutiny of the outside systems which usually provide a certain amount of control for deviant behavior. A number of writers (e.g., Finkelhor, 1978; Sgroi, 1982) have identified family social isolation as a major correlate to incestuous abuse. And although the stereotype of "mountain families" being particularly susceptible to incest is unfair, any family that is extremely isolated from the outside community's scrutiny is more vulnerable to incest than those families that are not.

Chronic Stress

As is the case for all vulnerability variables, the mere presence of chronic stress does not indicate incest. However, many sexually abusing families have experienced long periods of stress that are perceived as out of their control. An example of this might be the stress caused by long-term economic difficulties due to unemployment. Most families rally together during times of stress, but for some the chronicity of the stress may lead to a breaking down of their very foundations. This can lead to an exacerbation of all the vulnerability factors and increase the likelihood of precipitating events (like alcoholic episodes) and a breakdown of traditional coping mechanisms.

Strategies for Assessing

When assessing the socioenvironmental factors, there are a number of considerations the therapist must keep in mind. First, the family will not say, "Yes, we adhere to a male dominance model." Instead, the family therapist must infer this possibility from the interactions during family and individual sessions. For example, does the family look to father for approval before answering the therapist's questions? When the family is asked to make a decision, does father have the final say? Questions to the family about the process of discipline may elucidate the adherence to a male dominance theme, as will questions to the couple about sexual decisions. Questions such as, "What do you see as the man's role in the family?," or "When do you feel powerful?," or "When you feel like no one listens to you, how do you let people know you are upset?" can also provide important information about the family's acceptance of traditional sex-role stereotypes.

Second, the therapist should always ask questions concerning socioenvironmental variables in the *as if* mode; that is, to ask the question *as if* the behavior commonly occurs. So instead of asking, "Have you ever watched videos such as 'Taboo'?" the therapist should ask, "How often do you watch the 'Taboo' videos?" Third, the therapist must test these inferential hypotheses within a number of subsystems. The children can often provide more honest information about acceptance of male supremacy than the parents can; on the other hand, a session alone with the father can provide more information about his view of diminutive partners as sexually attractive.

Fourth, the therapist should be willing to abandon a common variable if it is indeed not present. Many therapists, for example, assume that the offender who was abused as a child is present in a family *even if the family assessment suggests otherwise,* simply because of the therapist's bias that this must be present for incest to occur. These are commonly reported variables, but not all families exhibit each possible variable. The purpose of the assessment is to "tease out" which variables contribute to a family's vulnerability and which do not.

With regard to objective tests, FILE and A-FILE (Olson et al., 1982) can provide useful information about the presence or absence of chronic family stress. Also, hypotheses concerning family isolation can be generated using FACES-III, along with the Clinical Rating Scale (Olson & Killorin, 1985), particularly for families scoring in the Rigidly Enmeshed quadrant (see Figure 6.3).

FAMILY-OF-ORIGIN FACTORS

One of the most commonly cited reasons for the incestuous abuse of daughters by their fathers has been that they themselves were abused as children (e.g., Summit & Kryso, 1978). As with many explanations for abuse, however, this one has not been fully supported by empirical evidence (Batten, 1983). Although actual data on the percentage of abusing fathers who were themselves abused is lacking at this time, we can say decidedly that it is not the profound causal variable once thought to be. And although to many clinicians it appears that most of the nonoffending mothers were themselves sexually abused, this too seems more illusory than real.

There is, however, evidence that the *perception* of parental mistreatment does in fact contribute to a father's vulnerability to abuse (Parker & Parker, 1986). And more important, family therapists have long been aware of the cyclical nature of parenting amd marital styles. In other words, abusing parents may have learned the factors contributing to their vulnerability to abuse, if not the abuse itself.

It is critical, therefore, to assess the offending and nonoffending parents' families of origin on the following dimensions:

1. *Family themes regarding roles of men and women, division of labor, and rules regarding male and female relationships.* Did the family, for example, support the notion, "A man is king in his castle, and women are there to serve"?

2. *The perceived quality of the relationship between the parent and his or her parents of both sexes.* For the offending father, it is particularly important to note if his relationship with *his* father was poor, which has been found to be correlated with sexual abuse of younger daughters (Gebhard et al., 1965).
3. *The incidence of sexual abuse in the offenders' own childhood.* It should be noted that the majority of offending fathers were not sexually abused (Groth, 1982; Kaufman & Zigler, 1987). For those that were, what seems most clinically relevant is their perceptions of their abuse. One father said, "My father used to not only sexually abuse me, but also sadistically physically abuse me as well. I swore I'd make amends for his life, but what do I do? I molest my own daughter!" In this example, ironically, the fact that he was *so* abused perhaps contributed to his great need for affection, which then contributed to his having sex with his own daughter when he was feeling particularly needy.
4. *The degree of perceived emotional neglect, abuse, or deprivation.* This factor may be the most critical, because it leads often to the profound affection seeking exhibited by many incestuous abusers and nonoffending parents, along with rage, devastated self-esteems, and impulsive and self-damaging behaviors.

There are two ways to assess family-of-origin contributions to a family's vulnerability to incest. One way is do genogram sessions with the parents to help elucidate the history and themes of the families of origin. Another way is to have sessions with the parents and *their* parents, which allows the therapist to have access to the "raw data" itself. These sessions furnish useful information about family-of-origin issues and also provide the therapist with information about the parents' parents' influence on the family. It is often impossible to get the families of origin to participate, as they may be dead, live in another city, or simply refuse to be involved. However, if at all possible, the therapist should attempt family-of-origin sessions, since the assessment information derived can be invaluable (see Chapter 12). A third way is to discuss, over time in individual sessions, the nature of the childhood traumas and their impact on subsequent adult behaviors.

FAMILY SYSTEMS FACTORS

Incest by definition is a family experience, and thus the family system in which it occurs must be fully understood if meaningful intervention is to transpire. Although viewing family abuse from an interactional perspective was once a more controversial notion, recent reviews have focused on the usefulness of such a framework (e.g., deChesnay, 1985; Wolfe, 1985). And although no one suggests a model of explanation that "blames the victims," an assessment using systems theory conceptualizations provides a more complete picture than merely centering on the pathology of the perpetrator (Alexander, 1985). What makes our program unique is the structured appraisal of the family systems factors contributing to the family's vulnerability to incestuous abuse.

The three major categories that we assess with regard to the family system are: (1) *family abusive style,* which provides an overall conceptualization of the function of the abuse; (2) *family structure,* which helps us define the types of interactional patterns a family possesses, and (3) *family communication patterns.*

Family Abusive Style

The concept of *family abusive style* is useful in understanding the function of the sexual abuse. Larson and Maddock (1986), based on their study of incest families in Minnesota, described four categories of incest families based on the underlying purpose of the abuse.

Affection-exchange. The affection-exchange family appears to be loving and caring, where there is a great need for nurturance on the part of its members. The incest occurs partially because of a need for affection on the part of the offending father, and often the victim as well. There is rarely if ever physical abuse present, and the offending fathers can be characterized as emotionally "needy." This is the most common type of incest family, and it often surprises the inexperienced therapist who expects to see more hostility, anger, and resentment. The affection-exchange family is most likely to wish to remain together, and the victim will often recant her disclosure when it appears her father will be incarcerated for the incest. These families can usually remain together during therapy from the start, and the prognosis for change is the best of all family styles.

Erotic-exchange. The erotic-exchange family is characterized by a sexualizing of most activities they engage in. This family may see family sexuality as a right and may even elevate their incestuous behavior to a philosophical level. This is the kind of family that might be involved with family "swinging"; that is, meeting other families through swinger magazine ads and other means for the purpose of group family sex. A rather notorious "nudist camp" (in quotes because almost no legitimate nudist group would condone family sex) operating until recently in Indiana was a well-known meeting ground for erotic-exchange families. To a less extreme degree, other erotic-exchange families engage in inappropriate touching, seductive tones, and sex talk with each other. Mother-son incestuous abuse is more common in this family style than in the others, as would be the encouragement of sex among siblings by the parents. These families are also rarely physically abusive and usually can remain intact for most of the therapy sessions. Prognosis for the erotic-exchange family is also good, provided the therapist can impact upon their cognitive distortion that family sex is philosophically supportable.

Aggression-exchange. In the aggression-exchange family, the incestuous abuse has a hostile intent. There is often physical abuse present, and the sexual abuse is often an extension of the physical abuse. It is common for an aggression-exchange father to sexually abuse his daughter after an argument has escalated as a form of punishment and humiliation. Sibling incest, particularly by an older brother to a younger sister, occurs most often in this family abusive style. And although power issues are a part of all incestuous abuse, they are most prevalent for this family style. The prognosis for these families is only fair, depending upon how much direct access the therapist has to the offending father or brother. These families are more likely to separate during the course of therapy. Finally, the aggression-exchange family often should not be seen in treatment together at the beginning if the daughter does not wish to be in the same room with the offending father.

Rage-expression. The rage-expression family abusive style is, gratefully, the least common, although it receives the most media attention because of its often dramatic consequences. The sexual abuse in these families is most akin to a rape, with much violence being perpetrated upon the child along with the sexual abuse. The sexual behavior is often sadistic and may lead to permanent physical damage. The offending fathers are most likely to display more extreme psychopathology, and the parents are most likely to engage in denial of facts to the extent that the child doubts her own reality-testing abilities. This kind of family should not be seen together, at least until the denial ends, the daughter feels comfortable, and the offending father is deemed psychologically able to be reunited with the daughter without "double-binding" her (requiring a direct response to a contradictory demand). The offending father will also need more intensive individual therapy, perhaps including psychiatric treatment if a psychotic condition is present. The prognosis is generally guarded or poor with these families.

It is relatively easy for the therapist to assess which of the four family abusive styles is operating by simply being aware of the definitions. Sometimes a family exhibits characteristics of more than one abusive style. For example, it is not uncommon for an affection-exchange family to have some erotic-exchange characteristics. Generally one style will predominate, however, and treatment can be accommodated to the presence of more than one style.

Function of the Incest

Another way in which we try to understand the meaning of the incestuous abuse is by using Alexander and Parsons' (1982) conceptualization of the function of a behavior. Put simply, we attempt to determine the degree to which the incestuous behavior has a *merging* function (one that produces contact and closeness) or a *separating* function (one that produces distance or independence). Since one aspect of incestuous behavior is interactional in nature, we attempt to understand the function of each family member's contribution. For example, in an aggression-exchange family, the father may attempt sex with the daughter as punishment (separating), the daughter may tacitly agree to have sex with her father as a way to please him and obtain his love and approval (merging), and the nonoffending mother may, although aware of the likelihood of the abuse, decide to look the other way to prevent a conflict (separating). Finally, the brother may alert the authorities to get his father thrown out of the house and off his back (separating). In each case, the behaviors of each family member are evaluated in terms of function. Of course, the function of the incest may change in a family; it does not serve only one purpose.

Although there are no formal tests that examine the functions of behavior, the alert family therapist can easily identify whether certain behaviors are separating or merging by: (1) observing in-session family interactions (e.g., the daughter is quick to defend her father and blame her mother for a conflict that arises during the session); (2) noting material obtained from direct questioning during individual session (e.g., "Why did you decide to tell on your father when you did?" "Because I wanted his ass thrown in jail, so he'd be off my back!"); and (3) examining test result data for the presence of either separating or merging functions (e.g., on FACES-III the daughter scores similarly to her father on both *perceived* and *ideal*, suggesting a merging hypothesis).

Family Structure

Family structure is one of those elusive constructs in the family therapy field which means something to everybody, but not necessarily the same thing. For our purpose, we define family structure using two common conceptualizations—those of David Olson and those of Salvador Minuchin.

Circumplex model. With the Circumplex model (Olson, Russell, & Sprenkle, 1983; Trepper & Sprenkle, in press), family structure is described using two interacting dimensions, cohesion and adaptability (see Figure 6.3). Cohesion refers to the degree of emotional bonding mem-

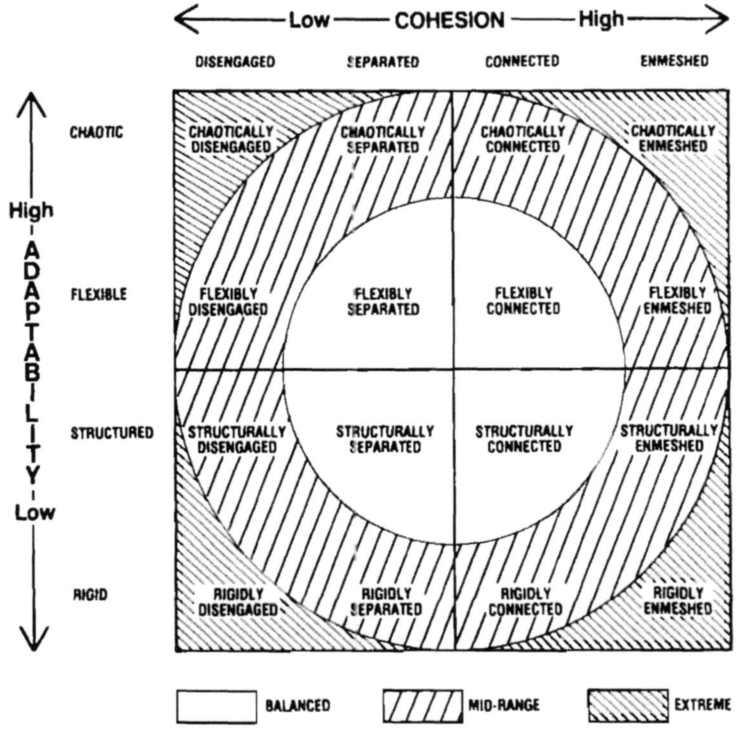

Figure 6.3. Circumplex model. (Reprinted with permission from David H. Olson, Ph.D.)

bers have with one another and is assessed along a continuum from "disengaged" to "enmeshed." Adaptability refers to the amount of flexibility to change present in the family system and is assessed along a continuum from "rigid" to "chaotic." A family is usually described combining the two dimensions, such as "rigidly enmeshed."

Family structure can be understood with the Circumplex in a variety of ways. A standardized paper-and-pencil test taken by the family, called FACES-III (Olson, Portner, & Lavee, 1985), can not only indicate a general family placement on the Circumplex, but also provide important information about the relative position of each family member from his or her perspective. This is highly significant information when developing hypotheses about subsystem interactions and the function of the incestuous behavior. This test can also indicate the family's overall level of dysfunction by comparing their scores to those of nonclinical families. There is also a Clinical Rating Scale (Olson & Killorin, 1985), filled out by the therapist, which asks a series of questions about the family's interactional patterns. Based on the results of the Clinical Rating Scale, a family can be placed more reliably on the Circumplex.

Although incestuously abusing families can be found anywhere along the Circumplex dimensions, the most common pattern we have found clinically is the rigidly enmeshed. For example, a firm adherence to the rule "do whatever daddy says" going unquestioned by the sexually abused daughter might be indicative of family rigidity. At the same time, the father's extreme need for affection, which culminated in his sexual advances to his daughter, and the mother's unwillingness to report it once she discovered the abuse could be seen as indicative of the family's enmeshment.

Interactional structures. Another framework that we use for assessing family structure is based upon Minuchin's structural family therapy (Minuchin, 1974). This model presupposes a functional family structure that allows for separation of generations through an imaginary "boundary," which is neither too permeable nor too rigid (see Figure 6.4). If children end up in the parents' generation, or a parent ends up in the children's generation, family dysfunction is inevitable.

We have identified five types of family structures that are particularly vulnerable to the development of incest. Families may fluctuate between any of the five structures at any given time. In all of the structures the key element is that the father and the child victim somehow end up in the same "generation" with regard to roles and boundaries. In fact, sex between two individuals can only occur within the same generational

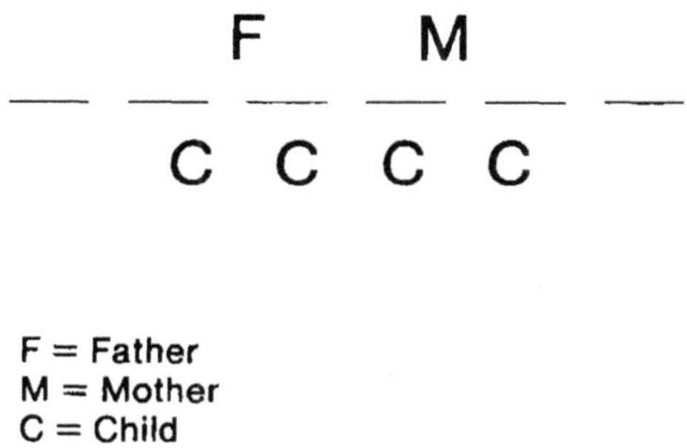

Figure 6.4. Functional family structure.

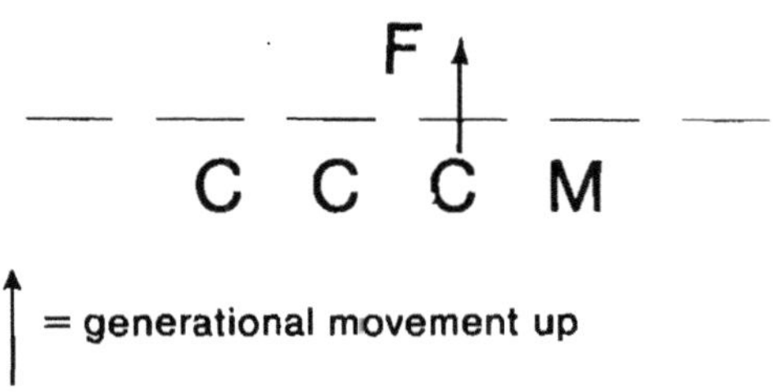

Figure 6.5. Father-executive structure.

boundary. Each of these five structures suggests a situation where either the child is "pulled up" into the father's generation or the father "falls down" into the child's. We are not suggesting that these five possible structures are all inclusive.

1. *Father-executive.* This structure (see Figure 6.5) suggests a family where the father is the dominant, powerful figure, who in effect "parents" the mother along with each of the children. He usually feels a sense of overresponsibility and rarely shares in decision making with his wife. The mother may feel dependent on and yet disengaged from her husband, and she may display a clinical "passivity." She may also exhibit a sense of relief when her daughter assumes many of the "wife" functions. The daughter indeed may be a parental child in this family, at times "mothering" her own mother, and may easily slip into the role of supporter and nurturer of her father. This structure leads to increased vulnerability to incest, particularly if the father is affection seeking, and views sex and affection as one and the same. He is also often enraged because he sees that he was the executive in his family of origin as well.

M

— — — — — —

C C C F

Figure 6.6. Mother-executive structure.

2. *Mother-executive.* With this structure (see Figure 6.6), the mother is the dominant, powerful figure and most likely "parents" the father along with the children. Similar to the father-executive, the mother-executive is overly responsible for decisions in the family, and feels a sense of isolation from her husband, to whom she may refer as "one of the children." The father may indeed appear to act out like an adolescent (excessive drinking, staying out all night with friends, etc.). His sexual contact with his daughter almost appears to be sibling sex play, but can also be more forceful, particularly if it occurs within an aggression-exchange or rage-expression family abusive style.

3. *Third-Generation Mother-Executive, and Third-Generation Father-Executive.* These structures (see Figure 6.7) more or less combine the previous two. In the first, father is a generational step below the mother-executive, and their marriage has all the problems associated with the mother-executive. However, he still manages to parent the children, and his sexual abuse of the daughter still involves an overtly parental action to obtain sexual favors. In the second, the mother is a generational step below the father but is still able to effectively parent the children. Father has, in effect, to meet the daughter halfway to have sex with her. In this structure, there is often siblinglike rivalry between the mother and daughter for the affections of the father.

4. *Chaotic.* This structure (see Figure 6.8) suggests a situation where all members of the family are within the same generational boundary. In these families, no one appears in charge, or the role of the leader fluctuates often. Incestuous fathers often report that they did not feel like their daughter's father, and given the blurred and confused roles this is not surprising. This structure is also particularly vulnerable to sibling or extended family incestuous abuse.

5. *Estranged father.* This structure (see Figure 6.9) is typified by a father who is uninvolved emotionally with the family, but when he temporarily reenters he does so in the same generation as the daughter. His

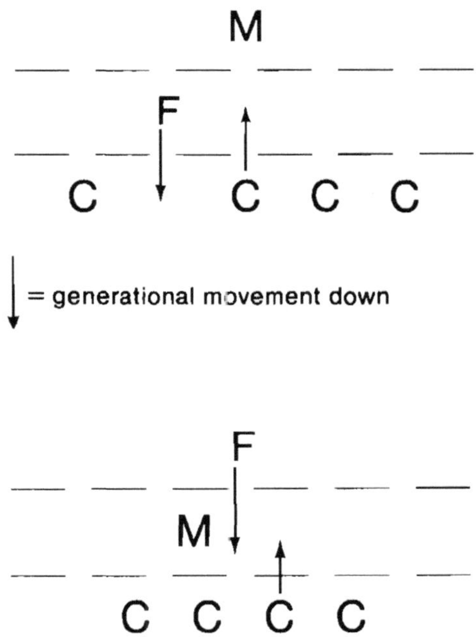

Figure 6.7. Third-generation structures.

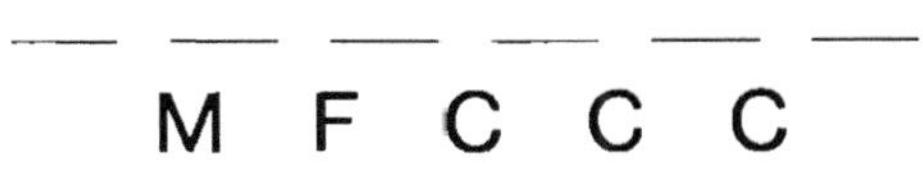

Figure 6.8. Chaotic structure.

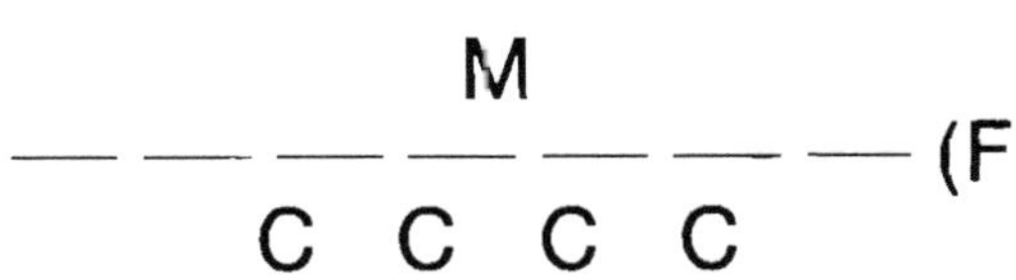

Figure 6.9. Estranged father structure.

reentries are often demanding and aggressive in nature. This is often the type of family structure found when there is a paramour.

Blended families. Blended families, which can appear structurally as any of the five described above, are particularly vulnerable to incestuous abuse. Finkelhor (1980a) reported a five times greater likelihood of sexual abuse within blended families, and Russell (1986) reported the incredible finding that 17% of girls raised by a stepfather were sexually abused by him.

There are a number of possible explanations for this. First, men with pedophile tendencies may seek out women with children in part because of their attraction to them (Russell, 1986). Second, sexual behavior with a stepdaughter may not be perceived as incestuous by the stepfather and thus can be cognitively accepted as less taboo and less detrimental (Russell, 1986). Third, since a key vulnerability factor is the degree of bonding and nurturing of the child that has occurred (Parker & Parker, 1986), it can be speculated that less bonding with blended families results in more sexual abuse. Fourth, there may be more opportunity factors and precipitating events in stepfamilies since more stepmothers work (Russell, 1986). Fifth, blended families are more vulnerable to the dysfunctional structures listed in the previous section, since they are newer and have had less time to solidify more functional hierarchies. Whereas non-stepfamilies have had years to develop appropriate rules, roles, and boundaries, blended families usually do not have the luxury of a protracted family evolution during which time these functional family components can emerge.

The structures operating for a family are usually assessed by the therapist in entire-family sessions. One of the best ways to obtain information about these structures is through *enactments* (Minuchin & Fishman, 1981). In this intervention the therapist purposely poses a difficult situation or problem for the family to solve, then encourages the family to solve it during the session. During the assessment phase, the therapist is not likely to intervene when the family has difficulties, but instead notes the interactional processes that are present with regard to the roles and boundaries. Another method for assessing these structures is to present the typical structures on a blackboard to the family and have *them* decide which ones fit them best (for a complete discussion of this technique, see Chapter 8).

Family Communication

Incestuous families experience similar communication problems as in other clinical families, and should be evaluated for both general communication strengths and weaknesses. Specific communication problems found with incest families include the following: (1) secretiveness; (2) inconsistent or unclear messages to one another; (3) infrequent discussion of feelings; (4) little attentive listening or empathy; and (5) lack of conflict-resolution skills. Entire-family sessions are essential for effective assessment of problematic communication patterns, but standardized family communication tests, such as the Parent-Adolescent Communication Inventory (Olson et al., 1982) may also be useful. The key is to appraise those aspects of the family's communication patterns that contribute to vulnerability to incest. For example, if discussion of feelings is discouraged in the family, the daughter is not likely to tell her father how she really feels about having sex with him. This may lead to his irrational belief that she enjoys the incest.

INDIVIDUAL PSYCHOLOGICAL FACTORS

The Multiple Systems model focuses on adequately assessing individual "systems," as well as social and family systems. There are specific individual characteristics and psychological states that have been identified both clinically and empirically as being correlated with incestuous abuse. Our program attempts to individually evaluate the offending father, the mother, and the daughter-victim, and any others whom we feel it would be critical to evaluate. Although not always possible, this assessment can best be accomplished by a family psychologist because evaluating the interaction between individuals and their systems falls best under the purview of that specialty.

Offending Father

Offending fathers have had more written about them in the clinical literature than any other members of incestuously abusing families. With all this attention, it is unfortunate that there is so little consensus concerning their characteristics. In fact, the descriptions provided vis-à-vis offending fathers is extremely varied and contradictory (Renshaw, 1982). However, based on recent empirical reports, careful literature reviews, and clinical descriptions from programs with large numbers of incest families, some common clinical patterns do emerge.

Psychopathology. Although most researchers have found severe psychopathology, such as psychosis, to be extremely rare among offending fathers (Meiselman, 1978), we nonetheless must rule out its possibility during the assessment. Occasionally a father will molest his daughter during a psychotic episode, or even more rarely, as a function of a multiple personality disorder. If this is seen at all, it is typical in the rage-expression family abusive style.

Personality disorders. There are a number of common personality characteristics cited for incest fathers. First, there is a sociopathic constellation, which includes the lack of impulse control, the need for immediate gratification, and lack of guilt (Summit & Kryso, 1978). Offending fathers usually present these characteristics to a lesser degree than would an individual with a diagnosable antisocial personality disorder. In fact, there is usually only a slightly elevated MMPI Scale 4 elevation present for offending fathers. Second, many incestuous fathers have difficulty with control of aggression and tolerance to stress (Herman & Hirschman, 1981). Third, many incest fathers are described clinically as narcissistic, having difficulty in showing empathy to others because of their profound focus on themselves (Justice & Justice, 1979). This must be carefully assessed, however, since incarceration is looming over many fathers during assessment. This may make them appear *narcissistic* when they are instead only responding to a very real overriding fear for their own future and safety.

Cognitive distortions. It is very important for the therapist to understand the way in which the offending father views the incestuous situation, its disclosure, and the subsequent ramifications for the family. Does he see himself as the victim, with the only real problem being the intrusion into his life by protective services and the therapist? Does he feel he has the right to "access" his child any way he wishes, because he is *the father?* Does he view the molestation as "sex education"? Does he see his daughter as being responsible for the incest because of her questions, behavior, or implications? Finally, does he see molestation as a form of punishment, deserved by his daughter when she is very bad? These sample questions are commonly answered in the affirmative by incestuous fathers, and indicate a cognitive view of incestuous abuse that will impede systemic change unless addressed during therapy (see Chapter 13).

Sexual orientation-fantasy. Although some have suggested that incestuous abuse is not so much *sexual* in nature as a reflection of other psychological needs (e.g., Groth, 1982), others have argued that a complete understanding of the sexual orientation and fantasies of incest fathers is critical (e.g., Frude, 1982).

Of specific interest is the degree to which the father is a pedophile; that is, the extent to which he is sexually attracted to young girls in general. Clinicians and researchers have been adamant in their belief that most incest fathers are not pedophiles (Batten, 1983; Justice & Justice, 1979; Meiselman, 1978). One could argue, in fact, that there is no more reason for a pedophile to want to have sex with his own child than for an adult heterosexual to want to have sex with his adult sister. And although an often cited penile plethysmographic study found incest fathers to be sexually aroused by scenes depicting sex with young girls (Abel et al., 1981), there were serious methodological problems with the study (e.g., extremely small sample and no control group). However, the possibility always remains that the incestuous abuse is partially a result of a generalized pedophile fantasy on the part of the offending father and thus should not be ruled out.

There are other aspects of the offending father's sexuality that should be assessed: his sexual attitudes and beliefs; the content of his fantasies; the quality and frequency of his sexual relationship with his wife and extramaritally; his body image; and his general sexual knowledge. We use a combination of a structured sex history using the Purdue Sex History Form (see Appendix) and the paper-and-pencil DSFI (Derogatis & Melisaratos, 1979). For example, a particularly vulnerable combination might be the father's rigid attitudes, incest fantasies, poor quality and low frequency of sexual behavior with his wife, poor body image, and little factual sexual knowledge.

Although there has been much attention paid lately to the concept of sexual addiction (Carnes, 1985), we have found few of our incest fathers to fall into this category. At the same time, if the father's sexual behavior with the daughter is part of a larger compulsive sex problem, the possibility of sexual addiction must be considered. If this is the case, then involvement in a sexual addiction self-help group will certainly be a useful adjunct to the program.

Involvement with child care and nurturance. It is essential to question both the father and the mother regarding the extent of the father's early care and nurturance with the children, especially the abused daughter. Recent research has shown this to be a very important contributor to an individual's vulnerability to abuse (Parker & Parker, 1986).

Nonoffending Mother

The assessment of the nonoffending mother must be accomplished without the process itself giving the unintentional message that she is somehow responsible for the abuse, since a philosophical theme of our entire program is that the offending father is ultimately responsible for the incest. However, the mother must be evaluated both for her contributions to the family's vulnerability to incest and for any psychological consequences she may be harboring as a result of the incestuous abuse. Also, the mother's own childhood traumas, if she experienced these, must be thoroughly explored during assessment and throughout treatment.

A number of characteristics of nonoffending mothers have been identified as possible contributors or concomitant factors. In particular, she should be evaluated for emotional absence or incapacitation from her husband or children, passivity and unassertiveness, and dependency issues. Sexual disorders are common, particularly inhibited sexual desire. Most cited in the literature is the appearance of a role reversal with her daughter, where the mother appears almost to need and receive parenting from her child (Meiselman, 1978; Zuelzer & Reposa, 1983).

Therapists should be hesitant to "overpathologize" the fact that a nonoffending mother did not report the abuse when she first discovered it. Although it is tempting to see this as collusion or denial, there are compelling reasons for a mother not to report the abuse of her daughter. First, she may fear her husband's physical retaliation, particularly in aggression-exchange or rage-expression families. Second, there is a certain amount of shame associated with the publicizing of incest, and the mother may feel embarrassed to admit that her husband and daughter were having sex with one another "right under her nose." Third, mothers may fear that once reported, her husband will either be removed from the family or incarcerated and that this will leave the family in economic ruin. Finally, mothers may wish to protect the rest of the children from the catastrophic disruption that will likely ensue if she reports the abuse. With all of these very sound reasons, it is no wonder many nonoffending mothers postpone or simply refuse to report the abuse.

Daughter

As with the nonoffending mother, the therapist should be concerned that the assessment of the daughter be done in a way that does not imply she is responsible for the incest. But as with the nonoffending mother, there are a number of dimensions that should be assessed to better understand the child's involvement with the abuse and its effect on her.

It is most critical to assess any psychological disorders present in the daughter. Although surprisingly rare (Scott & Stone, 1986), these problems must be identified if present. The most common of these are depression, social withdrawal, and acting-out behaviors. These are often situational and reflect the tremendous upheaval in the child's life as a result of the discovery as much as the incest itself (e.g., it is not uncommon for an incest victim to be placed in a foster home for her "protection"). It is a testimony to the resilience of children that in the face of the profound crisis and disruption present when the incest is discovered, the daughters fare as well as they do.

Another major psychological problem to assess is faulty reality testing. This is most likely in a family where there has been open denial of facts by both parents and where the child is younger. We have seen cases where a prepubescent child was sexually and physically abused by her father but was continually told by her mother that she was "a lying little slut" when she disclosed the abuse to her mother. She developed a rich fantasy life to defend against the abuse, but then displayed difficulty in separating fantasy from reality.

Incestuously abused adolescents more commonly display behavior disorders, such as running away and increased sexual acting out (deYoung, 1982). It is important to evaluate the girl's knowledge about sexuality, particularly reproduction and sexually transmitted diseases. Sometimes the daughters, especially in affection-exchange families, learn that sex can get attention, and they try to obtain this from their peer group as well as their family. Understanding this sex-for-affection cycle is important to determine how the daughter may have contributed to the family's vulnerability to incest (Justice & Justice, 1979).

Finally, it is essential to evaluate how the daughter's being sexually involved with her father has affected her relationship with the rest of her family. In some families the daughter has increased attention, favors, and money. There is often a *quid-pro-quo* relationship that results in the daughter clearly being the special child, usually to the resentment of the other children. This position of power is not only unsuited for a child, but isolates her from her siblings and even her mother.

Strategies for Assessing

As previously mentioned, our individual assessments are done by a family psychologist, or at least a psychologist who is specially trained in family systems assessment. We use both objective type personality tests such as the MMPI to assess for psychological disorders, and projective techniques such as the TAT and Kinetic Family Drawing to assess the way the individuals see themselves within their family. We also may use intelligence testing to better understand the cognitive styles of individuals. Other tests, such as the DSFI (Derogatis & Melisaratos, 1979), are employed to evaluate specific issues, such as sexuality, as necessary (see Table 6.1 for a complete list of tests typically used).

Much of our individual evaluation comes from separate sessions with the person during the assessment period. We have found that in order to obtain accurate information about things that are usually difficult to speak about, it is useful to talk "as if" the experience in question were true. For example, when questioning a father about possible generalized sexual fantasies of children (to assess for pedophilia), the therapist should ask "*How often* do you fantasize about other young girls?" rather than, "Do you *ever* fantasize about other young girls?" The assumption is made that he does, and it is then his responsibility to correct the therapist. This is also a useful strategy because there is not a judgment associated with the question itself. So, for example, saying to the daughter, "You know, many girls who were molested also enjoy having sex with boys their own age. How often do you have sex with guys you go out with?" is more likely to elicit an honest response because there appears to be no judgment involved.

It is a difficult yet critical task to gather the individual assessment information without implying blame, especially for the mother and daughter, and even to some degree for the father. After all, this is assessment, not intervention per se. The therapist wants to obtain accurate information *and* to engender the trust of the clients by joining. This will reduce resistance and allow for the intensive interventions that will come during Stage II of therapy. And at all times, the therapist must keep in mind what is and is not the purpose of the individual evaluation: It is not to *label* the family members, but to clarify which individual variables contributed to the family's overall vulnerability to incest.

PRECIPITATING EVENTS

Precipitating events are not vulnerability factors per se, but occurrences that may act to trigger an already vulnerable family into incestuous episodes. For the most part, precipitating events are idiosyncratic to the family. The challenge for the therapist is to identify those events under which episodes usually occur, so that interventions can be designed to reduce these events. Although there are numerous possible precipitants, the three most common will be briefly discussed.

Alcohol or *substance abuse* has been found to precede incestuous episodes in the majority of cases (Maisch, 1973; Morgan, 1982; Virkkunen,

1974). Intoxication does not in and of itself cause the abuse. Instead, it may act as a disinhibitor to the father already experiencing incestuous impulses (Finkelhor, 1984) and living in a vulnerable family. Alcohol or substance use also provides a mechanism for "Denial of Awareness" (see Chapter 7) by allowing the individual to "forget" having sex with his daughter. The father then does not have to deal cognitively with the reality that he has committed one of the most unacceptable acts, having sex with his own daughter.

Another often-cited precipitant is the *opportunity factor* (Batten, 1983). Vulnerable families often have incestuous episodes while the father and daughter are left alone for extended periods, such as when the mother works evening shifts. In our program, one of the most common times for incestuous episodes is when the mother is in the hospital for one reason or another. This may also reflect an acute stress period, also known to be a precipitant.

Acute stress may act as a precipitant by exacerbating the very factors that make the family vulnerable to incest in the first place. These stressors can include loss of a job, a newly manifested physical disability, or a change in the family composition, such as a new child being born. Acute stress may also reduce the family's access to previously utilized coping mechanisms. For example, when one father lost his job, the family stopped going to their church for fear of embarrassment. This isolated the family from its social support network, which may have helped prevent the incestuous episodes which now occurred for the first time in the family's history.

Precipitants can best be assessed by a thorough questioniong of the sequence of events that led to the incestuous abuse. This may be difficult to ascertain during this early period of therapy since the family members may be denying facts or awareness (see Chapter 7). However, the astute therapist, through careful questioning of all family members, will eventually be able to outline the sequence of events leading up to the incestuous episodes. For example, the degree of alcohol or substance abuse present is not difficult to assess if the therapist has access to the entire family (children are superb at describing the amount of substances consumed by the parents and under what circumstances).

COPING MECHANISMS

Assuming that a family is vulnerable to incest and that a precipitating event has occurred, does that mean an incestuous episode will occur?

Not necessarily. The last variable that we examine is the effectiveness of the family's coping mechanisms. If these are operating successfully, even a family vulnerable to incest and that has precipitating events present may not engage in incestuous behavior.

There are many possible coping mechanisms used by families to deal with all manner of dysfunctional behavior, including incestuous abuse. These, like precipitating events, are idiosyncratic to the family. However, there are some coping mechanisms that often are lacking in incestuous families.

Social Networks

The first important coping mechanism is a positive social network outside the family. This may include an extended family, friends, work relationships, and the like. If a daughter has a strong relationship with her grandmother, for example, one where she feels loved, safe, and trusted, then any inappropriate sexual advance made by her father is likely to result in her going to her grandmother, who in turn will "do something about it." Also, a father who is being hounded by sexual fantasies for his stepdaughter might feel safe talking about it with his brother if that is a strong relationship. A family with strong social network can use those networks to cope, even if vulnerable in other ways.

Religious Belief System

Although many incestuous families identify themselves as religious, for many the "fear of God" may be enough to thwart incestuous episodes and allow them to remain simply a fantasy. Also, the strong social network associated with some churches may add an extra coping mechanism for a vulnerable family. However, many use their religious beliefs to support their abusive behavior.

Use of Fantasy

For some offending fathers, the incestuous fantasy remains just that, a fantasy. Some have been successful in using erotic materials with incestuous content in masturbation, and in some cases this acts to inhibit the actual behavior. We would never suggest the use of such materials therapeutically, as that may run the risk of communicating acceptance of incest. However, the ability to use a *fantasy* to prevent it from becoming a *behavior* is a coping mechanism for many people (virtually everyone has sexual fantasies that they would never put into practice).

Therapy or Self-Help Group Availability

After completing our program, many of our incest families use their relationship with their therapist as a coping mechanism to prevent further sexual abuse or being further sexually abused. For example, one father who had completed therapy two years previously contacted us to discuss a problem he was having. He reported that his daughter, whom he had sexually molested, was now leaving the bathroom door unlocked while she was in there naked, and he had walked in on her once. He was concerned both that she was trying to gain power by acting "seductively" and that he could become sexually aroused again. We met with the family a few times to discuss sexual boundaries and helped them place limits on access to "private areas" such as bathrooms. Most important, however, was that the father called the therapist at the first hint of trouble. This was highly appropriate and demonstrated a new coping mechanism previously unavailable to the family.

Strategies for Assessing

We begin assessing coping mechanisms with a paper-and-pencil test called F-Copes (Olson et al., 1982). This provides information on areas of family coping, including social support, the ability to reframe problems in a positive manner, use of religion, and accepting help from outside sources. From this, the therapist can test other hypotheses concerning family coping strategies, using standard interview techniques.

PROBLEMS IN ASSESSMENT

A Family in Immediate Crisis

The formal assessment period usually begins with the first session and continues for about four to six weeks, during which time the entire family, relevant subsystems, and individuals are seen in session and tested. Sometimes, however, the crisis of discovery (see Chapter 5) precludes *formal* assessment. If this occurs, it should be recognized that *informal* assessment is ongoing. Most therapists could, after seeing the family in a crisis state for a number of weeks, fairly well appraise them along the vulnerability dimensions. In fact, viewing a family in severe crisis can provide the best look at their true systemic functioning because their collective guards are down, resistance is minimal, and the real underlying issues usually emerge.

One of the "rewards" for the family containing the crisis is the continuation of "formal" program therapy. As long as they are stuck, the family is told, therapy is not able to proceed. This reframing of a crisis as "understandable but an inhibitor to therapeutic movement" is used periodically throughout the program to motivate clients to successfully resolve their crises.

Entire Family Not Able to Be Present

This presents only a minimal problem in terms of assessment. Family therapists must often infer systemic functioning without having access to each family member or the family as a whole. Incest families are often separated because the father is incarcerated or the daughter is living with relatives who are uncooperative with therapy ("We don't want to subject her to any more of *that* family!").

It is important, however, to do whatever is possible to gain access to as many family members as possible. One of the goals of the networking process (see Chapter 4) is to have protective services ensure the daughter's involvement in therapy. When the father is incarcerated, we have sometimes been permitted to meet with him for assessment in jail. If that is not possible, we proceed with the rest of the family in the meantime and hope he will be available when his term is up (most of our fathers who serve time in prison do so for between six and 18 months).

Whenever possible, it is advisable to have the extended family present for at least one of the assessment sessions. It is not unusual for incestuously abusing parents to have severe problems with their own parents, who in turn may have an important impact on the family. This is particularly true if the grandparents have temporary custody of the abused child. It is not uncommon in these situations for strong negative messages regarding her parents to be communicated to the child via the grandparents, especially if there are old issues not yet resolved. That, plus the humiliation of incestuous abuse itself, may cause the final rift between grandparents and parents, and, of course, it is critical that this be fully understood by the parents.

Resistance to Assessment

As previously discussed in Chapter 3, resistance to therapy by incest families is to be expected and actually can be a "healthy" sign. Families may express resistance at this early stage in all of the usual manners, such as missed appointments, not cooperating during the testing, questioning the therapist's competence, and so on. The therapist should not take this as a personal affront, but use the resistance to his or her advantage to gain therapeutic control.

One strategy to counter the resistance to assessment is to reframe the resistance as positive. For example, when questioning his or her ability to competently assess the family, the therapist might say, "It is a good sign that you are questioning my abilities. That means not only are you a good consumer, but also you care enough about your family to only want the best for them." There are a number of other specific antiresistance techniques used in family therapy that can be used to disarm resistance to assessment; for a complete discussion of these see Anderson and Stewart (1983).

The ultimate weapon against resistance during assessment, however, is the control the therapist has over matters important to the family, such as visitation rights and a positive case review for the court (Anderson & Shafer, 1979). After encouraging them to maintain their resistance as long as they need to, the therapist might remind them that their counseling has effectively halted until the family proceeds through the assessment process. For example, the message is made clear that while no therapeutic movement occurs, there is no hope that the father will be allowed back in the home. Also, the family can be reminded that their progress report to protective services and the court will reflect this lack of movement.

Difficulty Accurately Assessing Degree of Pedophilia in Father

Although most incest fathers are not true pedophiles, there is some evidence that those who are will not honestly report either the degree or extent of their interest in young girls in general (Abel et al., 1981). If the therapist has access to a university or teaching hospital which uses plethmysography, it is possible that the father could be assessed using this objective physiological measure. However as pointed out earlier, this technique is not always reliable, and in fact some pedophiles are able to fake nonpedophile responses (Langevin & Lang, 1985).

The only "talking technique" that we have found useful is to directly question the fathers during their individual assessment *as if* they were true pedophiles. In other words, to say, "When you get aroused by other young girls, how do you make advances to them?" is more productive than to ask, "Do you ever become aroused by young girls other than your daughter?" Although easily seen through by some clients, it still puts the burden of proof onto them to convince you that they are *not* aroused by other young girls, and/or would not act upon those impulses if they were. Under these conditions, a father who is a pedophile may be able to be detected.

Agency-related Problems

There are number of problems that arise during the assessment process that are directly attributable to the structure of the particular agency providing the treatment program. These include the following:

Agency limits number of contacts per week. Some agencies under contract with a protective service agency are only paid for one contact hour per week per family. If this is the case, that particular contract should be renegotiated. In our opinion, an agency policy that inhibits the effective treatment of clients is unethical. It is clear that incestuously abusing families usually need more than one contact hour per week, particularly during the assessment period (which also, incidentally, is the time when the most severe family crises are likely to occur). Although every therapist must conform to agency policies to some extent, we believe this particular limitation places an undue constraint on therapy. The therapists at an agency who work with incestuously abusing families should meet with administrators to help develop a plan that will allow for as many contacts as necessary to adequately assess and treat the family.

Agency demands certain inappropriate tests. Occasionally, an agency has tests mandated for certain clients, regardless of their proven usefulness. For example, we have known of agencies that required a complete neuropsychological battery on every incest father, even if there was no suggestion of brain dysfunction from other psychological screenings. We have even known of one agency psychiatrist to routinely require a brain CAT scan on each offending incest father—this in spite of the fact that there was no evidence of brain dysfunction in any of the incest fathers.

Given the political and hierarchical realities of most agencies, there is little a nonmedical therapist can do to alleviate this problem. The only hope is for the therapist providing incest treatment to also provide training to the staff on appropriate assessment of incest families. This may be difficult, particularly if the therapist is not a psychologist or psychiatrist. Another possibility is for the therapist to share his or her concerns with the supervisor or clinical director. However, this may be one of those issues where the therapist will simply have to accept the political realities of mental health and do the best he or she can under the circumstances.

Agency demands contact with clinician who is not trained in incest work. Sometimes an agency requires each of their clients to be evaluated by a person other than the therapist who will be working with the client. They may—because of this clinician's lack of experience in treating incest families, dearth of sensitivity to the issues of sexual abuse, or inability to dissociate his/her own feelings about incest from his/her clinical work—unknowingly work counter to the program. For example, in one agency the staff psychiatrist had to evaluate each individual coming through the system. Inevitably, when incest fathers were evaluated, the psychiatrist diagnosed them antisocial personality disorder and stated in the report that they were untreatable. This was usually in direct contradiction of the social worker who ran the incest treatment program and who had been effectively treating incestuously abusing families for years. This situation inevitably led to conflicts, particularly when a report for the court was due.

The therapist working in such a system can often circumvent the problem by developing a close working relationship with *one* of these "required clinicians" (be it psychiatrist, psychologist, or intake worker), by training him or her in the treatment of incestuously abusing families, and by trying to get each of their families referred to that person for evaluation. An even better solution is to include that person on the "Incest Team" (or whatever it is called at the agency) so he or she can fully understand the complexities of the program and work with it rather than against it.

7

Denial

One of the most perplexing occurrences in Stage I of therapy is the tendency by family members to *deny* aspects of the incestuous abuse. Many therapists working for the first time with incest families are incensed when faced with a father who denies the abuse ever occurred; or when a daughter who previously reported the abuse recants her story to protect her father from certain incarceration; or when a mother continues to deny the possibility of her daughter being sexually abused even when the father and daughter both admit it happened. However, after working for a while with abusing families, most therapists come to expect a certain degree of denial, and may even learn to put it to "therapeutic use."

Reasons for Denial

Denial is a special case of a family's natural resistance to change, therapy, and the intrusion into their lives by social welfare agencies. Denial should be viewed not as a pathological or dysfunctional state, but as a protective device for the family members as individuals and for the family as a whole.

Denial can take one of two etiological forms. The first is *psychological* denial, where the denial is unconscious and the "truth" may be unavailable to the individual even if directly confronted with it. This form of denial is probably most akin to classical repression. With psychological denial, the individual does not cognitively experience the reality of the abuse as others would. For example, consider the child who denies responsibility by claiming she *caused* the abuse because she asked her father a sexual question (after which he "showed" her the answer). She does not truly believe that her father is the responsible one, even when the therapist confronts her with the reality of the situation.

The second form of denial is *social* denial. In this case, the decision to deny is *conscious* and made to protect the individual or the family. If the denial is continually confronted, it may be broken down, especially if doing so can be shown to be more useful than to maintain the denial. An example of social denial is when a father consciously denies that he molested his daughter for fear of going to jail; the therapist then convinces him that to admit to the abuse is an important first step in the therapy process and will allow the therapist to make a positive first report to the court. Because the denial is *social* (conscious), the father can then make the conscious decision to admit to the molestation.

In either form—psychological or social—the reason for the denial should be viewed as self-protective, guarding both the individuals in the family and the family as a whole. Therapists typically regard behavior that is protective as functional. Denial of incestuous abuse—whether to defend one's psyche from the reality of having engaged in the most taboo of behaviors or to defend against one's family being broken into pieces by the authorities—can be quite understandable.

Effects of Denial

Denial should never be encouraged by a therapist for a number of reasons. First, denial may appear to excuse rather than to protect. A theme of our program is the acceptance of responsibility by the offending parent. If a therapist allows denial to continue unchallenged, he or she may tacitly excuse the behavior. Second, if the *denial of facts* is maintained in spite of protests from the daughter she may eventually doubt her own reality testing, leading to more severe psychopathology in adulthood. Third, unchallenged denial communicates to children in the family that to *not* accept the truth and take the consequences is acceptable, a value few parents would wish children to learn. It would be intolerable for a family therapist to unknowingly model positive consequences for denial, and therefore he or she must be acutely aware of that possibility at all times during therapy.

FOUR TYPES OF DENIAL

We have identified four major types of denial which present clinically by sexually abusing families. Although most people present only one type of denial, sometimes two or even three are manifested at the same time by the same person. Any member of the family may deny any of the types of denial during the course of therapy. These four types of denial are: (1) denial of facts; (2) denial of awareness; (3) denial of responsibility; and (4) denial of impact.

Denial of Facts

An individual is said to demonstrate a *denial of facts* when he or she openly challenges the reality of the incestuous abuse. Either the abuse itself or the details of the abuse might be challenged, but in any event the person disputes the information as it is understood by the therapist. Denial of facts is happily not the most common, but it is the most pernicious form of denial and has the most therapeutic difficulties associated with it. In general, therapy cannot proceed beyond Stage I if there is a continued denial of facts.

The denial of facts by the father, mother, or child all take a similar form. For each, the occurrence of the abuse itself is said to be untrue, or the specifics are untrue. All three may collectively deny by corroborating an alternative story ("Oh, she just didn't get along with her father, so she made up a story that he messed around with her"). However, it is more likely that one person, usually the daughter, will accuse her father of the abuse and that he will state that *she* is lying. It is not uncommon, however, for a *father* to admit to the abuse, while his daughter (fearing the consequences for her father) denies its occurrence.

Unfortunately, in their understandable zeal to protect children from further abuse, some jurisdictions actually encourage denial of facts by pressing for criminal charges filed against all abusing fathers in spite of the recommendations by the therapists to the contrary. A father who has a criminal charge pending against him is often advised by his attorney (or figures it out for himself) that it is in his best interest to admit to as little as possible prior to the court date, often months or even years away. This in effect halts therapy in its tracks, particularly if the admission of facts is an important component of the counseling. A far better approach is to suspend criminal charges pending the outcome of therapy, or to make the condition of a probation to participate in the counseling process. This makes denial of facts disadvantageous for the family members and makes meaningful therapeutic change more likely.

Denial of facts by the father. Again, the most common form of denial of facts is a simple challenge to the authenticity of the abuse. Most denial of facts by the father is a *social denial,* where admitting to the abuse can lead to embarrassment, divorce, and/or incarceration, and therefore it appears only prudent to lie. Dad states, "It just never happened," or some more nasty variation such as, "She's a lying little whore with a dirty mind, who is trying to do me in." The father may also deny the extent of the abuse, such as, "I only fondled her that one time when I was drunk," when indeed the incest had involved intercourse and on a number of occasions.

Denial of facts by the mother. The nonoffending mother denies the facts of the abuse more often than most would imagine, and often for reasons that could be considered protective of her and her family (see Chapter 6). Usually, her denial occurs in tandem with her husband's denial ("If he says he didn't do it, he didn't do it!"). And occasionally the mother refutes the admission of the incest by *both* father and daughter ("They are just making this up to get back at me!").

Denial of facts by the daughter. Although most therapists assume that the daughter will not deny facts, it is quite common for her to do so. She may deny the abuse from the onset, such as when it was circumstantially discovered by another family member ("Grandma doesn't know what she's talking about, she's just trying to get back at my dad!"). More likely, she will recant the admission at a later time ("I don't know why I said it happened; I guess I was just trying to get my stepdad into trouble with my mom").

What If the Abuse Did Not Occur?

With denial of facts, there is always the unsettling possibility that the incestuous abuse being denied may not have actually occurred. This is especially troublesome if both the father and the daughter are claiming that it did not happen and if the evidence presented is circumstantial.

It is an accepted notion that almost all reported abuse ultimately turns out to be true (which is a corollary to another accepted notion that "children do not lie about sexual abuse"). Although we have seen no empirical data either accepting or refuting this claim, we can state that in over 10 years of working with sexual abuse cases we have known of only a few cases where a denied report of child sexual abuse was indeed false. In almost every other case, the denying family member came to admit to the abuse or continued to deny it in spite of evidence clear enough to convince a court to convict the father. In any event, it is rare indeed for the authenticity of the incest to remain in doubt very long.

It should be kept in mind, however, that there will be those rare occurrences when the father did *not* molest the child and that the denial was valid. It is difficult to balance the need to protect a child from abuse with the rights of a father to be safeguarded from ungrounded accusations. And while our system of jurisprudence guarantees innocence until guilt is proven beyond a shadow of a doubt, most men accused of incestuous abuse are seen as guilty *ipso facto*.

In cases where the father continues to deny that the abuse occurred, while his daughter maintains that it did, we usually give the following "speech":

Therapist: We understand that you say you did not abuse your child, and yet she still claims you did. We should tell you that in our many years of working with incestuous abuse, it is *very* rare for a child to lie about being molested, and there is no reason now for us to doubt her report. We should also add that protective services, who work with hundreds of abuse cases a year, also believe your daughter. However, we are not a judge. If you have indeed not abused your daughter, you should get an attorney to represent you, and you should fight the charges. Since we are not in the business of discovering who is telling the truth, and because we generally believe the claims of children unless there is reason to doubt them, we will not be able to work with you in family therapy, although we can continue to work with your daughter. We should also tell you that if we must testify in court, we will tell the judge what we have told you here, namely, that we have no reason to doubt that abuse occurred. We do wish you the best of luck, however.

The purpose of this speech is twofold. First, if the father is indeed innocent of the charges, we do not wish to encourage him to lie and "admit" to abuse he did not commit. We always try and put ourselves in the position of an individual falsely accused of sexual impropriety (something which conceivably could happen to a therapist!), and then advise that an appropriate defense be mounted through an attorney. Second, if the father *is* lying, this speech effectively isolates him from the family and from any possible assistance that the therapist may be able to provide if he were to admit to the abuse.

Denial of Awareness

A family member who states that *if* the abuse has occurred it has happened without his or her cognizance is *denying awareness*. Denial of awareness is more likely to be *psychological* than social; that is, the lack of awareness is usually reflective of repression more than a conscious decision to lie. Denial of awareness is considered less serious than denial of facts because the individual at least maintains the *possibility* that the abuse occurred, giving the therapist a toehold to work with. Denial of awareness subsumes another type, *denial of responsibility*, since one is not truly "responsible" if one does not remember the action.

Denial of awareness by the father. The most common way an offending father denies awareness is by claiming that he was intoxicated at the time of the abuse ("I guess I did it if you guys tell me I did, but you know, I have this drinking problem, and when I get drunk I don't remember a thing"). Although there is no doubt many people do black out if sufficiently intoxicated, we do question the father's ability to achieve and maintain an erection if he is so drunk as to not remember having sex with his daughter.

In a recent version of denial of awareness, offending fathers who were also Vietnam veterans claim that they experience "post-traumatic stress disorder blackouts," during which time the abuse "may have occurred." It is possible for an already vulnerable father in a family vulnerable to incest to sexually abuse his daughter during a precipitating post-traumatic stress episode. However, the father should be carefully assessed to see if he indeed suffers from this disorder. It is more likely that with the current publicity given to post-traumatic stress syndrome an abusing father has simply found a convenient "social" denial of awareness.

Denial of awareness by the mother. It is quite common for a nonoffending mother to claim she did not know of the abuse when it was happening. We often hear, "I cannot believe I didn't know about it when it was happening right under my nose!" Even more curious is the situation where the mother is directly told by her daughter that the abuse occurred and the mother continues to maintain that she was unaware, saying, "She may have told me, but I don't remember." This is heard with such regularity that it cannot be assumed outright to be lying or social denial. Instead, this is probably a psychological denial of awareness, where the reality of the abuse is so potentially disabling that a mother must block the reality of it from her awareness.

Denial of awareness by the daughter. Incestuously abused daughters usually deny awareness by claiming to have been asleep when the molestation took place. Some may also maintain that they simply do not remember. Another version finds the daughter saying, "I didn't know that what he was doing was sexual," usually in response to fondling. Finally, very young girls may deny awareness by turning the experience into a dream or fantasy, and when questioned they will not be able to understand the molestation as a fact. In this case, the denial is almost always psychological rather than social.

Denial of Responsibility

An exceptionally common form of denial, *denial of responsibility*, arises when a family member admits to the occurrence of the abuse and is also aware of it happening. What *is* disputed, however, is the offending father's ultimate culpability. Instead, the blame is placed on another person ("I wouldn't have to touch her if my wife would give me some sex now and then!") or other external events ("It's all because he lost his job . . . he just hasn't been the same since the mill closed"). Denial of responsibility can be a form of protection of the offending parent by other family members who believe (or wish to believe) that "father can do no wrong." It may also reflect the societal view that men are "forced" into abusive sexuality by seductive, cunning, teasing, or sexually withholding women.

Denial of responsibility is particularly baneful since it *justifies* the abuse, making its recurrence under some other "acceptable" conditions possible. For example, if the mother excuses her husband's having sex with their daughter because "he was drunk," she is reducing the abuse to a justifiable consequence of a socially acceptable behavior. Is committing any crime defensible because it occurred while "under the influence," or must the individual ultimately take responsibility for all his actions?

Denial of responsibility by the father. A father can deny responsibility in a variety of ways. He may claim that his daughter was seductive, that she wanted to be sexual with him, and that after she aroused him he could not help himself. A common variation of the seduction theme occurs when the father says he had sex with his daughter in response to a sexual question: "She asked me what a blow job was and I showed her," with the implication being that if she had not asked he would not have been "forced" to show her. As noted above, a father may deny responsibility by blaming his intoxicated condition for the abuse. Finally, a father might believe that the sexual difficulties he is having with his wife *made* him seek sex with his daughter.

Denial of responsibility by the mother. A mother might ascribe the responsibility for the abuse to the same factors as her husband. For example, she may blame her daughter, either for overt seduction or at least for not halting his advances when they were made ("She must have really wanted to do it if she let him; hell, I have no problem telling him *no*!"). The mother might also blame herself ("If I had only been there for him sexually, he wouldn't have had to do this"), and, of course, the ubiquitous alcohol ("When he gets real drunk, there's no telling what he'll do").

Denial of responsibility by the daughter. It is particularly sad but common for the daughter to take the responsibility for the abuse. There often is an irrational belief present that because she was unsuccessful in stopping him, she is therefore to blame for the incest. A number of daughters who were molested in response to asking a sexual question feel that *the asking of the question* made them responsible. And many daughters deny their fathers' responsibility by blaming their mothers; this is especially true for adolescent girls who may already be experiencing conflicts with their mothers.

Denial of Impact

Denial of impact means that, while admitting to the facts, awareness, and responsibility, the family member lessens the intensity or meaning of the incestuous abuse, in a sense suggesting that "it wasn't really very abusive at all." This is probably the least serious of the four types of denial for a couple of reasons. First, denial of facts and awareness deal with the *reality of the abuse*, and confrontation by the therapist can basically be seen as calling the person a liar. Denial of responsibility focuses on the ultimate *blame* for the abuse, and the process of "blaming" usually produces a hostile response. Denial of impact, however, is merely a *softening* of the facts and locus of responsibility. Second, no major cognitive shift is necessary, nor is there an admitting to something new that might land the offending parent in jail. For these reasons, denial of impact is also the easiest upon which to intervene.

Denial of impact by the father, mother, and daughter. For all three of these family members, the denial of impact takes on a similar form. The incest is seen in terms of *onlys:* "It was *only* fondling"; "I *only* touched her, she didn't have to touch me" (or the converse, "She *only* touched me, I didn't touch her"); "We *only* did it a few times"; "He *only* had intercourse with her once." Denial of impact can also apply to the consequences, or rather the lack of consequences, of the incest: "It doesn't bother me at all that he and I messed around"; "She's real young, it won't really affect her that much"; "She might even have gotten something out of it . . . after all, some parents don't spend any time with their daughters."

TREATMENT OF DENIAL

The ultimate goal is for the denial to end and for all family members to accept the reality of the abuse. At the beginning, however, the therapist should understand the denial as a necessary defense mechanism and treat it with the respect afforded other dysfunctional family coping styles. Denial, as previously discussed, is yet another form of resistance to therapy and should be viewed as an added therapeutic challenge rather than a personal affront.

There should be no or minimal denial present by the end of therapy, because denial in and of itself is a factor that can contribute to a family's vulnerability to incest. However, some types of denial are worse than others and should be of most therapeutic concern. For example, denial of the facts about the abuse is so serious a problem that therapy cannot proceed into Stage II until it ceases.

There are no certain methods to ending denial. Denial tends to be very tenacious and difficult to shatter, particularly when there are good reasons to maintain it. For example, it is understandable for a daughter who does not want her father to go to prison to recant her disclosure that he fondled her twice. As far as she is concerned, it wasn't serious enough to warrant that strong a response, and thus she now claims that she lied. And certainly few would not understand an incestuous father denying the facts of the abuse if doing so might prevent his incarceration. In these examples, the therapist must often wait until those actions are settled before the family members can reduce their denial. A

TABLE 7.1
Interventions for Denial

I. Denial of Facts
    A. Separate denying father from rest of family
    B. Hold individual sessions with father
    C. Make paradoxical statement: "I wouldn't admit to the facts just yet if I were you"
    D. Reframe that to admit to the facts as in *his* best interest
    E. Speak "as if" the abuse occurred
    F. Suggest the father may have to risk jail to do a "selfless act" for the family

II. Denial of Awareness
    A. Accept substance abuse as a "reason," but insist on intensive treatment for it
    B. Suggest the possibility that the "memories might come back spontaneously"

III. Denial of Responsibility
    A. Constantly confront family on misplaced responsibility.
    B. Model accurate statements concerning responsibility.
    C. Reframe for family how it is in their best interest to place responsibility accurately with father
    D. Spread the responsibility to entire family for making the family better in general
    E. Hold Apology Session

IV. Denial of Impact
    A. Use all of above interventions
    B. Explain negative consequences of giving-up denial
    C. Confront use of euphemisms for abuse and replace with accurate terms.

number of interventions have been used to reduce denial (e.g., Hoke, Sykes, & Winn, in press). A partial list of these interventions is presented in Table 7.1.

Intervention for Denial of Facts

As previously noted, denial of facts is the most serious type of denial because it questions the validity of the child's reality, and ultimately the validity of therapy itself. After all, if the abuse did not occur, why is the family meeting with the therapist? Therapists can get mired early in therapy with denial of facts, getting into an "I didn't do it!" "Yes you did!" interaction.

When the father is denying facts, the first therapeutic intervention is to separate him from the rest of the family during therapy sessions. This is done for two reasons. First, the therapist does not want to put an abused child in the position of defending herself from the denial of the father; the possibility for intimidation, mystification, or confusion is simply too great. Second, the offending father typically wants to be reunited with his family, and the first step to achieving this is "cooperation in therapy." The therapist can set up a powerful reward for the father by making entire-family sessions contingent upon his admitting to the facts of the abuse; conversely, the therapist can "punish" the denying father by withholding entire-family sessions.

Another intervention is for the therapist to have a series of individual sessions with the offending father, the purpose of which is to gain his trust and respect. As such, the therapist should not enter into a power play with him, but instead use the joining techniques common to all family therapy. Sometimes a paradoxical statement is useful at the beginning of the individual sessions: "I wouldn't admit to the facts concerning the abuse just yet if I were you. . . . You don't know me, and you don't know what I may do to you if you were to stop denying." This intervention is productive for a couple of reasons. It forces the father to accept the sincerity of the therapist by suggesting the possibility of insincerity. It also implies that the therapist knows the "truth," but accepts the underlying *function* of the denial, making the father less nefarious for not admitting. It also provides a time frame for the ending of the denial ("not just yet" implies "soon").

A very important intervention is for the therapist to provide a framework defining that it is in the individual's best interest to admit to the facts of the abuse. For example, the therapist can remind the family that as long as denial of facts is occurring, therapy can proceed only so far, and this, of course, will have to be communicated to the court; however, when the denial ends, then the family can get back to the work change that everyone involved so much wants. A daughter who has recanted her disclosure to protect her father might be told, "Your daddy may never get to return home if the court thinks you are lying to protect him."

An intervention that we use periodically throughout the program, the *negative consequences of change*, can be quite useful in stopping the denial of facts. Some of the common negative consequences of "giving up the denial" include conflict with the family, pain, suicide attempts, embarrassment, depression, guilt, and, of course, incarceration. The therapist should address the negative consequences of giving up the denial with the father, mother, and daughter:

Therapist: (*to the father*) Your daughter initially said that you abused her. Now she is saying that she was very angry at you and was trying to punish you. You know that I think there is a great possibility that she is saying this as a way to protect you. Pretend with me for a while; you have to be here, you might as well indulge me. Let's pretend it's true, and you admit it to me now. What are all the bad things that could happen to you if you told me you abused your daughter?

Father: Well, that's obvious, I could go to jail, my wife would leave me, I'd lose my job, my family, my parents, my friends, my entire life.

Therapist: Yep, maybe, but maybe not. But what will your daughter lose if in fact it happened and you never admit it?

To a mother who is denying the facts about the abuse, the therapist might say:

Therapist: Even if your husband never admits it, but you would decide to believe your daughter and consequently protect her, what do you stand to lose?

Mother: My marriage. I would have to leave him if it were true.

Therapist: Why? Who says you have to leave him? You would have to make a choice, true enough. But a choice implies options; options imply you could stay with changes or leave.

Mother: Everyone would say I'd have to leave—my family, my friends, the church, everyone.

Therapist: You know your husband said that if he ever admitted it he would lose his life, his family, his friends, his parents, the church. Now I see that you agree, and maybe this is helping him to continue to deny. You know if you and your husband ever admitted this, we could move on in therapy and then you *might* be able to have a better life and family than you had before. You will have to convince him that it's okay with you that he admits to the abuse. He needs to know that you don't need him to protect you from the truth. Do you need protecting from the truth?

Mother: I don't know.

Therapist: Then we need to talk about that, because until you are convinced yourself that you can bear to hear the truth without killing yourself, him, your daughter, or all of you going crazy, or any of the other things that you are worried about, then you can never convince him to tell us the truth.

For some families that are not very solidified in their denial of the facts (e.g., the stories keep changing, and sometimes various family members "slip" and admit to the known facts of the abuse), another simple intervention can be used: The therapist can continually speak "as if" the abuse did occur. Using the term "when it happened" rather than "if it happened" in a consistent manner may throw a family's shaky denial of facts into enough confusion that the only way out is to accept the unvarying statements of the therapist.

Through long, tedious, and repetitive sessions, the therapist slowly chisels away at the denial of the facts. The clinician, through questioning, challenging of facts, pointing out discrepancies, preying on the client's sense of decency, and upholding the therapist's own sense of truth, can often break through the denial.

Therapist: (*to the father*) Tell me again how it is possible that you don't know if in fact you sexually abused your daughter or not. You do say sometimes you fell asleep while putting her to bed? (*waiting for an answer*)

Father: (*after long pause*) Yes.

Therapist: I know this is hard and I'm sick of it, too. But humor me, I just don't seem to get it. Anyway, you don't know if you touched her. Do you think you ever had wet dreams?

Father Yes, I suppose I could have.

Therapist: Then maybe that is when you were rubbing up against her.

Father: Yeah, maybe, but is that abuse?

Therapist: Yes, that's not very responsible behavior by a father. Susie says you touched her all over and made her touch your penis . . . and you know I believe her.

Father: Right.

Therapist: You love your daughter, that is obvious. It is also obvious that you want the best for her and want to be a good father. I believe you want her to grow up and have a happy normal adult life. You have the power to make that happen or not, do you realize that?

Father: Yes, I guess I do. You keep reminding me of it.

The following is an example of how direct challenges and repetition may be used to confront the denial of facts by the daughter:

Therapist: I know it's difficult for you to keep talking with everyone about the abuse and the fact you have changed your story.

Daughter: I told you it never happened. He wouldn't let me go out with my boyfriend so I got him back.

Therapist: You know, that right there makes me think he abused you. You know why? First of all, fathers who abuse their daughters are often overinvolved with their social lives and their boyfriends. They behave many times as jealous boyfriends. The fact that he would not let you go out with your boyfriend, who from what you have told me sounds like a decent enough guy, makes me suspicious of your father's motives. It's like he didn't want to lose you. Also, if it was just a simple father and daughter fight, that he wouldn't let you go out for a night. You certainly went to some dangerous extremes to get back at your dad. You don't seem like that disturbed of a person, but maybe I am wrong. Maybe we are barking up the wrong tree here. Maybe it's you who has some real psychological problem that causes you to be so destructive to yourself and your family. To make up such a lie is a pretty serious problem. On the other hand, to tell the truth and then take it away as a way to protect your family is not sick; it's understandable.

There are many fathers who, in spite of all of the preceding interventions, will not budge on their insistence that the abuse did not happen, despite all evidence to the contrary. Again, this is most common when criminal action is likely. Sometimes what can work here as a last resort is a plea to his paternal side to do one good thing for his family, maybe the only good thing he has done for them in a long time. We sometimes refer to this as the "It's a far, far better thing that I do than I have ever done" intervention, after Sydney Carton's final words in Dickens's *A Tale of Two Cities*. During an individual session the offending father is told:

Therapist Yes, if you admit it, you may go to jail. And if you don't, you may get off. But your daughter, who is the true victim here, will have to live with the scars of sexual abuse for the rest of her life, scars *you* caused. Here is your chance to do one selfless thing for your child and your family. I wonder if you are "man enough" to do it?

Interventions for Denial of Awareness

Denial of awareness by the father is generally a little easier to address than denial of facts. If it is based on the father's alcohol or substance abuse, the therapist might "accept" that explanation, provided the father begins intensive substance abuse treatment. This should include regular attendance at AA or NA meetings—"After all," the family is told, "if father becomes so intoxicated that he molests daughter, he must have quite a substance abuse problem!" If he refuses, therapy for him comes to a halt, since he himself has admitted the problem related to substance abuse and yet he spurns treatment for that component.

If the denial of awareness is a social denial (i.e., the father does indeed remember the incident but is using lack of awareness as an excuse), it is important for the therapist to understand the reason underlying the denial. Rarely do incestuously abusing fathers use lack of awareness as a way to prevent legal action. Instead, the fathers are afraid of the consequences for their family: "If my wife thought I knew what was going on when I did it, she'd divorce me!" is commonly heard. In this case, the therapist might provide an "out" by which the father can stop denying awareness without focusing on whether he was aware of it from the beginning. Saying something to the effect of, "Usually during the course of counseling the memories about the molestation come back spontaneously," often allows those memories to "involuntarily" emerge. Some may argue that this intervention actually supports the "lie" that the father does not remember the abuse, and therefore should not be encouraged. However, since the outcome (if this intervention works) is to stop the denial, this is a compromise position a therapist might be willing to take.

Finally, at all times during the period that the family member denies awareness, the therapist should continually talk *as if* the molestation occurred. At no time should the therapist say, "*If* the abuse happened," but instead say, "*When* the abuse happened." Also, the denying family member should be confronted often with statements such as:

Therapist: You may say you don't remember, but between you and me (you did want me to be honest with you, didn't you?), I think you remember just fine; you just have some very good reasons why you want to 'forget.' Maybe we should focus on some of these reasons. . . .

Interventions for Denial of Responsibility

It is not difficult to help incestuously abusing family members to *say* that they now know who was responsible for the abuse; almost all verbalize within the first few weeks of therapy that the father was ultimately at fault (probably because they are feeding the therapist what they perceive he or she wants to hear). However, helping them to *internalize* it is a different story. If a therapist views attitudes as following from behavior (i.e., if people behave a certain way, their attitude toward that behavior becomes more positive), then he or she can use various strategies to get the family to verbalize that father is responsible for the molestation, and can then hope that ultimately father and the rest of the family will believe it.

These strategies include: (1) correcting family members when they state anyone other than the offending father was ultimately responsible (e.g., if the daughter says, "It was my fault for asking the sex question," the therapist responds, "No, it was really your dad's responsibility to not let that question turn into having sex"); (2) modeling for the family accurate statements about responsibility (e.g., "Joe, since you, as the father and the oldest, were ultimately responsible for the sexual abuse, why don't you tell Mary what she should do if you were ever to try and touch her again?"); (3) showing the family why it is to their advantage to place the responsibility appropriately (e.g., "I like how, Joe, you are now taking the responsibility for the sexual abuse; that is a good sign, and I think an important step in the family's therapy"); (4) spreading the responsibility for making the family a better place to live over the *entire* family (e.g., "Dad may have been responsible for the sexual abuse, but what can the rest of you do to make sure these things don't happen again?"); and (5) the Apology Session, which is a formal ritualized session that encourages the offending father to apologize for the molestation and the consequences it has had on the family.

Interventions for Denial of Impact

The therapist will most likely use many of the interventions described above to eliminate denial of impact. These include especially correction and modeling by the therapist, and showing the family where it is in their best interest to accept the seriousness of the abuse. The therapist may also didactically present material on the long-term negative consequences of incest on abused girls, and may also provide reading material. The Structural Session (Chapter 8) provides information on the negative consequences of incest on families and family structure in a way understandable to all. At all times the therapist must be careful not to unintentionally minimize the abuse, which may reinforce the denial of impact. Finally, the therapist should be cautious not to accept the euphemisms for sexual abuse (e.g., "When daddy and Mary *messed around*" or "When she and I *did things*"). Instead, the therapist and the family can agree on one of the following terms: *incest, sexual abuse, abuse,* or *molestation*.

8

The Structural Session

One of the most common and important questions an incestuously abusing family can ask is: How did this happen to us? Most family members know that the answer to this question is complex. However, even when the Vulnerability to Incest model is explained to them, it is rare for a family to have a clear "picture" of what caused incest in their family. The Structural Session, which is a psychoeducational procedure that is presented didactically in the middle of Stage I, was designed to help the family understand how incest happened in a way that they can use as a basis of change. The structural session is usually held after the initial crisis has been managed and a therapeutic relationship has been established.

GOALS OF THE STRUCTURAL SESSION

There are five major goals of the Structural Session: (1) to create an atmosphere for the family members that is conducive to therapy; (2) to provide a common language between the therapist and the family which can be used throughout therapy; (3) to at least partially answer the question: How did this happen to us? (4) to provide a visual metaphor of the symptom and the changes that will be necessary for change to occur; and (5) to continue to assess the family's structure.

Creating a Positive Atmosphere

The incestuous family's view of themselves after the discovery is usually quite negative. Family members are often angry at each other and at the outside "intruders." Once the taboo behavior is no longer a secret they may see themselves and the situation as hopeless. Through the Structural Session the therapist helps the family comprehend the severity of the problem, yet simultaneously realize that change is possible. The therapist helps the family change a deficit view to one that is based on strengths. The Structural Session allows the family members to see themselves as able to change, to give them "a light at the end of the tunnel."

The therapist explains to the family during the Structural Session that incestuous behavior is partially the result of confused generational boundaries and their choice of family roles and rules. This is not meant to minimize or normalize the sexual abuse. On the contrary, this removes the problem from the realm of "illness" and reframes it into one of "responsibility." Through this intervention the family can connote incestuous abuse in terms of "choice," which implies the ability to change, rather than "sickness," which implies hopelessness.

Providing a Common Language

During the Structural Session the family is supplied with the words the therapist will use to describe their interactions and individual dynamics. The family is taught the meaning of such words as "boundaries," "generations," "family roles," and "rules." The therapist and family now have a common language with which to communicate throughout the remainder of the treatment. The family members begin to put words to the feelings they have about their position in the family. For example, the incest victim during a Structural Session might say, "Oh, that's why I always felt like the mother in the family," or the nonoffending mother might say, "When he was drinking, it felt as if I had three children instead of two." Family members who previously lacked the words to describe how they felt can now share their feelings with a mutual understanding.

Offering Answers

The recurring question, How did this happen to us? begins to be answered during the Structural Session. By viewing the diagrams, learning the new language, and observing their own interactional process that takes place during the session, the family begins to fully appreciate how their *system* operated to maintain the incest. The therapist should communicate to the family that a dysfunctional family structure is not the primary causal factor in the expression of incest, but is merely one factor in their vulnerability to incest (see Chapter 2).

Providing a Visual Metaphor

During the Structural Session the therapist draws or distributes the six possible family structures contributing to the family's vulnerability to incest, along with an example of family hierarchy in which incest would be virtually impossible (see Figures 8.1 to 8.6). These diagrams provide

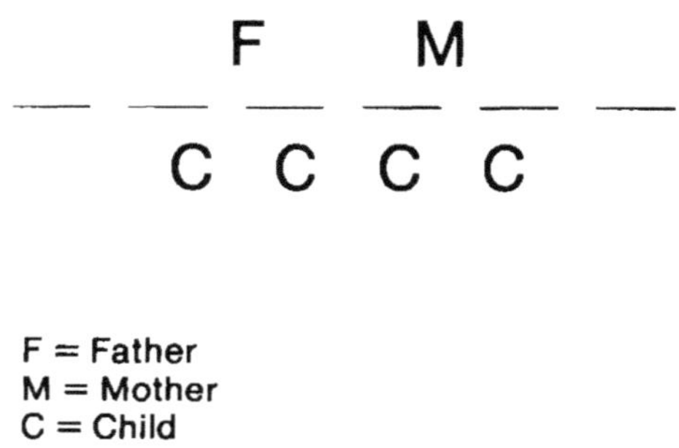

Figure 8.1. Functional family structure.

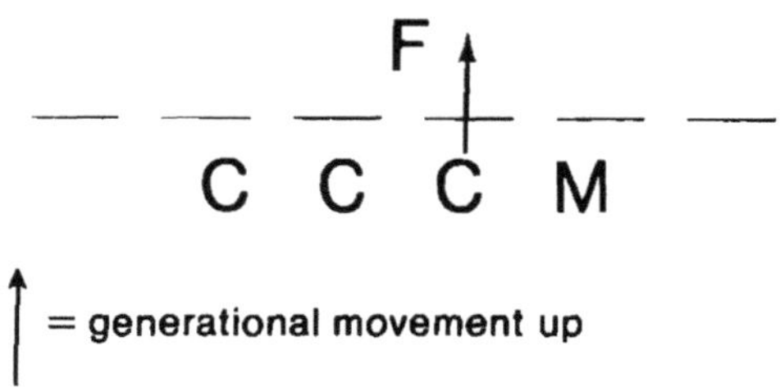

Figure 8.2. Father-executive structure.

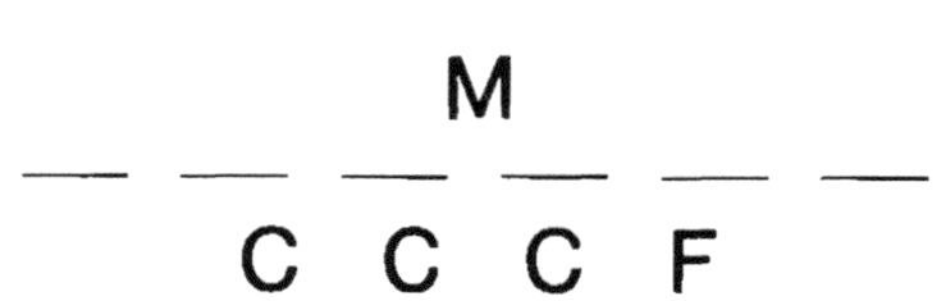

Figure 8.3. Mother-executive structure.

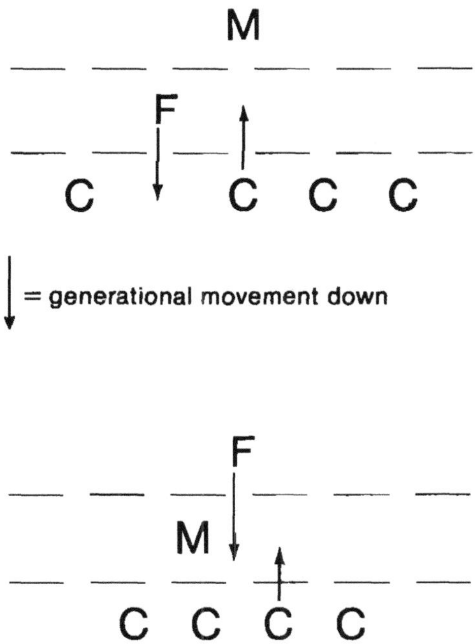

Figure 8.4 Third-generation structures.

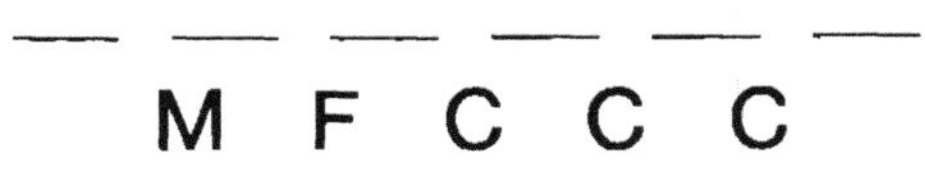

Figure 8.5. Chaotic structure.

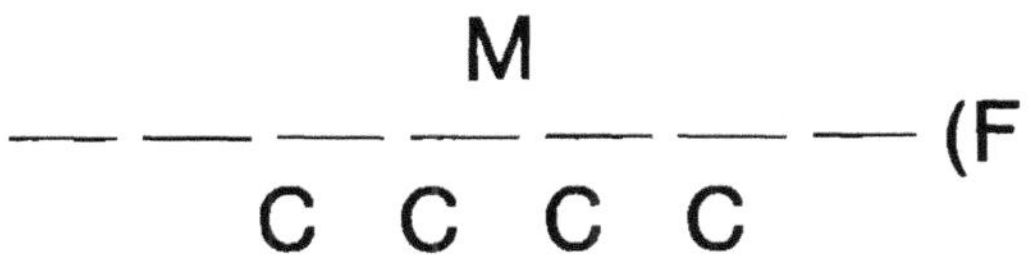

Figure 8.6 Estranged father structure.

the family with a visual representation of the possible hierarchies present in their family. These diagrams act as visual metaphors for both the "problem" and the "cure." The family, for instance, can "see" how in the chaotic structure (see Figure 8.5) all members of the family operate in the same generation with no one consistently in charge. This highly abstract concept becomes easy to follow through the visual metaphor.

Using the Structural Session for Assessment

Because the Structural Session is easily comprehended and has such a practical orientation, clients tend to relate the figures immediately to their own family and to discuss them openly. This openness allows the therapist to assess a number of possible vulnerability factors that may have been concealed before. Some family system characteristics that usually emerge during the Structural Session include: power and control; conflict resolution or lack thereof; the family's communication style, such as who speaks for whom, who cuts off whom, who does not listen to whom; and what dysfunctional nonverbal communication may be present.

DESCRIPTION OF THE STRUCTURAL SESSION

The approach to the Structural Session is basically educational, where the family is taught about "normal" family functioning and dysfunctional interaction. The Structural Session begins with the therapist explaining the concept of family structure (Minuchin, 1974, 1981; Rosenberg, 1983). Each of the structural diagrams are described in detail and drawn on a blackboard. Examples from normal family experiences are given, as well as from other families with which the therapist has worked. The family is encouraged to discuss the different pictures and to ask questions as the session progresses.

Therapist: When families fail to work well together and begin to have problems, either moderate or severe, one of the reasons is because they are no longer functioning well in their family structure. Let me show you, and it might make more sense. I am going to spend the next 20 minutes or so kind of teaching you about these different pictures and how these confused family structures caused problems for your family and how these problems contributed to the sexual abuse. Please let me know at any time if this is not making sense or if I am going too fast. Then when I am done we will talk together about how all of this applies to your family.

(*Showing them Figure 8.1*) This first picture is an example of when a family is working well together. Notice there are two adults on top of the dotted line and the children underneath. A family is working well when there are two adults in charge. The important point is that the adults don't ask a child to help them do the parenting. The line is dotted because it is important for normal families to be flexible and to let communication flow between the two generations. Also the line is dotted because there are times when parents and kids behave in the same generation and it isn't a problem, like a day at the amusement park. But if something goes wrong or someone gets hurt, then immediately an adult must act appropriately and raise above the line.

With me? Good. Anyway I don't want you to get the idea here that any family can be functioning perfectly at all times. Many times in my own family my husband and I do not work well above the line as an "executive subsystem." Like when I want to put the kids to bed and his way of "helping" is to begin wrestling with them and to wind them up so bad that the whole procedure takes twice as long. Then my husband has crossed the line to join the kids' generation. I become a "screaming mimi" parenting my husband as well as the kids. My husband resents me and the evening is shot. So you see, the smallest problem in a family can be looked at in terms of these structures that I am going to show you. A family works well when they recognize that they are in pain or having problems, see they have been crossing the lines, and reorganize themselves so they once again look like this: parents on top, kids on the bottom. If they can move from these dysfunctional structures back to this functional one, then things improve and the problem doesn't become cemented. If they simply bounce between dysfunctional structures and very rarely see this one (referring to the diagram), then problems get worse and more rigid—all sorts of problems from getting kids to clean up their room to sexual abuse.

In the following example, the therapist presents one specific structure, the mother-executive (see Figure 8.3) to the family:

Therapist: This one is mother-executive. This is when the mother feels like she is solely responsible for the family and even has to parent her husband. For example, this might be where the husband doesn't have kids of his own. This is the wife's second marriage, and she's attempting to not inflict her kids on her husband, but he feels he has no way of having any relationship with the kids unless he acts like them. Maybe from his own family he never learned much about responsibility or the role of a father in a family. He acts like one of the children and she treats him that way. When she needs help, support, or maybe companionship, she calls on one of

> the kids to come up to her generation and parent with her. When he needs companionship—someone he can relate to—he turns to someone in his generation, since he is now in the kids' generation. This might be one of the times the sexual abuse happens. I know a family where the only time the stepfather had any interaction with the kids or was even permitted to be with them was during Saturday morning cartoons. The kids would lie around in bed watching the cartoons in their pajamas while their mother slept in the other room and the stepfather would join, and that is also the time he sexually abused the child.

Once the family understands each structure, the therapist encourages them to discuss how the structural diagrams presented apply to their family. Sometimes family members will disagree with each other as to what structure fits them best. This merely indicates how individual family members can experience a family situation differently from one another. Sometimes family members create variations of the six diagrams. This is all perfectly acceptable; the purpose of the session is not to reach a consensus, but for the family to understand how incest is related to the breaking down of intergenerational boundaries *when an adult or child crosses the intergenerational boundary*.

During this portion of the session the therapist must attend to both content and process. The dysfunctional structures that are identified can often be illustrated with the family's own behavior during the session. For example, the offending father identifies his wife as "not acting like a wife, and behaving much more like a child," when explaining why he believes the father-executive structure is operating in the family (see Figure 8.2). As he describes her childlike behavior, she cowers in the corner of the couch. All her attempts at making herself heard are thwarted by his verbal degradation of her. Their interaction can be pointed out as evidence of the very problem that was being described.

Once the family members have identified the structures that seem to contribute to their vulnerability to incest, they then discuss the changes they think will need to take place for them to look like the nonabusing family. They identify the ways that family members cross generational boundaries, not only through sexual abuse but also in other ways. After that, the therapist assigns the family to record the different ways they cross these imaginary boundaries during the next week. In future sessions they continue to track these interactions and also take note of how they feel when the boundaries are crossed.

Therapist: So Sue (*incest victim*), you feel like everyone treats you like the mom and that you have a lot of responsibility in the house. How old do you feel?

Sue: Sometimes in this family I feel a lot of different ages. Sometimes I feel like I am 30 and sometimes I feel 5. They want me to run the house and then they won't even let me go out with my boyfriend. I never feel 16.

Father (offender): Sometimes you act 30 and sometimes you act 5. You can be very helpful and you can be very bossy. Sometimes I feel like you are the parent and your mother and I are the children.

Therapist: I'd like all of you to do something for me. I'd like you to each keep track of all the times you feel like someone else has crossed the line or that you have willingly crossed or been forced to cross the generational boundary. Don't discuss this assignment with each other, just keep track. It helps to write it down. This assignment has a tendency to put you all on your good behavior and consequently there is a chance that no one will cross the line in the next week or so. If that in fact does happen, then keep track about how it feels to have people respecting each other's boundaries and generations.

Teaching the family to track when they "cross the boundaries" is a natural outgrowth of the structural sessions. Once they can identify its occurrence, they can then learn new ways to prevent the behavior that has contributed to incestuous abuse.

There might be times when a number of structural sessions take place. Rather than have a Structural Session with the entire family, the therapist can instead first present the material to the parents, and then in another session have the parents teach what they have learned to the children. This would take place if the children were young or if the therapist wanted to establish clearer boundaries between the generations. The therapist works with the parents, explaining the diagrams and having them discuss them together. After the parents demonstrate they understand the structures and how they apply to their family, the children join in the next session. It is important that the therapist is comfortable with the parents' rendition before the children are permitted to join. In following sessions, the parents then explain the family structures to their children in a language they can understand.

Therapist: (*pointing to the diagram, shown in Figure 8.5*) This first structure is what we call the chaotic family. Everyone knows a family like

> this, where it seems that there are no parents. The kids and the parents are in the same generation. This is the kind of family where, when I make home visits, there are 15 different people running through the house, and when I ask whose kids are those or where are their parents no one seems to know. This is also what teenage parents and their kids look like. Children parenting children. Maybe your family looked like this when the two of you would go on those drinking binges you told me about. You two would feel close for once, while drunk, but no one was in charge of the family. Sue, you'd come home and pass out after the two of you would argue, and then Jerry would be with the kids, drunk too, and he would sexually abuse Sharon after the others were in bed. Sometimes in these families the kids have to rise above the line to do the parenting because the parents are stuck down there in the kids' generation. Now I am not saying this is your family; maybe sometimes it is and maybe not. Let me go through the rest and then we will talk about it.

OTHER CONSIDERATIONS

The greatest problem of the Structural Session is that family members tend to use the information to support their denial of either the responsibility or impact of the sexual abuse. Many families try to convince themselves and the therapist that what they have learned about dysfunctional structures is the *entire* basis for the problem and there is nothing else to explore therapeutically. This, of course, is untrue. A dysfunctional family structure is but one factor contributing to a family's vulnerability to incest, and it would be unwise for the therapist to accept the insights gleaned during the Structural Session as the family's only causal explanation. The therapist must balance the notion of crossing the boundaries with the insistence that other patterns in the family's life will also have to be changed for incest to never emerge again.

When the Offending Father Denies Facts

Many offending fathers continue to deny the known facts about the abuse at the time the family is ready for the Structural Session (see Chapter 7). Although it is inadvisable to have an entire-family Structural Session in this case (given our rule: Never put an abused child in a session with a parent who is denying facts), the session can still be held.

In this case, two structural sessions or a series of sessions are held for the father and family members separately. When and if the family is brought together in future sessions, then much of the same material will have already been covered, and the family will have established a common ground without having yet met as a unit.

The following illustrates an introduction to a father-only Structural Session:

Therapist: Can you see how any of these family pictures reminds you of your family?

Father (currently denying incest): Yeah, the one that has the man on top and wife with the kids. That looks a whole lot like our family! I have to do everything because Jan is always being so spacey.

Therapist: You have to take charge of the house and kids by yourself?

Father: Yeah, everything. Jan always turns away with her tail between her legs.

Therapist: That is a lot of work. You have no one to help you? How about the kids, friends, or relatives?

Father: Well, no family or friends. They are just more trouble, always nosing in your business, telling you how to run your life. That's no help. Maybe sometimes Suzy (*the incest victim*) helps. Then she starts acting like her britches are too big and I have to put her back in her place.

Therapist: I would imagine you don't like the feeling of being alone up there above the line (*referring to the diagram*) and maybe you would like to spend less time being angry. You do sound angry to me.

Family of Origin

Many times the parents' families of origin are intricately involved from the beginning of therapy (see Chapter 12). If this is the case, it can be very helpful to include the grandparents in a Structural Session. The grandparents can meet alone or with their adult children, depending on the comfort levels of the client and the therapist. During these meetings the offending and nonoffending spouse examine their own family of origin's structural diagrams and identify recurring patterns. They also examine how the structures of their families of origin impact upon their current family situation.

A therapist might refer to the diagrams to help clients discuss their own family of origin concerns.

Therapist: Can you let your mother know, Stacy, how it makes you feel when she parents your kids? Help your mother find other ways to be helpful to you without the two of you crossing the lines and getting the generations all confused. Maybe it will help if you draw your family using the diagrams, since we are familiar with them.

Other Uses of the Structural Session

The Structural Session and terminology can be used throughout the treatment process and in each of the different modalities. In group therapy it is common to hear the members talking about "crossing the lines" in their families, as well as how they are attempting to "draw boundaries" in the work and social environments. Many therapists have reported that they use the structural language and diagrams when discussing the case with other professionals or at case conferences. Finally, mental health agencies have found having an "Institutional Structural Session" helpful to understand their own staff relationships and to provide a metaphor that can lead to change.

9

The Apology Session

The line of demarcation between Stage I and Stage II of therapy is artificial and somewhat blurry. For example, families *do* change faulty behavioral patterns during the Stage I of therapy, even though that period is conceptualized as "Creating a Context for Change." And although a "context for change" may have been created, many times families become resistant again during the intensive interventions which occur during Stage II. When that happens, a repetition of some Stage I interventions becomes necessary. However, for conceptual, educational, and practical purposes, it is useful to make the line between the two therapeutic stages clear to the family, and in fact to ritualize that therapeutic crossing into the next stage.

We have developed a ritual a family can perform that will act as a "rite of passage" from Stage I to Stage II. The Apology Session (Justice & Justice, 1979; Trepper, 1986; Trepper & Traicoff, 1985) is a powerful intervention that effectively accomplishes a number of aims at the same time.

First, the Apology Session acts as a consolidation of what the family has learned during Stage I of treatment. For this stage to be completed, family members must each accept the *facts* concerning the abuse. They also have a conceptual understanding of what *caused* the abuse, including what factors contributed to the family's vulnerability to incest, what precipitants occurred prior to abusive episodes, and what coping mechanisms their family was lacking. They have a common language to describe their own dysfunctional interactional patterns, learned during the Structural Session. And they are quite aware of the possible positive and negative consequences of changing these dysfunctional patterns. The Apology Session allows the family to actively integrate each of these.

Second, the Apology Session forces the offending father to formally take responsibility for the incestuous abuse. He is compelled to say in no uncertain terms that, even though there are many contributing factors that made their family vulnerable to abuse, *he* and he alone is ultimately *responsible* for having sex with his daughter. Although many of the fathers have said this to their daughters and families during previous sessions, this is a formal and public admission of this important point.

Third, the Apology Session is a significant structural family therapy intervention. The therapist uses a "manipulation of space" technique (Minuchin, 1974) by moving the parents next to each other, and the children across from them. In fact, by virtue of *both* parents apologizing to the children for their piece in the problem (but not asking the children to apologize for anything), a firm parent/children boundary is erected. This boundary says metaphorically that: (a) parents and children are different; (b) parents have certain rights and obligations that children do not have in a family; and (c) parents are ultimately the managers of the family and thus have the ultimate responsibility when problems arise, although the entire family can help to make things better.

A fourth aim of the Apology Session is to act as a milestone for the family. Often during the course of Stage I treatment the family has asked, "But what do we need to *do* to change (understood as, 'to get my kids back,' or 'to get to go home,' or 'to get through with this therapy,' etc.)?" Usually the answers to this question are rather nebulous because the therapist is working more to assess and set the stage for intervention than to actually change the family system. The Apology Session is different. It is something the family, especially the parents, can *do* to prove that they can change and that they will change. The session is presented to the family as a landmark in their therapy: the preparatory stage of therapy having been completed, and now the "real work" is about to take place.

DIFFERENT STAGES OF APOLOGY

Although the mother is an important part of the Apology Session and does indeed apologize for her part in the family's problems, this session is clearly the father's show. He has many things to apologize for besides directly having sex with his daughter. For example, he can apologize for his own emotional, attitudinal, and sexual problems. He also must apologize for his own *denial* of the abuse and the problems that were caused in the family because of it.

Like therapy, however, the Apology Session has been shown to be most effective when it is done *in stages*. That is, there are Stage I, II, and III Apology Sessions, corresponding to those stages of treatment. During the Stage I Apology Session, the father apologizes for the *facts* of the abuse, the problems it has caused, and for those controllable aspects of his life that contributed to the abuse. The Stage II Apology Session's purpose is for the father to apologize for the *impact* of the abuse on the future life of the daughter and the rest of the family members. The Stage III Apology Session is a review of the previous two, and a summary by the father of what was wrong in his life that contributed to the abuse, the problems for the family that resulted from these, and how he is now different. It should be noted that Apology sessions can still take place even if the parents have divorced. Each parent would conduct his or her own Apology session separately.

APOLOGY SESSION FORMAT

Pre-Apology Sessions

There are usually weeks, and sometimes months, of preparation for an Apology Session. Because it is a therapeutic ritual, it is important that the family can accomplish the session with as few surprises as possible. In some respects, since the Apology is the punctuation for Stage I of therapy, we could consider all of the "Creating a Context for Change" sessions as pre-Apology Sessions. However, the sessions immediately preceding the Apology should be structured and have specific goals.

The father, mother, and daughter are seen individually to discuss what to expect from the Apology Session, what each of their goals will be, and to anticipate how they might react to each other. The father and/or the mother are then seen for a session or two prior to the Apology so that they can role play what they intend to say and be coached for what *not* to say. Finally, the rest of the children are seen for a session to prepare them for what will transpire. These pre-Apology Sessions are essential to protect against messages being communicated which might make the situation worse, such as the father stating that his wife was really to blame for the abuse because she wasn't there for him romantically.

The father and the mother are each told to write down everything they would want to apologize for, what each of these apologies means to them, and all of the possible responses from the daughter and the rest of the family. The father is told that he is expected to apologize for the facts of the abuse, and what it has done to his daughter and the rest of the family. He is also told that he should avoid focusing on the reasons for the abuse here, but instead focus on his own responsibility.

In the following session, the therapist is helping the father prepare for his daughter's possible responses in the apology session.

Therapist: (*to father*) You have done a great job in deciding all the things you want to say to your daughter and talking about all the feelings you might have regarding this session. Let's take a moment and prepare for her responses. Just like when you prepared for what you were going to say, it's important to think of every possible response she could come up with. Even the ones you think she would never come back to you with. Any ideas? Will she accept the apology?

Father: I don't know. I suppose she can say, "Dad, let's not talk about it, what's done is done. Let's move on with our lives."

Therapist: I'll bet there is a big part of you that would like to hear that. You used to tell me that all the time a few months ago, remember?—"Why do we keep hashing over all this? I made a mistake, so let's move on." I think you know it's a bit more than a mistake. Even though it would be nice if she says that, you can't let it stop there. So how will you respond?

Father: Well, if she says that, then I'll tell her, "It's not that easy and we have a lot more to understand and change before we can completely move on. Right now I just want you to know that I am sorry for what I did. I can't make it up to you but I can make sure you know it is not your fault. But we just can't pretend it didn't happen and move on."

Therapist: Good. What else might she say?

Father: "I won't forgive you, I never will. You have ruined my life and now I'll ruin yours."

Therapist: There is probably another part of you that wishes that she'd say that, too. Then maybe if she punishes you enough you can feel guilty, repent, and move on. Remember, this session is not to absolve you of anything. It is to restate responsibility and move on to Stage II. What will you say to that?

Father: "You don't have to forgive me. I know you will never forget what happened to you. I just want you to know that I am clear that it is my fault and I will do whatever it takes to make sure everyone is safe with me and I control my problems. I hope you don't spend your whole life trying to punish me because then you'll keep punishing yourself."

Therapist: Fantastic. I'll help her see how punishing you in certain ways can revictimize herself in the world. I don't mean by testifying in court, but spending her life centered on revenge.

The mother is told that she should apologize to her daughter for those problems in her relationship with her that prevented the child from coming to her mother when the abuse began, or if this were the case, for not believing her when her daughter first disclosed the facts about the sexual abuse. The mother is carefully instructed during these pre-Apology Sessions, however, to avoid taking the responsibility for the abuse (e.g., she should not say, "It was my fault because I was working and wasn't there to protect you").

The therapist should help the daughter to anticipate what her parents might say when they apologize and what she would like to tell them in response. She, of course, is told *not* to apologize for the sexual abuse in any way. This is true even if she had a direct role in the maintenance of the abuse, even if she actually initiated incestuous episodes. The reason for this is clear: An important purpose of this session is to solidify the reality that the *adult* must take the ultimate responsibility for sexual abuse in a family; that is, there is an important difference between *responsibility* and *cause*. If the daughter did initiate the incestuous events, or she could have told her mother but didn't, or agreed to have sex with her father in return for special favors—if any or all of these were the case, they are important and will be dealt with in Stage II of therapy. However, she should not be expected to apologize for these because, in the philosophy of the program, she was ultimately not responsible.

Stage I Apology Session

Once everyone is prepared for the session and the therapist is convinced that the family will benefit from it, the Apology Session can be held. It usually takes the entire hour, and it is often useful to videotape the session so that the family can view it at a later stage of therapy. The parents are seated next to one another, the children across from them, and the therapist near the parents but in a position to be able to move near the person who is speaking.

The father usually begins the session, explains to the children why they are all there, and what they hope to accomplish. He then formally apologizes to the daughter for his actions in the sexual abuse and to the rest of the family for what has resulted. He then summarizes what he has learned from therapy so far and what he hopes will happen in the future. The mother then apologizes for her role and summarizes what she has learned thus far. They both tell the children how things will be different and what they should do in the event of further inappropriate sexual advances or innuendo, and then end on a positive note by saying what good things they expect to come from this. The children are then encouraged to respond and ask questions. They usually formally accept their parents' apology, or at least on the condition that it does not happen again.

The therapist coaches the family through the session by encouraging each parent to do the tasks they have prepared for. It is important for the therapist to keep the session on track, and of course to watch for any inappropriate accusations, denial, or hostility. If these should occur, the therapist must point it out and move them back on track. If hostility or denial should continue, the session may have to be "officially" ended. This rarely occurs if there has been adequate pre-Apology planning.

The following is an excerpt from a Stage I Apology Session:

Father: Well, this is pretty hard for me, as you probably know. I don't really know where to start . . .

Therapist: Tell them all what this session is all about.

Father: (*hesitating*) I guess you pretty well know what happened, what with us coming to counseling all this time, but just as a beginning, let me say that what we are doing here today is for me to apologize to you all, especially you Linda (*the abused 11-year-old*) for what happened. I guess you all know that it's because of me and what I did that made it so I'm living with Uncle Bob and Aunt Nancy now. I just want to say that I am really sorry about all that happened and that thing about . . . doing sexual things and all with you, Linda . . .

Therapist: You mean the incest?

Father: Yah, I am really sorry about the incest. You've heard me apologize to you lots of times, but this is a public version of that, and I want to say in front of you all how sorry I am. You know what happened to me when I used to get drunk, and this is just one more thing. But I'm getting help for the drinking, and we're coming to counseling, and you know I won't try nothing with you again.

Therapist: Tell her why you won't.

Father: I won't because it's wrong, it's just wrong. I always knew it was, you always knew it was, but I just didn't know how not to. And I won't anymore because I'm not drinking, and I won't because we're here now. . . . And I hope I won't because you'd never let me!

Therapist: You're not saying it's Linda's fault, are you?

Father: Oh, God, no! She was just a kid . . . I mean I hope that she wouldn't let *anybody* touch her when she don't want to . . . I mean, she should be in charge as to what happens to her about sex.

Therapist: So summarize to Linda what you are apologizing for.

Father: OK, I am apologizing for the incest stuff, and for our family being split up like this, and for all the problems I've caused . . . (*starts to sob*) . . . this is so hard . . .

Therapist: (*moving over and touching him*) You're doing excellently. Tell Linda what you'd like from her.

Father: (*still sobbing gently*) I'd like . . . I'd like her to forgive me, to give me another chance, to let us all start over . . . I want everyone to . . .

Therapist: (*moving over near Linda*) Linda, you heard your Dad, what do you think?

Linda: I told him a lot that it's OK, that I still love him.

Therapist: Is it really OK?

Linda: Yes.

Therapist: Just tell me so I know.

Linda: That he feels bad what he did and everything, and that he won't do it anymore.

Therapist: And what does he want from you?

Linda: Oh yah, that he wants me to accept his apology?

(Therapist nods.) Well, yah, I said I did.

Therapist: Linda, you look a little uncomfortable.

Linda: Well, it's just weird having your Dad apologize to you.

Therapist: I know, but this was real important and you did real good. Dad, do you want to say anything to the others, to Mom and Bobby?

Father: Well, yah, that I'm really sorry for all that's happened 'cause of me, and if they'd forgive me, I'd really . . .(*starts to sob again*) . . .I'd really like that.

Therapist: (*looks to the eight-year-old brother*) Bobby, what do you think?

Bobby: I don't know . . .

Therapist: Do you know what your father is talking about?

Bobby: (*looking a little uncomfortable*) Yah, about him and Linda doing that stuff they weren't supposed to?

Therapist: Yes. Dad, tell Bobby what you want to tell him.

Father: That I know he misses me (*therapist directs Father to Bobby with her hand*) . . . I know that you miss me and want me to come home, and I'm sorry that I'm not, but I hope to be soon, and I'm sorry for all the trouble that all this . . . that *I've* caused, and hope you forgive me.

Therapist: What do you think, Bobby?

Bobby: (*brightening up*) Yes, I do.

Therapist: Mother, you've been pretty quiet. What do you want to say?

Mother: (*slowly and deliberately*) Well, like Dad said, I'm sorry too for what's happened. I feel real bad about our family being apart like this, and I know I've been grouchy to you kids lately . . . (*starts sobbing*) . . . but it's real tough doing all this by yourself and not knowing what's gonna happen . . .

Therapist: "And so I'd like to tell you . . ."

Mother: And so I'd like to tell you, as part of all this, that I want to apologize to you Linda for not believing you the first time you told me, and for not doing nothing about what happened with you and Dad, the incest stuff. I told you already why, that I didn't know what to believe, that I didn't want to believe it, that it was just easier for me to think you were making up fibs again. . . . But I want to say here now that I'm sorry for this and that you can always come to me anytime something's wrong, about *anything*, not just sex stuff . . . . And I'm sorry that you have to grow up so fast . . . (*begins to cry*).

Therapist: (*touches Mother*) You're doing very good, very good. Ask Linda and Bobby what you'd like?

Mother: (*still crying*) I'd like them both, especially Linda, to accept my apology for not being there when they needed me, and my not believing her, and for the troubles Dad and I have.

Therapist: Kids?

Linda: Well, yah, I do Mom.

Bobby: Me, too!

Therapist: I just want to say that you, Mom, aren't saying that your troubles with Father made the incest happen. I want to make it clear from my point of view that you aren't responsible for the incest, just like Linda isn't. Father already said *he* was ultimately responsible. I just want you all to make sure you heard that.

Mother: Well, yes, right. I just want to apologize for not knowing, for not believing.

Therapist: Linda, what would you like to say to your parents?

Linda: (*hesitating*) I don't know . . . . Well, just that I want us all to be a family again, and I love them both.

Stage II Apology Session

The Stage II Apology Session occurs toward the end of Stage II of the treatment program. Like the Stage I Apology, this session is prepared for with a number of pre-Apology Sessions, is ritualized in terms of format, and acts as a rite of passage for the family, this time to Stage III of therapy. The goal of this session is for the parents to apologize for the *impact* of the abuse on the family. This is different from the previous apology, which is primarily a focus on the *facts* of the abuse. And whereas the Stage I apology often sounds somewhat "forced" and even somewhat insincere, the Stage II apology is usually much more spontaneous, natural, and heartfelt.

Perhaps reflecting the changes in the structure of the family, Stage II Apology Sessions tend to be more direct and even confrontational. This Apology Session also tends to be less formalized and expresses the specific needs of the family at this point in their counseling. For example, if the therapist is working with the family to strengthen the mother-daughter bond, then the mother is told to sit next to her daughter and help her confront the father.

The child victim is encouraged during the pre-Apology Sessions to challenge her parents more than in the Stage I Apology and to state directly how the incestuous abuse affected her. She often talks about the regrets she had—for example, in not having a "normal relationship with a real father" or in feeling estranged from her mother. And the mother, too, is encouraged to discuss how the incestuous abuse had an impact on her life—what it was like to be torn between her love for her husband and her desire to protect her daughter.

Although it might seem that this Apology Session would be more difficult because it is more confrontational, in practice it is not. This is most likely because the family has been focusing on these very issues during the entire Stage II of therapy, and so this session is more of a summary than a "surprise attack." The family also knows that the completion of this session indicates their moving into the last stage of therapy.

The following dialogue illustrates a Stage II Apology Session where the father has abused the oldest *son* but not the younger two daughters. The parents are in the process of divorce, but still meet together periodically in therapy to discuss issues relating to the children. In this session the father talks with the children about the impact of the abuse on their lives.

Therapist: Sam (*the father*), why don't you summarize the agenda for this session?

Sam: In therapy lately we've been talking about how sad it is that our family missed out on a lot of normal things because we were all wrapped up in keeping the secret that I forced on everyone. I never really was the kind of father or husband I always thought I could be. If I missed out, then there is no telling how you felt about what you missed out. I know how your mother feels; we talk about it a lot in our counseling. But I'd like to hear more about your regrets. I want to hear how the sexual abuse really affected all of you. Believe me, it is safe to tell me anything. There is nothing you can say that I have not already thought of. But if nothing else, this therapy has convinced me that it's important to talk things out.

Therapist: Why don't you start a specific conversation with one of the kids. Not necessarily Scott (the victim). I know all of the kids were affected by the abuse and your behaviors and absences.

Sam: How about you, Cindy (*the 10-year-old not sexually abused*)? What regrets do you have about us and me in the family? Like what do you wish would have been different?

Cindy: We have talked about this before. I hated the fighting. I hated how Scott was always so sad and angry and how you would walk around so angry. I hated how Mom was always so sad. We just didn't have a family that was any good.

Sam: I know . . . .Tell me more about how you would have liked to see Dad different? Think about things you wish we would have done together.

Cindy: I wish you had wanted to be around me more and that I had wanted to be around you. I just never wanted to be around you. Nothing ever felt normal in our family. I wanted a normal mother and father. I wanted you to act like a normal couple and do normal things. We never did normal things and now you are getting divorced so we won't ever be able to do normal things.

Sam: Is it possible to try to be a normal divorced family? That probably sounds pretty weird but a lot of families today are divorced and there are some things that can be normal about it.

Cindy: Like what do you mean?

Sam: Well, considering that most of the time when I said I was going to do something before, I never did it. Like if I was supposed to take you somewhere, then I never showed up or was late or was angry or some such thing. So isn't it more normal that when I come to visit you, I am on time, I have a plan, and I really do want to be with you.

Therapist: Sam, all those things are very true, and in fact you are right, there are some norms about being divorced and you really are trying to adapt to that new type of family. However, you and I wanted this session for the kids to have an opportunity to voice regrets and sadness, not for them to have a regret and for you to change their minds. Sounds like some of that old control creeping back in there. Remember, a lot of times when you felt sad or like you had let someone down or done something, what did you used to do to feel better?

Sam: You're right, I didn't even catch it. I tried to control them, to change their minds so that it could change how I felt inside. Absolutely, I did it. Guess I'm not done yet. Sorry.

Therapist: Hey, don't get carried away. You are human and you always forget that. Just try again.

Sam: Cindy, you're right. It probably feels like I just keep screwing up your life.

Therapist: How does it make you feel when you have that thought.

Sam: Well, Cindy, I get so mad at myself and then I want to change your mind so you won't feel like I screwed up your life, but you know what I did. Yours, Scott's, Mom's and mine. But I didn't end it for any of us. I want to have a better relationship. I am trying. I feel sad 'cause I can see you are sad.

Cindy: Will I ever not remember how weird all of this is and how sick our family seems? (*looking at both Father and the therapist*)

Therapist: (*responding to Dad's glance*) You go first Sam.

Sam: I'm not sure of that one, honey. I can only guess that if we do enough things together that are not weird then one day you will remember those, too, and they will be equal to or maybe even outweigh the sick stuff.

Therapist: Could not have said it any better myself. See if she understands what you mean. It was too important to get lost.

Sam: Does that make any sense to you?

Cindy: Yes, I think so. You mean so many bad things happened that's all that is in my brain, but when more good things happen then both will be in there.

Sam: Absolutely.

Therapist: I know this family is going to be all right just listening to how well you are be able to talk and understand things right now.

Then the father talks with Scott, the victim.

Sam: You and I have talked a lot in our sessions. But I guess we need to summarize about your regrets.

Scott: I regret a whole lot of things. I regret that I was embarrassed by you so that I never wanted to be seen with you, which meant I never had a father at any games or anything with me. I regret that you made me feel like the sick and crazy one all those years. I regret that you made me confused about myself, my life, and my mother. I just wanted to be normal and never could be me. I regret that nothing was ever good enough for you so I always felt like shit. I regret that I couldn't get out of mind what happened to me a long time ago and that you still kept trying. I regret that I never got to be a kid and have fun and now it's too late. I wish I didn't have to say all of this.

Sam: But you do because I sexually abused you and now you have a lot of regrets. I regret that I did it all and caused it all. But there is one thing therapy has helped me realize that I don't regret and that is I don't regret that that suicide attempt didn't work. Because if it had worked then that would have been another way to abuse you and another thing this family would have to live with and feel crazy about. And now that I'm alive I can't take away what I did or give you back a good childhood, but I can be a different kind of dad for as long as I am able. I really want to Scott . . . do you believe me?

Scott: (*after a pause*) Yeah, I do.

Sam: Do you think it'll help at all?

Scott: Well, I used to think that no dad at all would be better than the one I got, but I don't feel that way anymore so . . . I . . . yeah, I guess it's helped.

Their conversation continues with a discussion of how the family can be normal now. Scott's major concern is that he wants to stop feeling "crazy" because of having had sex with his father. He is afraid he can never feel "normal" around his father, no matter what has changed. The father's response to his son follows:

Sam: I can understand how you can feel so strange and so scared. I felt crazy a lot of the time, too, when the sexual abuse was going on. I am not sure if this'll help but I want you to know that people can't tell what happened to you by looking at you.

Scott: Sometimes it still feels like they can.

Sam: I know. Also, maybe if you just tell me out loud that you are starting to feel weird when we're together, that might help. Remember what we talk about in therapy—only a "part" of you is feeling weird or worrying about everyone knowing or hating me, the other "parts" of you can take care of you and talk to me about it. Right (*looking at the therapist*)?

Therapist: Right. That was really well put. I'm impressed with the change the two of you—the entire family for that matter—have made. Is it starting to be like this outside of therapy?

Finally the father talks with his youngest daughter, the six-year-old:

Sam: Jessie, do you understand any of what we have been talking about?

Jessie: Yeah, kind of.

Sam: Well, what are you angry at Daddy for?

Jessie: I'm angry that you get mad a lot. And that you and Mom don't live together. And that Scott's always mad. I just want us all to be happy and a family.

Sam: I can't promise you anything. Mommy and I aren't going to be living together again. But I can try to help Scott be less angry. What kind of things do you want you and me to be doing with each other? If you could make us be a different dad and kid, what would you do?

Jessie: I want us to play more. I want you to go to Indian Princesses with me. I want you to be funny with my friends like the other daddies. We never did any of those things and I want to do them.

Sam: I am sorry, honey, that we didn't do those things. You are right, we didn't. But now that Daddy is thinking and feeling better, I think we will be able to do those things without much problems. OK?

Jessie: OK.

Stage III Apology

Stage III of therapy consists of a number of ritualized sessions (see Chapter 15), and the Stage III Apology is one of those sessions. Where Stage III represents a reviewing, summarizing, and cementing of all the changes made during therapy, the Apology during this stage also is a reviewing, summarizing, and cementing of the other Apology Sessions. This last Apology is more of a ritualized ending to the apology process, with a review of how the family members are going to do things differently so that they will not have to apologize for the rest of their lives. It can be a very powerful experience for the family to view the videotape of the first Apology Session and to let them discuss how they are different and how they plan to continue to make changes for the better.

The following case illustrates a Stage III Apology Session. The family has been in therapy for two years. The stepfather sexually abused two daughters, and one daughter and one son were not sexually abused. Here they review their treatment and the changes they have made:

Therapist: We just reviewed (*on videotape*) the two Apology Sessions that you've had. The first one had Tom (*stepfather*) taking responsibility for the act and Kathy (*natural mother*) apologizing for the fact that you kids did not feel she was available to you and her trying to help you understand her fear of Tom. The second one has all of you talking about how sad it was to not feel normal all those years and making some agreements about what you might try to feel normal.

I guess now what I want you to do is to talk about all that. For example, Do you still feel like your parents are taking responsibility for what they did or did not do as parents? Where are you all at in terms of forgiving? Did you accomplish anything in respect to feeling more normal? Basically summarize anything you are thinking or feeling based on those two sessions we reviewed. Go ahead, Kathy, you get it going.

Kathy: (*to kids*) Well, you guys seemed to understand at the time that I wasn't afraid of Tom physically, but that I was real afraid of just being without a man. We have spent a lot of time, particularly the girls and me, trying to figure out who we are without always thinking of ourselves as someone's woman. You know it was me having to be his woman that made me pretend there weren't problems and act like I wanted to choose him over you all. You know I just didn't want to choose, period. Now we know how not to have to. Do you think I act as afraid?

Kelly: No, especially when you were separated from Tom during that time. You did real good. Now you guys seem like you want to be together. You are more fun to be around. And I am not always feeling bad for you. It seems like you can take care of yourself.

Laura: I think you really want to take care of us and be married to him, too. It's very different. It's like there is enough of you to go around now, and you are no fatter (*laughter from the family*).

John: He can't push you around anymore. I like that.

Kathy: Are you guys acting different with your boyfriends and girlfriends? (*The kids nod their heads yes very enthusiastically.*)

Kelly: Believe me, I have learned a lot about what my relationships are going to be about.

Kathy: (*to son*) Are you going to push girls around?

John: I hope not. I don't want my family, if I ever have one, to go through this shit.

Stepfather: How about me?

Therapist: Feeling left out again? Is that still happening?

Stepfather: Sure, it happens.

Bonnie: Yeah, but now he's always telling us how he's feeling about being left out (*said mockingly, but with obvious benevolence toward stepfather and treatment*).

Stepfather: Yes, to quote a famous therapist,"I know how to take care of myself now in a way that people can hear me."(*Again they laugh.*) Well, what about me? From that first Apology Session, do you think I am more sincere about being sorry for what I did? Do you think I could do it again?

All the children: Oh, God, no!

Kelly: You would never do it again. The family is too different. You would never get away with it. Plus I don't think you would even want to.

Stepfather: You're right. It makes me sick to think I did such a sick thing and caused so much trouble to you guys. It's amazing that you still want me in the family.

Kathy: Do you, guys?

Laura: Yeah, we have had a lot of chances to decide to get rid of you but we like having you around now that we know it is safe.

John: We have always liked "parts" of you (*again mocking therapy*).

Stepfather: So you believe I am sorry? (*They all respond, "Yes."*) Do you think we act more normal? Have we started to do the things you all wanted to do to help normalize this group? (*He is referring to the second Apology Session*)

Kelly: Yes. I am really beginning to feel much more normal and sometimes even proud to be in this family. We certainly have gone through a lot and probably now communicate better than most families.

Kathy: I know none of us will ever forget what happened but now I don't think about it 24 hours a day. But I also don't go to the other extreme and pretend it didn't happen. Do any of you pretend it didn't happen?

Patty (*one of the victims*): I know I was sexually abused, but it doesn't make me so crazy to think about it as it used to. I definitely can feel normal a lot of the times.

John: Yeah, I think you and me, Tom, have done a lot of the things that we said we were going to do to try to be more like a stepfather and stepson. Now I feel like I can even be OK around my real dad. I am less confused about the whole thing now.

The son and daughter verbalize for the family how therapy has helped them feel less "crazy" and confused not only about the sexual abuse, but also about the many aspects of their lives.

SECTION II

10

Introduction to Stage II: Challenging Behaviors, Expanding Alternatives

During Stage I of treatment the *context* for change was created for the family and individual family members. Although much change in family interactions and feelings occurred as a result of *Stage I* interventions, this period primarily addressed: early case management concerns: assessment of the factors contributing to the family's vulnerability to incest; dealing with the family's resistance to therapy; reducing initial denial; and creating the reality that the family can and will eventually make significant enough changes so that incestuous abuse will never again occur.

Most of the interventions to specifically reduce the family's vulnerability to incest occur during *Stage II* of the treatment program. In Stage II, the therapist takes the dysfunctional behavior patterns, belief systems, and interactional sequences that were identified in Stage I and designs interventions to interrupt them. More important, the therapist offers alternatives for those behaviors. By *Stage III* of the program, the family members themselves should be able to come up with alternatives to this dysfunctional behavior without the help of the therapist. At that point, formal therapy is considered complete.

STAGE II THERAPY SESSIONS

Stage II is the longest of the three stages. Whereas Stage I lasts approximately four or five months, Stage II typically lasts over one year. The family and/or its individual members have contact with the therapist at least twice a week. Some have referred to this as the "meat and potatoes" part of treatment, where the therapist can use his or her own talent and creativity to elicit change. Therapists use a variety of family and individually oriented interventions, usually based upon their own clinical backgrounds. At all times, however, the therapist's goals are to challenge behaviors and expand the alternatives available to the family. This long stage can be the most interesting and fulfilling for the therapist, particularly if the resistances of Stage I were properly managed.

Like all "middle phases" of therapy, however, this can be a most seductive stage and an unwitting therapist may find him- or herself faced with unexpected resistances. These resistances are typically neither as overt nor as hostile as during Stage I. On the contrary, the family usually believe that they have changed, that all is now well, and that they really do not need any more therapy. The challenge here is for the therapist to keep the family committed to the program and to be prepared for the series of "honeymoons and crises" that inevitably arise. Also, it is not uncommon for the offender to remain in Stage I because of his denial, while the rest of the family progresses to Stage II.

A therapist might describe Stage II to the family with the following analogy:

Therapist: Stage II of your therapy is really a lot more like your real life than Stage I. In Stage I, you'll remember, it felt like you were in crisis all the time, that things were never going to get better, like a deep, black hole in which you were drawn deeper and deeper. In Stage II, you'll see it will feel like a middle ground and generally less extreme. There will be intense and intimate moments, but those will be mixed in with repetitious and mundane experiences. Just like real life.

Depending upon the family's vulnerability to incest, the focus of Stage II may be entirely on sexual abuse, or the incest may get brought up only periodically. Once the Apology Session has been completed, and if the family is not engaging in denial, the therapist usually elects to focus on the nonsexual family factors that have contributed to their vulnerability. For example, dysfunctional power hierarchies, problematical communication patterns, and relationship problems between the father and mother may be the primary therapeutic focus during Stage II of a family's therapy.

One of the most difficult aspects of Stage II is that it can feel boring to the family. The therapist, in challenging the family's behavioral patterns, often must be repetitious and tenacious. It is not uncommon for family members to say, "But we've gone all over this before," when an assignment is made. However, it is essential that if a dysfunctional pattern is to be broken, it must be interrupted and replaced *often*. One way to keep it more interesting is for the therapist to make the interventions through in-session *enactments* and homework assignments as often as possible. In this way, the therapist does not simply talk about changing something, but encourages the family to *do* something about it.

The therapist is far more active and directive during Stage II than the previous stage of therapy. It is not uncommon for a therapist during Stage I to let a problematic sequence or statement pass without comment, or to simply identify that it happened for the family. In Stage II, however, the therapist does not let an identified problem belief, behavior, or sequence go without comment; instead, he or she interrupts it and makes some appropriate intervention. For example, if the abused daughter during Stage I says that she cannot easily talk to her mother, this will be discussed and even positively connoted (e.g., "Sometimes mothers and daughters, when they love each other very much, have difficulty communicating for fear of hurting each other"). During Stage II, the reasons behind the daughter's fear might be challenged; she might be encouraged to openly discuss her feelings with her mother during a mother-daughter session, or assignments might be made to increase their time together. The therapist will not stop intervening until this particular problem is resolved, particularly if the mother and daughter's communication problem was assessed to a be factor that contributed to their vulnerability to incest.

As Stage II progresses, the therapist should become less and less direct, and instead insist that the client take on more and more of the responsibility for challenging their own problem behaviors and finding their own alternatives for those behaviors. For example, at the beginning of Stage II, the therapist might start an enactment of this identified situation:

Therapist: You know, I've just noticed something I think is real important. Whenever John (*the father*) wants something, he pouts and becomes silent, which ultimately leads to the family doing what he wants. See, Mary, you just did that . . . John wanted you to consider getting the boat, but instead of asking what you thought about it directly, he just became silent and "pouty." Then you started to agree about the boat.

Mary: Ya, we've talked about that before in here.

John: I wasn't really pouting . . .

Therapist: I'd call it that, when you make that face (*mimicks the pout, John laughs*). This time, Mary, I want you to try something different.

Mary: OK.

Therapist: (*whispers to Mary in her ear so the rest of the family cannot hear*) Tell John you'll be happy to talk to him about getting a boat if he asks you directly what you think about it and agrees to discuss it without pouting.

Mary: John, we can talk about the boat . . . but I want you to talk to me like an adult—you know, two people just talking, without pouting.

John: I wasn't pouting.

Julie: There you go, Dad, you're pouting now (*whole family laughs*)!

John: OK, what do you really think about our getting a boat?

Mary: I really think it's too expensive right now.

John: I don't think so.

Mary: How much are they?

John: I haven't really gotten all the prices.

Mary: Well, why don't we get the prices, and then we can decide.

Therapist: OK, John, here would be a great time either to pout or to show your new style!

John: I won't pout! I think she's right, we should get the prices. Maybe it would be too expensive, but we don't know till we get the prices.

Therapist: Seem fair to you all?

Julie: Yah, a boat could be fun!

Mary: We are just going to get the prices.

Therapist: I like the way you talked about that without doing your usual thing, you know—John looking sad until everyone gives in. Remember, we talked about how some of the incest occurred when you pouted and looked sad, and then Julie "gave in." This time, it sounded more like a real family, where the parents talk things over equally like adults, and you, John, didn't need to pout. Good job!

By the end of Stage II, however, the family should be able to stop the "pouting leading to acquiescence" sequence as it occurs, and then to alter their responses without the aid of the therapist, or only with minimal assistance. In fact, their ability to accomplish this determines when the family will move into Stage III.

STAGE II TREATMENT MODALITIES

Stage II is characterized by not only a variety of treatment techniques to challenge and alter behavior, but also a variety of treatment modalities. Family, marital, sibling, individual, and group therapy are all used extensively during Stage II (Barrett, Sykes & Byrnes, 1986), and it is not uncommon for a father, for example, to have an individual, family, and group therapy session in the same week.

Family therapy sessions address the dysfunctional repetitive interactional sequences that maintain the symptoms associated with incestuous abuse. *Marital sessions* serve to establish functional boundaries around the marriage, help the couple make pragmatic decisions about the future of their relationship, and encourage them to improve the quality of their relationship. *Individual therapy sessions* for the abusing father, mother, and daughter allow each to explore, in relative safety, feelings of victimization; how they use and misuse power and control; their sexual feelings, behaviors, and problems; and what contributes to their lowered self-esteem. *Sibling sessions* are used to help the nonabused children allay their fears, confusion, anger, and concerns regarding the molestation; they reestablish the children into their generational ranks and relieve them from any guilt or responsibility they are feeling. *Group therapy* for the father, mother, and daughter is used to expand and intensify the issues and alternatives developed during family sessions.

Guidelines for the Use of Each Modality

In all of Stage II, the therapist has a great deal of flexibility with regard to interventions and modalities. An obvious rule of thumb could be to use whatever modality makes the most sense in working on a particular problem. If one of the vulnerability factors is a sexual relationship problem for the father and mother, then marital sessions should be the primary modality for a period of time. If an inappropriate sexual belief system is present for the father—for example, that sexual experiences between adults and children is philosophically supportable (including his sexual experiences with his daughter), then ongoing individual sessions will be necessary to confront this belief through cognitive restructuring.

As in Stage I, the therapist will find it helpful to switch modalities when he or she feels therapeutically "stuck." This may be when family members become angry or confrontive; or conversely, it may occur when they "improve" so quickly that the therapist suspects a "flight into health" as a way of defocusing from the issues that really bother them (e.g., a fear of divorce). In either of these extremes, the therapist can usually gain important insights by switching to another modality.

The therapist can and should use material extracted from one modality of therapy in another. For example, feelings of inadequacy that were articulated by a father during his group session might be incorporated into his family sessions. We make it clear to the family at the beginning of therapy that, unless they absolutely refuse to allow it, information may be shared with the entire family when the therapist believes it to be appropriate and after discussing the option with the particular family member.

11

Family Sessions

Sessions with the entire family are held throughout all three stages of the program. The main purpose of Stage I family therapy is to identify the dysfunctional systemic interactions and behavioral sequences that contribute to the family's vulnerability to incest. The main purpose of Stage II family interventions is to intercede with and disrupt those dysfunctional interactions and sequences. A list of common family interventions is provided in Table 11.1.

There are three additional goals of Stage II family sessions. First, the therapist assesses change in the family's style of interacting over a period of time, rather than the more static assessment accomplished during Stage I. Second, the therapist integrates information gathered from individual and group sessions into the family sessions. For example, if the therapist learns during individual sessions that the abused daughter still feels unable to open up to her mother when her father is there, the therapist can encourage a mother-daughter dialogue while keeping the father out of the conversation. A third goal of the Stage II family sessions is to recognize and change new problem areas that will arise as the family makes significant changes. For example, as the communication improves between the abused daughter and her mother, it is possible that the other, previously "favored" sibling now becomes ignored. This situation can be identified and the therapist can make appropriate interventions during the family sessions.

TABLE 11.1
Family Interventions

I. *Direct Interventions*
   A. Therapist and family agree on a dysfunctional sequence of behavior; family permits therapist to challenge that sequence and provide alternatives
   B. Enactments
   C. Homework assignments designed to disrupt dysfunctioning structural patterns and behavior

II. *Indirect Interventions*
   A. Positive connoting of understanding meaning of a dysfunctioning sequence of behavior
   B. Restraining change
   C. Negative consequences of change
   D. Symptom prescription (not of abuse)
   E. Use of metaphor

FREQUENCY OF FAMILY SESSIONS

The relative frequency of the sessions is always at the therapist's discretion. To have regular, entire-family sessions is the ideal, whether that means scheduling them on an average of once every two weeks or once every month. However, whether family or subsystem sessions should be utilized depends upon which particular dimension of the family's vulnerability to incest treatment is focusing. For example, if power and control are the current issues, family sessions will certainly be more useful; conversely, if the sexual problems of the parents are of concern, marital sessions will be most appropriate.

There are certain criteria a therapist can use to discern when to employ family versus another type of session. First and foremost, entire-family sessions are *contraindicated* if either of the parents is denying the facts about the abuse. In this case it is possible to see the daughter with the nondenying parent, or the whole family minus the denying parent (who would be seen by the therapist individually). However, the abused child should not be subjected to the further abuse of having to face a parent who challenges her truthfulness.

The therapist might decide to forego family sessions for a while if one family member is particularly "stuck," and the intensity of having the entire family present becomes counterproductive. A therapist might further elect to have fewer entire-family sessions if the abused child is an older adolescent. In this case, an important developmental issue for the adolescent is to separate from the family in an appropriate fashion. For the therapist to see the adolescent alone communicates her imminent independence and adulthood to the entire family, while providing an appropriate adult relationship with a person with whom she can safely discuss feelings and choices (Haley, 1980). Finally, if the therapist has been focusing on one subsystem (e.g., marital) and an impasse is reached, it is helpful to expand the unit of focus to include the entire family to regain therapeutic momentum.

PHYSICAL ARRANGEMENT OF SESSIONS

The use of space can be a powerful intervention tool, as has been demonstrated by structural family therapists (e.g., Minuchin, 1974; Minuchin & Fishman, 1981). Most family therapists physically arrange their office in a way that is comfortable and practical. We usually have an office arrangement which allows the most flexibility in seating, so that subsystems can be physically altered during the session, and so that the therapist can easily place herself in between people if necessary. For example, a coalition between the father and the daughter against the mother may physically manifest with the daughter sitting in between her parents. A simple yet powerful intervention is to ask the parents to sit together, and to move the daughter closer to her siblings.

It is also useful to periodically divide the therapy sessions between subsystems; for example, to see the entire family for the first third, the marital subsystem for the second third, and the siblings for the last third of the session. In addition to permitting the therapist to discuss matters relevant only to that subsystem, this division also communicates the new structural boundaries now being encouraged by the therapist. Families will often resist this, particularly if the children have had an inordinate amount of power in the family. It is important, though, for the therapist to continue this "boundary-marking" intervention, particularly *if* there is resistance from the children.

INTERVENTIONS DURING FAMILY SESSIONS

Both direct and indirect interventions are used with the families. *Direct* approaches are usually insight-oriented, overtly confront dysfunctional sequences and patterns of behavior, provide the maximum amount of information to the family about what needs to be changed and how to change it, and are usually considered obvious and understandable to all.

Indirect approaches are strategic interventions designed to encourage change, but these are usually paradoxical, provide less or even counterintuitive information to the family about the problem and how to change it, and are often considered inconsistent or confusing. Both direct and indirect methods are used throughout the family sessions, although the proportion of each is dependent upon how the case is proceeding and on how resistant to change the family is. Generally, if the family is making progress and is not resistant, then direct approaches are used to a greater extent than indirect approaches. Conversely, if the family is moving slowly and/or is resistant, then indirect approaches are used proportionately more frequently.

When an intervention is planned, the therapist is usually concerned with stopping or reducing a dysfunctional behavioral pattern or sequence. In addition, however, the therapist should also be cognizant of the *function* of this pattern or sequence so that an appropriate alternative can be introduced. A dysfunctional pattern or sequence may operate to *increase intimacy* among family members; or, it may operate to increase the *emotional distance* among family members (Alexander & Parsons, 1982). For example, if a particular dysfunctional behavior is assessed to have a distancing function, then the alternative suggested by the therapist should allow for increased distancing. As an illustration, if the abused daughter's current experimentation with drugs is seen as a way of obtaining distance from her parents, the therapist may encourage the family to provide her with more time out with "straight" friends in return for not using drugs (Piercy & Frankel, 1987).

We will discuss the common classes of interventions that can be used during Stage II family sessions that correspond to each of the three major family system vulnerability factors. These three, as will be recalled, are: *family abusive style; family structure;* and *communication* (see Chapter 6).

Interventions for Family Abusive Style

Larson and Maddock (1986) have suggested that incestuous abuse serves one of four basic functions in interpersonal exchange: (1) *affection-exchange,* where the incest is a result of affectional needs on the part of the father and/or daughter that are not met through more appropriate means; (2) *erotic-exchange,* where the family sexualizes most relationships and sexual meaning is attached to all behavior; (3) *aggression-exchange,* where the family sexualizes its anger and hostility rather than expresses it appropriately; and (4) *rage-expression,* where the offending parent acts out his psychopathological rage upon the least resistant family member in a sexual fashion, most akin to a violent rape.

There is usually only one family abusive style present, although it is possible that two overlap or that different family members are operating under a different style. After the therapist has assessed which style is present, the focus of the interventions is to redirect the family to meet the underlying *need* without sexually abusing anyone. For example, if the style is affection-exchange, the goal is for the father and daughter to be able to exchange affection and feel loved without having sex with one another.

Direct interventions. The general sequence of direct interventions to redirect the family abusive style is as follows: The therapist and the family agree upon the style they display and the different way they would like to meet their needs. The therapist might highlight some examples of behavioral patterns evident during the family sessions that clearly demonstrate the problematic style. The family members then agree to attempt the alternative behaviors designed with the therapist when inappropriate behaviors occur. The therapist consistently and tenaciously challenges the family whenever the "old" abusive style arises. The therapist actually encourages this to occur through enactments during the family sessions so that the family's behavior can be "shaped" and the family will eventually come to choose the alternative pattern.

Indirect interventions. Similar to an individual's "personality," a family's abusive style is quite pervasive and resilient to change, no matter how disheartening it may be even to the family. Indirect interventions may be useful to alter the most entrenched of abusive styles. The therapist should from the beginning *positively connote* the underlying meaning of the abusive style (but, of course, not the sexual abuse itself). For example, an aggression-exchange family might have their style described by the therapist as serving to protect or take care of the family and show love; however, the therapist will also point out that this style has not been effective for the family. The therapist may also *restrain change* by reminding the family throughout Stage II that abusive style is difficult to change, maybe impossible (which usually results in the family's disagreeing!). The therapist may *prescribe the symptom* by encouraging the mother to act "incompetently" for a specified period of time so that the father can practice a different style.

Interventions for Family Structure: Cohesion and Adaptability

Direct interventions. The therapist first identifies with the family the behaviors that place them in the extremes of cohesion and adaptability (see Chapter 6). For example, a common type of enmeshed behavior in incest families occurs when the daughter is forced to comply with the sexual advances of her father, with the threat that if she were *not* to do so she would be emotionally abandoned by the rest of the family. Also, the daughter is sometimes told to keep the incest a secret, with the threat that its disclosure would lead to the breaking up of the family. This threat is quite terryifying to a member of an enmeshed family, or of the kind of family described earlier that oscillates between enmeshed and disengaged. A daughter in a purely disengaged family might not particularly care and, in fact, might even find the separation of the family preferable to continued abuse.

The next step is to introduce the concept of middle ground. Extreme families appear to live in an all-or-nothing world and cannot conceive of life in shades of gray. This is one reason why incest families may fluctuate between enmeshed and disengaged. The therapist can point out how the extreme positions of both cohesion and adaptability have not worked for the family, and have probably contributed to the sexual abuse. Once this concept has been explained and accepted, the therapist obtains from the family an agreement that a middle ground is preferable and more workable, and then requests permission to interrupt extreme cohesion and adaptability sequences when he or she sees it occurring. Finally, the therapist directly challenges extreme behaviors as they happen during enactments, and suggests alternatives that fit more into the middle-ground category.

Indirect interventions. The intent behind a family member's extreme-range behavior can always be *positively connoted.* An obvious example is to reframe enmeshment as extreme love and caring (which should be easy—the family will probably connote it that way themselves), only in this case *too* much love and *too* much caring. A family can also be *restrained* from moving to the middle ground too quickly; the therapist might cite as a reason some of the *negative consequences of change* inherent in changing too fast. A *symptom prescription* might be made, where a father is told to be as rigid and inflexible with the rules as he can for a week, and the children and mother must ask permission for everything; then the next session family members are asked to discuss how this felt, and to suggest other (usually less extreme) options.

Finally, *metaphors* can be offered which describe enmeshment and rigidity in a language that the family can understand. Living in a rigid family may be described "like living at a bad military school," and enmeshment may be described "like the family living alone on a small ship, with no privacy, nobody else to talk to, and no way out." The extreme version, where the family is both enmeshed and disengaged, may be metaphorically pictured as "that island family, viewing any challenge as disloyalty and mutiny, that casts a family member into the sea."

Interventions for Family Structure: Hierarchy

Direct and indirect interventions. The interventions to alter the family's hierarchy and boundaries come directly from information provided during the Structural Session (see Chapter 8).

During Stage II family sessions, the family members are encouraged to identify for themselves when they have "crossed the line." This, of course, does not just refer to sexual abuse. Sexual abuse is viewed as one dramatic outcome when boundaries are crossed, but many other smaller examples occur each and every day. For example, the therapist might first remind the daughter that she has "crossed the line" when she begins to discipline one of her younger siblings while her parents sit next to her. Next, the therapist might stop the action, and ask the family, "Are any lines being crossed here? What could your daughter do differently? What could you, the parents, do to help your daughter so that she can stay on her own side of the line?" Eventually, with persistence and with the passing of time, the family will come to recognize hierarchical problems, stop them during the session, and alter their behavior.

The structural session and the vocabulary used (e.g., "crossing the line") is a metaphor itself, and thus the whole intervention can be viewed as an indirect approach. The other indirect interventions, such as restraining, the negative consequences of change, and symptom prescription, can all be used to support the metaphor of "keeping the lines clear and separate."

Interventions for Family Communication

Once communication is recognized as the vehicle through which dysfunctional behavior is expressed, it becomes an isomorph of the dysfunctional behavior itself. Therefore, a therapist could conceivably *not* intervene upon the family's communication at all, but instead wait until the dysfunctional sequences of behavior change the communication. However, to use a double-pronged approach and intervene at both the behavioral *and* the communication level usually is the most effective.

Direct and indirect interventions. Most often, family therapists use direct approaches to change problematic communication in the following areas: listening skills, self-expression, making requests, providing positive and correct feedback, and clarification of intended messages (Stuart, 1980). This follows the general sequence of: (1) *identifying* the dysfunctional communication style; (2) *obtaining the family's acceptance* that it is indeed a problem; (3) *getting the family into an enactment* that will force the dysfunctional communication to the surface; (4) *stopping* the action; and (5) *suggesting alternatives* to the problematic communication.

Some indirect support for these interventions may be used. For example, before allowing the family members to change a particular type of communication, the therapist might *restrain* them from the change and/or go over the *negative consequences* of making the change. The family could also be encouraged to practice extreme versions of their dysfunctional communication as a *symptom prescription*.

CASE EXAMPLE

In the following case example, the family and therapist have agreed that their style of interacting is exemplary of the aggression-exchange family abusive style. At this point in the session, the therapist observes the father behaving angrily toward the mother and then attempting to draw the daughter into the conflict. When the daughter does not behave in the manner that he desires, the father begins to react in an angry, immature way.

Therapist: (*to the father*) Tell Louise (*the mother*) what it is that you are so angry about.

Father: She never understands me. She'll just sit there with this blank look and say nothing.

Therapist: What do you think you do that stops her from talking? She knows how to talk and she knows what she thinks. I have seen evidence of this time and time again.

Father: I don't know what I do, damn it. I don't think I do anything. She just wants to act stupid so that I have to make all the decisions and run the house. (*turning to his daughter*) What do you think I do that stops your mother from talking?

Darlene: (*looking back and forth between both parents*) I'm not sure.

Father: You live with us. You know, what do you think I do?

Therapist: Joseph, you're doing it right now!

Father: Doing what?

Therapist: You're abusing Darlene.

Father: What? You're sitting right here. How can I be abusing Darlene?

Therapist: (*moving closer to the daughter*) Darlene, do you understand what I mean?

Darlene: Yeah, I think so.

Therapist: (*to the mother*) Louise, are you with me?

Mother: Yes.

Therapist: Louise, see if you can find out from your daughter what felt abusive and how she would want it different. (*to the father*) Joseph, you look like you are starting to pout. Stick in there. It might feel like you're getting picked on, but I want to help you get what you need from your family without hurting them. I've told you before, I often agree with what is in your heart, but the way you get it out, the style, is hurtful . . . and you get hurt, too.

Father: I know you say that, but I just don't get it. You have to get angry if no one will listen. It's the only way I can get anyone to hear me.

Therapist: Louise, go on. Find out from your daughter.

Mother: What just felt bad to you about what went on between Dad and me and you?

Darlene: I'm in the middle. I can't win. If I answer Dad, then I lose with you, and if I answer you, then I lose with Dad. It's where I always end up, so I don't do nothing or just get upset.

Mother: Well, you should just tell us to leave you out of it.

Therapist: No, it's not up to her. If *she's* the one who has to get herself out of the middle, then *she's* over the line and in your generation. You two have to take responsibility for your own pulling her in the middle and for getting her out of it.

Father: So how is being in the middle abuse?

Therapist: Darlene, can you answer that?

Darlene: Yeah, I think so. I'm always between the two of you. And making someone do something they don't want to do is hurting them and that's abuse (*starts to cry*).

Therapist: Is that how it feels to you?

Darlene: Yes.

Therapist: Joseph, when you sexually abused Darlene, you made her do things she didn't want to do. She's made to pick between you and her mother by your forcing her to keep a secret. When she's placed in the adult generation by having to perform tasks or give opinions that are not appropriate to her age, then that is abusive, too. I guess what I'm trying to say is that when you use power inappropriately, then that is abuse. And you do have a lot of power over Darlene.

Father: Well, she has a lot of power over me, and I should have some power anyway.

Therapist: I know it feels that way to you, and what we are trying here is to get some of those power problems straightened out. Louise, what are you thinking about all of this?

Mother: It makes sense to me but I'm not sure when it happens. I don't know what to do.

Therapist: Maybe you and Joseph can talk to each other now and figure out a plan to keep Darlene out of your marital dilemmas. (*turning their chairs to face one another*) Go ahead, try now to come up with some temporary solution.

Mother: Well, Joe, what do you think? How can we keep her out of the middle?

Father: I'm not sure that she is in the middle. (*turning away from wife and toward daughter*) It really feels that bad to you when I ask you your opinion?

Darlene: Yes, and aren't you supposed to be talking to Mom right now.

Father: (*now turning to the therapist*) See how she has power over me? She is telling me who to talk to and when to do it.

Therapist: This is amazing to me, I wish I had this all on videotape to show how you keep repeating the same dance over and over again. Let me draw it for you. (*drawing on the blackboard*) I ask the two of you to talk. Louise turns to Joe and asks a question. Joe turns to Darlene, bringing her into the marital conversation. Darlene, then, is the parental generation and parents her father. This has to stop and I know you can do it. Do it NOW!!

Mother: Joe, how can we stop this picture from happening?

Father: I don't know.

Mother: I have an idea, do you want to hear it?

Father: Sure.

Mother: Maybe we should ask Darlene to leave the room when we are having a conversation or we can go for a walk. Yah, that's something we both like to do and she hates. Maybe if we can't see her, we won't always ask her opinion.

Father: Maybe so. I guess when she's sitting there I'm just used to always asking her opinion.

Mother: Maybe if you heard mine once, you wouldn't think I was so stupid. I guess I always feel like I have to fight to get my two cents in, so I just give up. I'm getting tired of giving up.

Therapist: And your giving up isn't helpful to you. It can make you feel bad about yourself and incompetent. It doesn't help your daughter to see you give up because that's probably not the role model you want to be. It makes it easier for her to be drawn into the middle if you give up. I can see why you are tired of giving up, and I think it is great that you are wanting to do something about it. Darlene, are you going to be able to stay out of the middle? Tell your parents about how it will be for you if they go for these walks and do not talk in front of you.

Darlene: I think I'll love it if you two don't talk anymore in front of me. And I also would like to stop talking to both of you separately about the other one. I hate it.

Father: Do we do it that much?

Darlene: Yes, it really drives me crazy.

Therapist: Great job! Get an agreement from them.

Darlene: Will you do that?

Father: Do what?

Therapist: Darlene, you look upset. What just happened?

Darlene: How can I believe they'll change or get an agreement from them when they don't even know what I'm talking about?

Therapist: Both of them? I haven't heard anything from your mother on this topic. (*turning to the mother*) Does Darlene lump you and Joseph together much?

Mother: Yes, it seems that way to me.

Therapist: Maybe that's another problem that is an outcome of you giving up.

Mother: Yeah, maybe you are right.

Therapist: Don't give up now. Do you want to be lumped with Joe? (*Mother shakes her head no*) Then tell your daughter that.

Mother: I know what you're talking about when you say we talk to you about each other. I'll stop doing that, but I need to know that your Dad isn't talking to you about me. I'll stop doing it. If you feel bad, you have to let me know.

Darlene: Sounds good. Dad, what about you?

Father: Sure, I'll try. I won't talk to you about your mother and I'll try to keep you out of the middle.

Therapist: Have the two of you come up with an agreement?

Father: Are we going to take a walk?

Mother: Yeah, I think so.

Therapist: I guess all your ideas aren't bad, huh Louise? We need to talk more about this in your marital sessions.

Many changes take place during this session. Through some indirect interventions the therapist attempts to seal these changes and prevent further symptomatic behaviors.

Therapist: You did a lot of great work in this session. In a way that makes me nervous. I know you have heard me say this before, but it's scary to maintain that much change after doing things one way for so long. It's like climbing a mountain. The higher you get, the further you get from the ground where you were nice and safe. You all are getting higher and higher. It is getting further from your base camp and things are getting riskier.

Mother: We could never go back to the ground, not after we came this far.

Therapist: I know it feels like that but, believe me, I know a lot of people who say that but become afraid the further away they get from the old family. Let's talk about the negative consequences of the two of you talking to each other more and asking less of Darlene. What do you all stand to lose? Joe, what about you? How will things change for you if you don't rely on Darlene's opinion as much? What will happen between you and your daughter, and you and your wife?

Father: I know that if I say nothing bad will happen and only good can come from it you'll say no, right?

Therapist: RIGHT!

Father: Well, I'll miss her. Darlene always seems to understand me. I'm not sure what we'll have to talk about. I guess I never talked to her about stuff most Dads talk to their daughters about. I am not even sure what that is.

Therapist: Then this could be a big loss for you?

Father: Yes, I guess so.

Therapist: Anything else you can think of? How about with Louise?

Father: The same thing as the other times we have talked about this. We might find out we don't like each other and don't want to be together. That's probably the worst.

Therapist: Yes, and maybe you two could never agree on anything and those walks could turn into huge fights. What about you, Mom?

Mother: I suppose I'd have to find a new way to be a mother to Darlene, too. I'd have to find some new friends to confide in and not my daughter.

Therapist: And those new friends might threaten Joseph, and then that might cause further marital problems. See, there is a long way to fall down the more changes you make. You two will have to figure out a way to break your isolation that will not threaten your positions and still help you expand.

Mother: I might end up giving my opinion on those walks and Joe won't like it and then I'll feel bad. Or maybe he'll get mad and then hurt me.

Therapist: I guess we need to talk about that possibility now and renegotiate the No-Violence Contract, and update it.

After a new No-Violence Contract is established, the therapist resumes her discussion of the negative consequences of the daughter being extricated from being in the middle:

Darlene: I'm going to be pretty lonely. I'm going to have to worry about my own life, if I'm not worrying about theirs so much.

Therapist: Yeah, you might have to go to school and try to be sober long enough to see what it is really like out there.

Darlene: You're being obnoxious . . . but I guess you're right. Plus, I'll worry about Mom's safety. Sometimes she doesn't seem like she can protect herself.

Therapist: Check it out. See if she thinks she still needs your protection.

During the final moments of the family session, the therapist restrains the family from too abrupt a change and prescribes the old way of interacting as a way to protect the family from "failure."

Therapist: Because we all can now see the potential pitfalls from these changes, I'd like to suggest that you only attempt to take this walk, or ask Darlene to leave the room, once during the week. Every time you pull her into the conversations, observe how it feels. Does it feel safe and reassuring? Does it feel painful and abusive? You'll pull her into it, and that's OK . . . just notice it.

Father: What happens if we don't? I mean, I'm trying not to hurt her. Isn't that what we are here for?

Therapist: I know. But we also just agreed that too much change too fast is scary. Don't set yourselves up to be perfect. At least acknowledge when you're doing the old communication. Take it slow.

Mother: I think I know what you mean.

Here the therapist is helping the family slow down their pace. Many times the family will attempt to change so quickly that the change does not become integrated into the family structure or interactions.

12

Subsystem Sessions

One of the most powerful aspects of Multiple Systems therapy is the ability to access the various subsystems of the incestuous family. In individually oriented therapy the client can usually only talk about the problems he or she is having with a spouse, or a mother, or a sibling. In a family-oriented program, on the other hand, problems among family members are confronted directly by those members experiencing the difficulty.

Incestuous families, because of their tendency to blur generational boundaries, their penchant for secrecy, and the overall severity of their family problems, can particularly benefit from subsystem therapy. Although any functional subsystem can be having difficulties, the *marital, parents' family-of-origin,* and *sibling* subsystems almost always will require special attention from the therapist. The *social networks* that help maintain the incestuous abuse or could be used to change it can also be accessed in subsystem sessions. A list of common subsystem interventions is presented in Table 12.1.

MARITAL THERAPY

Direct therapeutic intervention for the marital subsystem is one of the pivotal components of Stage II therapy. The marital unit, as the Execu-

TABLE 12.1
Subsystem Interventions

I. Marital Therapy Interventions
   A. Communication skills
   B. Conflict resolution
   C. Structural interventions
   D. Intimacy-enhancing interventions
   E. Sex therapy
   F. Enactments
   G. Confronting affairs
II. Family-of-Origin Therapy
   A. Preparatory sessions with the parent
   B. Negative consequences of meeting with family of origin
   C. Meeting with family of origin
III. Children's Sessions
   A. Conflict-resolution among siblings
   B. Reduce children's guilt, fear, shame through open communication
   C. Play therapy techniques

tive subsystem, is without doubt the most influential constituent in a family system, and thus needs to have the most attention paid to it (Minuchin, 1974). It is difficult to imagine a fully functional family where the marital subsystem is dysfunctional. In a sense, the style and tenor of a family are set by the parents, and how they interact can affect the interaction of each and every other subsystem component.

It is not surprising, then, that one of the most common reports among those working with incestuously abusing families is that the marriages are often riddled with conflict, communication problems, sexual difficulties, and general marital unhappiness (Anderson & Shafer, 1979; Giarretto, 1978; Justice & Justice, 1979; Renshaw, 1982; Rist, 1979; Zuelzer & Reposa, 1983). Marital therapy, therefore, becomes crucial to helping the couple improve their relationship, which will also have a positive effect on other aspects of family functioning.

There are many possible goals for the couple's marital therapy, depending upon the specific problems noted during Stage I. Generally, the therapist works to make the couple more flexible, interdependent upon one another, and comfortable with the culturally prescribed boundaries that separate them as a couple from their children. In addition, however, the therapist will likely focus on the following issues which are commonly found to be problematic in the marriages.

Areas of Focus in Marital Therapy

The future of the relationship. For many couples, a quick decision was made in Stage I (after the disclosure of the incest) as to whether they wished to remain together or to separate. This decision was obviously made under great stress and may now need to be reexamined. Some wives who had initially decided to remain with the abusing husbands have had the opportunity to reevaluate their feelings about the marriage, partially based upon how committed to change they feel their husbands are. On the other hand, some wives who had previously decided to separate because of the abuse have now changed their minds and wish to reunite with their spouses with the help of therapy. Either way, it is during these early marital sessions that reevaluation decisions are made.

If the couple decides that their marriage cannot continue, then marital therapy becomes divorce therapy. In this case, important issues must be resolved, including how they plan to maintain a parental relationship, how they will manage their legal difficulties, who will retain the custody of the children, how visitation will occur, and so forth. Often the therapist ends up performing the role of divorce mediator. This is certainly a role consistent with the overall family goals of the treatment program. However, the therapist may wish to refer the couple for specialized divorce mediation if it appears that the therapist cannot effectively do it and family therapy at the same time.

Communication. It is important to help the couple learn to communicate effectively so that they have the requisite skills to resolve other potent difficulties later in marital therapy. Most incestuously abusing families have specific communication difficulties that have contributed, at least partially, to their vulnerability to incest. These include double-binding exchanges, lack of clarity in both affective and instrumental communication, and noncongruence between verbal and nonverbal communication. The therapist must help the couple improve their style of communication so that they can "teach" the rest of the family what they have learned, both directly and through modeling.

Conflict resolution. Almost as basic as communication, the ability to successfully resolve conflicts is a skill that a great many couples lack. Many report *never* reaching a conclusion to an argument, but instead that it just "goes away" without ever being resolved. This leaves an unfinished feeling in a relationship. It may ultimately prevent intimacy because the couple is afraid to become too close lest they have to "start all over again with the same old argument."

The "structure" of the marriage. Just as the entire family system has structural components (e.g., power, boundaries, hierarchy), so does the marital subsystem. The therapist must guide the couple through an examination of and change in their balance of power and control; their disengagement from or overdependence upon each other; their isolation from others outside their family; and exploration of sex roles and gender-related differences.

Sexuality and sexual problems. Although the assessment of sexual disorders takes place during Stage I individual sessions, the interventions for sexual problems are presented in Stage II marital therapy. Also, many important sexual issues must be examined with both husband and wife present. Examples of sexual problems that need to be addressed include any discrepancy of sexual desire; difficulties asking for or postponing sexual activity; confusion between affection needs and sexual needs; and, of course, any of the possible specific sexual dysfunctions, such as erectile dysfunction or inorgasmia.

Codependency. A pattern has been identified in many couples where the husband has incestuously abused his daughter that is akin to the *codependency* profile in couples where one spouse is alcoholic (Bepko & Krestan, 1985). Within this framework, the husband and wife are both dependent upon the other's dysfunctional behavior to maintain the role of each in the relationship. For instance, a nonabusing wife appears to be dependent upon her husband's abusing behavior to meet certain psychological and social needs of her own; therefore, she subtly allows the abuse to occur, maintaining her victimization.

In another example, the husband is "overcompetent," while his wife complimentarily acts "incompetent." The husband is dependent upon his wife's continued victimization and incompetent behavior as a way to maintain his power in the family and to distract him from his abusive behavior. However, after he abuses his daughter, he feels guilty, depressed, loses his job, and so forth. Now his wife becomes the "competent" one, going back to work, taking care of him psychologically, and so on. This pattern is repeated often enough to a point where a "delicate balance" forms between the husband and wife, resulting in a continuation of the abuse. An important function of marital therapy, then, is to identify and ameliorate this potentially devastating pattern.

Other issues. There are a number of other important issues that should be addressed during the marital therapy. First, the link between each of the pair's family of origin and their current marriage must be examined, particularly in terms of communication style, how they resolve conflict, and inappropriate boundaries between parents and children. Each of these current marital problems may have been "learned" via their own families as the husband and wife were growing up. Second, the couple's overall parenting skills should be evaluated and improved as necessary. Not surprising, many of these couples have inadequate or inconsistent parenting abilities, particularly when they must concur with one another. Third, the therapist has to prevent the couple from maintaining other family problems (including, perhaps, the sexual abuse) as a way of distracting themselves from focusing on their marital problems.

MARITAL THERAPY INTERVENTIONS

There are five classes of interventions we use in the marital therapy component of Stage II treatment. We recognize that there are many more possible interventions; at the same time, those we use seem to encompass the most relevant problems experienced by marriages in incestuous families. These five are communication improvement, conflict resolution, changing the structure of the marriage, increasing intimacy, and improving the couple's sexual relationship.

Communication Improvement

The first class of interventions for the couple is communication improvement. The therapist, through a series of exercises both in and out of session, teaches the couple four basic but essential communication skills described by Stuart (1980). These are:

1. *The ability to listen.* Couples are taught to provide the physical appearance and readiness to listen to each other. They are confronted by the therapist when they interrupt each other. Finally, they are instructed to paraphrase each other to make certain that what was said was understood. This can feel cumbersome to clients, and the therapist must continue this exercise vigorously until the clients can paraphrase the other almost automatically.

2. *The ability to use self-expression successfully.* One of the most important communication tasks is for the couple to learn to use self-expression effectively. Stuart (1980) suggests teaching the couple six simple rules:

a. The "I" rule is that all self-statements should begin with the pronoun "I" rather that "you" ("I feel angry" versus "You make me angry").
b. The "say-ask" rule requires the couple to make a self-statement before asking a question ("I would like to talk about my getting a job. Would you like to talk about it?").
c. The "how" rule suggests that it is safer to begin a question with "how" rather than "why" ("*How* are you feeling?" versus "*Why* are you feeling bad?").
d. The "two-question" rule requires that a second question be asked after the first, to indicate to the other person a true interest and to avoid using the first question as a way to lead into a self-statement.
e. The "now" rule emphasizes that all self-statements be made in the present tense.
f. The "simplicity-speaks-the-truth" rule asserts that all self-statements be made simply with a minimum of added verbiage.

3. *The ability to make requests constructively.* Many couples are uncomfortable making requests from their partners and thus do so in an oblique manner. This leads to confusion and, most important, the request going unnoticed or ignored. Couples should be taught to make requests directly to one another, with the term "I want" being used rather than the less intense "I need," and to make these requests at a time when they are most likely to be carried out (Stuart, 1980).

4. *The ability to give positive feedback.* Couples in incestuous families seem to be like most other dysfunctional families in that they exchange a high degree of negative feedback with each other. An extremely important task is for the couple to learn to provide each other with positive statements and to do so in a nonjudgmental fashion (Stuart, 1980). Finally, the couple should be encouraged by the therapist to provide this positive feedback as the behavior occurs. Examples of positive feedback statements include: "I liked the way you cuddled with me last night"; "You sure were good with the kids just now;" and "You were so smart in how you figured out that payment problem!"

Secrecy. Since secrecy is one of the most common vulnerability factors in incestuously abusing families, secrecy must be confronted in all subsystems receiving treatment. Obviously, certain aspects of a person's life are private, as are aspects of the couple's life private from the children's (e.g., the details of the parents' sex life should be private from the children as a way of maintaining appropriate boundaries). However, it is generally a sign of a dysfunctional family when important facts are kept secret from other family members. And it is particularly harmful if one parent keeps a major secret from the other parent, especially if this secret is shared with one of the children.

The therapist should make a "no-secrecy" rule with the couple that states that no important secret will be kept from each other. An "important secret" is defined as one that the other would want to be or should be aware of. For example, the father who plans a secret surprise birthday party for the mother would not be in violation of the rule; however, the father who is secretly making and selling pornographic movies would be.

Enactments. Once the communication rules are described to the clients, they practice them during real-issue discussions during the marital therapy sessions. The communication rules are more likely to be incorporated into their lives if they occur naturally. Therefore, few formal "communication exercise sessions" are done, except at the very beginning of marital therapy. Instead, the couple is led into an *enactment* by the therapist. During the discussion or argument that ensues, the therapist interrupts them when they demonstrate poor communication, reminds them of the communication rule, and then makes them do it again, this time substituting the appropriate rule. This process is repeated throughout marital therapy, until the couple uses these rules effortlessly without therapeutic intervention.

Conflict Resolution

One of the most frustrating feelings is to experience a conflict without a resolution. Couples with a variety of presenting problems endure this feeling often; therefore, a common element of most marital therapy programs is training in conflict resolution. This is especially vital for couples in incestuously abusing families, since the propensity for conflict is so great and the consequences so grave.

As with communication exercises, conflict resolution can be practiced during the marital sessions by the therapist encouraging a conflict and then making suggestions about how to change the interactions to avoid it. Although many techniques are used to resolve conflicts, the three guidelines described by Stuart (1980) have proven particularly useful. These are to: (1) teach the couple to search for the solution in the present, not in the past; (2) have them adopt a "conciliatory set" (i.e., teach them to seek solutions where both husband and wife are "winners"); and (3) encourage the couple to solve problems in small steps rather than to let a conflict spill over into a secondary or even tertiary fight. Consider the following example:

Wife: He doesn't take charge of anything in the house without me yelling at him. I have to get furious for him to do anything. Your picture is right, I've told you that. He's just one of the kids.

Husband: I try to do things. Nothing is ever good enough for you.

Wife: Like what? You're just like the kids. You do something so half-assed that it makes me have to do it. I know it's planned. Don't do it right and the she'll have to do it.

Husband: It isn't a plan. According to you, nothing is right unless you do it.

Wife: Not true. I'd give anything for a little help.

Therapist: OK, wait a minute. I see the same old pattern happening here. Let's try to identify the sequence and then pick one area and try to resolve it satisfactorily to both of you. We'll start with you, Sue. Sue asks Roger to do something.

Husband: Tells me is more like it.

Therapist: OK. Maybe that's something to look at. Sue asks or tells you to do something. You then do it?

Wife: Half-way does it.

Therapist: OK. I know what you two are saying. Sue demands and then Roger acts like a kid, just ignoring you or saying he'll do it and then doesn't. Right? Sue, you see Roger as a kid. Roger, you see Sue as a parent. Roger, do you want Sue to be your mother?

Husband: No, absolutely not. I don't need another mother. If she would stop, then maybe I could stop being a kid.

Therapist: Exactly. Do you need Roger to be another child?

Wife: Definitely not.

Therapist: So you'd both be "winners" if you both acted differently?

Husband: You bet. I hate it.

Therapist: Let's try to solve one little problem you two are having, OK? Sue, pick a specific situation, a problem you two have.

Wife: Easy, whenever you get the kids ready in the morning, the kitchen and the house are a mess. The clothes are everywhere, the dishes are filthy, the house is a wreck, and I have to clean it up. I really think you should be in charge in the morning, since you're home and I work then.

Husband: OK. I can do that, but I need some help from you.

Wife: Then I'll just do it if I'm going to have to help. This is what you always do.

Therapist: Wait, let's keep this in the present. In other words, what's important is that you two solve this problem *now.* Roger, tell your wife how she can help you. Use the skills for talking that we have been working on.

Husband: I would like to be able to get the kids ready without leaving you more work. But you have to let me do a few things my way. You can't control how I do everything. Like if I decide to use the dishwasher, it would help if you didn't tell me I was lazy. If I give the kids cereal—not all the time, but sometimes—then I don't want to get yelled at when you come home. In other words, work with me, like a team, you know. Like if you hate the clothes I put on the kids, maybe you can put out what you think they should wear the night before.

Therapist: So what you're saying will help solve this problem is that when you are in charge at a prescribed time, like in the morning, you will do the work and Sue will not criticize?

Husband: Right.

Therapist: And if there is really something she would like to see different, she can make a suggestion?

Husband: Right.

Therapist: Nice job. What do you think, Sue? Will this solve the problem for you?

Wife: God, yes. If he'd just do the morning work, it'd be great.

Therapist: He says to do that he'll need you to give him some "margin of error."

Wife: Yes, I'll stay out of it.

Therapist: Might not be easy. With that parent-child pattern and all. Let's try it this week. I'll call you during the week to see if you are both doing your end of the bargain.

Structural Interventions

There are a number of interventions that can be made that are designed to help the couple alter their problematic boundaries, power, hierarchy patterns, and gender imbalances.

Boundary marking is a structural intervention that reinforces certain subsystem boundaries while it diffuses other inappropriate boundaries (Minuchin & Fishman, 1981). One could argue that simply to hold formalized and timely *marital* sessions during the course of *family* treatment for incestuous abuse is a form of boundary marking, since it offers the message to the family that the marital unit is distinct, significant, and separate from the other subsystems. Marital boundary marking can also occur when the therapist makes assignments for the couple to spend time alone with each other, to go on "dates," or to take a vacation with one another without the children.

Parenting skill improvement can actually be considered a type of specialized boundary marking. Assignments are made that will force the couple to make parental decisions together, and to resist their children's natural "divide-and-conquer" approach to getting what they want by forcing the parents to dispute one another. Marital sessions are used to discuss and role play possible parenting problems and solutions with the help of the therapist.

Examining and changing the couple's *balance of power* with one another can be accomplished in a number of ways. First, the therapist didactically presents a number of different types of unbalanced relationships. For example, a couple may have an unbalance of power if the wife is afraid to tell her husband "no" directly because he will yell at her; instead, she agrees to do something but then conveniently "forgets." The therapist then asks which of these sample relationships exemplify them. Once the couple can identify their own balance-of-power patterns, they can then engage in directed enactments, with the therapist interrupting and challenging those patterns as they occur.

Isolation from other marital couples is a hallmark of incestuously abusing families. An important intervention is to encourage the couple to contact and maintain relationships with their couple friends; or, if they do not have any (which is quite common in incestuously abusing families), to engage in activities that will allow them to make new friends. There are many possible resources for this, and the assignments should be made with the couple's interests and history in mind. Thus, encouraging a religious couple to become more involved with church activities would be more successful than encouraging a nonreligious or atheist couple to do the same. On the other hand, the therapist must take care not to advocate activities that may contribute to other related problems. So a couple where the family sexual abuse style was *erotic exchange* should obviously not be reinforced by the therapist for becoming involved with a local swingers club as a way of reducing their isolation.

Interventions Around Intimacy Issues

Once a couple have the ability to communicate effectively with one another, can resolve conflict in a manner acceptable to both, and have strengthened their relationship structurally within their larger family and external systems, they are then ready to face the most difficult issue a couple can face—intimacy with one another. Whereas clinical change in the other three areas is observable and apparent to the therapist, changes in intimate feelings are phenomenological in nature and are more experiential than measurable. Also, what indicates intimacy to one person may not to another. Therefore, interventions to increase intimacy in couples are far more personalized than for any other aspect of the program.

It is common for couples to fear an increase in intimacy. The therapist should discuss the negative consequences of intimacy. There are some typical negative consequences that clients raise: loss of control and power; discovering after they become more intimate that they really do not like each other, which might lead to divorce; feeling the pain and hurt that may materialize when opening oneself up; and the most typical of all, leaving oneself vulnerable if the intimacy offered is not reciprocated. After the clients have shared their anticipated negative consequences of intimacy, the therapist can then use the technique of restraining to paradoxically aid in their commitment, as is shown in the following example.

Therapist: I understand how real these negative consequences are, and it indeed seems as though you have some good reasons not to become intimate with one another. In fact, even though it is one of the most important things a couple can have, it just may be too risky at this time for you two to chance it.

Husband: But I'm confused. If it's so important, why shouldn't we have it?

Therapist: Oh, I'm not saying you shouldn't have it . . . just the opposite. I think it is essential that you eventually are more intimate with one another. It's just . . .

Husband: I know I want it.

Therapist It's just that it's risky, especially after those negative consequences you came up with.

Wife: I think what Bob's saying is that we want to take that risk.

Therapist: That's great, that's great. . . . Only if, as we're doing some of the things necessary for you two to become more intimate, it gets tough and you need to back away, that'll be OK. I'll understand why. With those negative consequences and all.

An important discussion the therapist has with the clients helps them to examine how much intimacy each can tolerate. Just as everyone has his or her own "personal space" that permits others to get just so close without discomfort and social stress, everyone has a different "psychological space" that permits others to get just so close without psychological stress. Clarifying the parameters of intimacy for both kinds of space and normalizing the difference between the two can be a useful intervention.

Another intervention is to draw the connection between perceived loss of intimacy and the appearance of symptomatic behavior. A prevalent pattern in incestuous families is for the father to make sexual advances to his daughter after he perceives his wife distancing herself from him. The couple are asked to explore ways that they can distance themselves from their partners in a way that says, "I still love you, I just need some space," rather than, "Get away from me, I don't need you."

Many clients, particularly but not exclusively men, cannot effectively differentiate affection from sexuality. To them affection *means* sex, and vice versa. Consequently, the rebuking of a sexual advance is experienced as a rebuking of intimacy. On the other hand, for some, true intimacy and affection mean *not* to have sex, or at least to not "dirty up the intimacy." The therapist should first help the clients clarify each spouse's cognitive beliefs about affection and sex. The therapist should then help each spouse to mediate his or her extreme position. Finally, the couple should be taught how to communicate directly what they really want with regard to affection and sex, and how to distance themselves in ways that do not hurt the feelings of the other person.

Because the therapist also sees each of the clients in individual sessions, he or she knows the levels of risk each is willing to take. The therapist helps the clients to try new risk-taking behaviors in the individual sessions; if these go well, they can be included in the marital sessions. The therapist can encourage the clients to say risky things to one another, things that expose their most visceral vulnerabilities and that may eventually lead to deeper intimacy.

Empathy is one of the most crucial elements of a marriage. We have found that having the couple discuss with each other some of their myths, messages, and belief systems helps them develop a heightened sense of compassion and empathy for one another. One way to stimulate such a discussion is to have the couple answer the following questions, first individually, and then together.

1. How did you two get into this relationship? Do you feel like you had a choice? Were you forced by some situation, person, or feeling?

2. Did getting into this relationship serve any another purpose?
3. What did you expect this relationship to be like when it first began? What were some of your dreams and wishes about the relationship?
4. What messages have you gotten from society about relationships? What have you learned about relationships from the movies? What do you think your friends think about marriage?
5. What did you learn from the world, friends, movies, magazines, etc., about *your* role in marriage and family?
6. What did you learn from those same sources about what the role of a spouse should be?
7. What did you learn from your family about marriage, about men in marriage, and about women in marriage?
8. What did you learn from seeing your grandparents' marriage about what to expect in marriage? What to expect from the other person and how much to give?
9. What are the messages you got about control in a marriage? What sort of things should you control? What sort of things should your spouse control? What should you control in yourself and what should you control in the other?
10. How should you gain and keep this control? What is permissible when trying to effect change?
11. Did your expectations about a marriage get met? What are your major disappointments about marriage and this one in particular? What are your major joys about the marriage?
12. Do you feel in or out of control?
13. Looking over your answers, what sort of things do you feel are realistic messages and beliefs and what are unrealistic?

In the case of an affair. It is never easy for a marital therapist to manage the information that one of the clients is having an affair unbeknownst to the other spouse. It is especially difficult for a therapist treating an incest family since the issues of boundaries, intimacy, and secrecy are so entwined with the family's vulnerability to incest. There are really no completely satisfying solutions, and more often than not the therapist must make a decision that makes the most sense for that couple at that time.

At the beginning of therapy it is useful for the therapist to announce to the entire family in a family, marital, or individual session the following:

> During the course of counseling you may want to confide in me about something that is going on in your life. In most cases I regard

> what people tell me in therapy to be totally confidential. However, given the incest and the secrets surrounding it, I feel that it would be inappropriate for *me* to keep a secret with any member of the family. So I just want you to know that if you do want to tell me something privately, I reserve the right to help you tell other people in the family as I feel is necessary.

The result of this may be that the therapist is *not* told about an affair; however, many therapists are willing to risk nondisclosure rather than be forced to participate in another family secret.

If the therapist has not offered this dictum at the onset of treatment and the husband or wife does divulge an affair, then the therapist can explore the meaning of the affair, discuss the negative consequences of giving up the affair, and encourage him or her to give up the affair (citing the emotional distractions that an affair causes in a marriage, the need for both spouses to be able to give 100% to working on the marriage during therapy, etc.). However, if the husband or wife still refuses to put an end to the affair *and* refuses to tell the spouse, the therapist will most likely have to say:

> There is really nothing left for me to do. You have told me something that I believe will have a detrimental effect on our work, and yet you refuse to do what needs to be done: either give up the affair or tell your wife. This forces me to keep a secret, which I find unhealthy for your family. That puts me in such an awkward position that I don't think I will be able to treat you folks anymore. Therefore, what I will have to do is terminate therapy; I won't, of course, say why; just that I have encountered information that makes my continuing with you impossible. I will give you a week, however, to decide if you can come up with a better alternative.

Quite often, the client comes back the next week having either told his spouse, or ended the affair.

Sex Therapy

If clients are assessed to be in need of therapy for a specific sexual dysfunction, the therapist has two options: He or she can refer the couple to a sex therapist or provide the treatment him- or herself. If the therapist has no specialized training in the treatment of sexual dysfunction, then the ethical choice is to refer the couple. However, many family therapists have received enough training in sex therapy to provide competent treatment for all but the most difficult of sexual problems. Also, because of the intensive therapy in which the family has already taken part, including family, couple, individual, group, and possibly alcohol and substance abuse treatment, it just may be too much to ask the couple to begin another treatment with another therapist. Therefore, whenever possible it is recommended that the family therapist also provide the couple's sex therapy. There are a number of excellent sourcebooks in sex therapy that should be of help to the clinician, including those by Kaplan (1974, 1979, 1983), Leiblum and Pervin (1980), and LoPiccolo and LoPiccolo (1979).

The sexual dysfunctions most frequently seen include erectile dysfunction, ejaculatory incompetence, and premature ejaculation for the man; and vaginismus, dyspareunia (caused by a lack of vaginal lubrication), and inorgasmia for the woman. These dysfunctions often respond to a program combining the following components (after LoPiccolo, 1979):

1. *The acceptance of mutual responsibility.* Whereas the responsibility for the sexual abuse of their daughter has been clearly placed upon the father during therapy, the responsibility for the sexual dysfunction the couple may be experiencing is framed as a shared responsibility between the husband and wife. Sexual problems certainly do not arise without the influence of and effect upon the spouse. And most important, both will be needed to work to alleviate the problem.
2. *Basic sex education.* The therapist uses sex therapy sessions to provide basic sex education for the clients. Readings are assigned from a basic college-level human sexuality text (for example Denney & Quadagno, 1988) and then are discussed with the clients. Topics usually include basic sexual anatomy and physiology, of which clients are generally woefully ignorant; the range of sexual expression; techniques of sexual arousal; research on love and intimacy; sexual fantasies; and sexual variations.
3. *Reducing sexual anxiety.* Most of the specific sexual disorders are either a direct or indirect function of anxiety. Anxiety has been shown to be reduced through the *sensate focus* exercises, described first by Masters and Johnson (1970). The clients engage in mutual kissing, touching, caressing, and massage for a number of weeks before they are "permitted" to include genital sexuality. Sensate focus is most akin to systematic desensitization and is quite effective in relieving the performance anxiety associated with the sexual dysfunction.

4. *Improving sexual communication.* As a rule, most "normal" couples do not communicate adequately about sexuality; it is no surprise then that dysfunctional couples also have difficulty expressing their sexual needs, wants, and limits in an effective manner. It is useful to apply some of the communication rules learned earlier to the sex therapy. Couples are assigned "talking sessions" at home, to discuss a variety of sexual topics suggested by the therapist. For example, they may be assigned to talk about what they enjoyed about the previous sensate focus session, and what they would like added to it in the subsequent session. We find it useful to have them tape record these "talking sessions" to help them comply with what is often the most difficult component of sex therapy—sexual communication.
5. *Specific sexual skill improvement.* Some dysfunctions are partially caused by what can best be termed a "skill deficit." For example, men with premature ejaculation have often not "learned" to recognize the point of ejaculatory inevitability which, if identified, could help them to prevent the orgasmic reflex. Learning the "squeeze technique" (Masters & Johnson, 1970) can help them acquire that skill so that eventually they can control the reflex in a more natural way. In the same way, women who have not experienced an orgasm can be taught to do so fairly easily (Barbach, 1975).

FAMILY-OF-ORIGIN THERAPY

One of the unique elements of Multiple Systems therapy is the inclusion of the parents' families of origin in our treatment. It is not always an easy task to engage the family of origin of either the offending or nonoffending parent, but it is well worth the effort. In our experience, therapy is greatly enhanced and expedited when the extended family is included. Within these families the high level of cooperation in helping one another is amazing.

There are a number of reasons why it is important for the parents of the parents to be involved when treating incestuous families. First, the extended family has undoubtedly been severely affected by the disclosure of incest, and their own pain, guilt, and humiliation should be addressed. To not include them in therapy is, in our opinion, a cruel neglect. Second, they deserve to know, just as the nuclear family has discovered, how incest occurred in their family.

A third reason to include the families of origin is that incestuous abuse is often part of a long transgenerational pattern, and it is possible that the inclusion of the parents' parents will open up old secrets that can be finally addressed. Fourth, there is sometimes an unconscious attempt made by the families of origin to sabotage the changes made by the nuclear family during their therapy. These problems can often be dealt with if the therapist has access to the extended family as well.

There are other reasons to include the families of origin in the therapy. Many incestuously abusing parents have felt victimized in their own families. These sessions allow them to confront those feelings and experiences of victimization with their own family, and to hopefully develop realistic expectations about their future relationship with their parents.

Sometimes an abusing father has grown up taking the responsibility for the abuse that was inflicted on him when he was young. This is similar to when *his* daughter accepts the responsibility of the abuse and all the subsequent family problems were all her fault. The therapist encourages them all to understand how each person must be culpable for only that which he has control. The abusing father is no more to blame for his own childhood abuse than his daughter is for hers.

Finally, the parent and his family of origin must decide on what type of relationship they want and can reasonably expect to have in the future, and on how they are going to achieve it. They must recognize that some long-standing interactions will probably never change. To paraphrase the "serenity prayer," they must learn to change that which is changeable and to accept that which is not.

Family-of-Origin Interventions

These interventions refer to sessions held with either the abusing or the nonabusing parent and his or her parents. Other extended family members, such as the parent's siblings, might also be present. The clients set the goals of these sessions. A goal may be to simply gather more information about their families of origin. Another goal might be to confront the past with their parents, such as their own experience of abuse or neglect. However, direct confrontation of families of origin is not always the most appropriate goal. Many clients prefer to try and change how they currently interact with their own parents and siblings.

The therapist, in helping the client decide which tack to take, must consider what the outcome is likely to be. That is, will the client be successful and feel stronger and more independent from his or her family? Or will he or she be revictimized and experience a psychological regression. In any case, the therapist can serve an important role in confirming the client's reality about his or her family of origin, a reality that may have been obscured since childhood.

It is important to be aware that the majority of clients do not want to have family-of-origin sessions. We begin in Stage I to "drop the hint" that there may be a time when they will need, for many reasons, to talk with their parents. Throughout therapy, when issues regarding the family of origin come up, the therapist may suggest that it may be helpful to include the parents once or twice in the session. If the therapist is persistent and convincing enough over time, the resistance to family-of-origin sessions usually diminishes. If the therapist is convinced of the importance of this type of therapeutic empowerment for the client, the client soon becomes convinced of its importance.

The client must first have a series of preparatory sessions prior to meeting with his family. There are a number of concerns that must be explored and prepared for. First, the negative consequences of having these family-of-origin sessions are examined. Some typical negative consequences offered are the following:

1. These sessions will stir up old feelings and problems.
2. I will not be able to "protect" my parents, as I have done in the past, if I am the "accuser."
3. I may have to give up my fantasy that ours was the "perfect family," a fantasy that has served me well to protect against the reality of living in an abusing family;
4. I will have to "grow up" to meet my parents as an adult, and I'm not quite ready to grow up.
5. I might go crazy (literally) if I were to realize that my mother: was an abuser; didn't love me; loved my father more than me, etc.
6. My parents may still deny: their abuse of me, our family problems, etc.
7. My parents might reject me after this session.

After the negative consequences have been explored, the client, should he* still wish to have the family-of-origin sessions, then plans the "strategy" for the session. He plans everything he will say, everything

*or she. We do not mean to imply that it is *only* abusing fathers who are in therapy with their families of origin.

that his parents could say in response, and how he may feel after these things are said. The therapist should present extreme examples of responses from the parents (e.g., they will deny every experience he claims he has had), and ask him to role play how he will respond. This can go on for a number of weeks or even months. The goal of this continued practice of responses to his family of origin is for him to be in control of the session and for there to be as few surprises as possible.

The following illustrates a segment of a session where the abusing father is confronting both of his parents on how he wants his relationship with them, which has been one in which he was overly responsible for everyone in the family (a pattern that continues into his current family) to be different.

Mark (*the abusing father*): We have talked about how my role in the family has caused problems for me. I hope you know that I know you didn't mean to do anything that was going to cause problems. Now I want to do things differently. I really want you both to stop talking to me about the other one, putting me in the middle. I know you have no one else to talk to, but you have to find someone or don't talk at all. Maybe you could start telling each other what you don't like.

Therapist: You can only talk about yourself, Mark. Your parents have been married a long time. You are trying to be too helpful again, by telling them what they need to do differently. Tell them what you need to do to help yourself and your family.

Mark: I need to worry about you less. I need not to be involved in all of your problems or all of the problems of my brothers and sisters. I want to still see you and I love you and the whole family. I just don't want you to think that I am ignoring you or am mad but I have to set my limits. I have to worry about my own family. I have felt like I have had two families to take care of all these years. I know you take care of the kids, Mom and Dad. You have always worked hard to support so many people and I respect you for that but I felt like I had to do an awful lot and you turned to me for a lot of things. I can't do it anymore.

Mary (*his mother*): We never meant to do this. You always just seemed to fix things and call people up and keep the family together, you know. Your father doesn't want to hear about it.

Joe (*his father*): I don't see what any of this has to do with sexual abuse.

Therapist: (*to Mary*) I know this feels like a huge loss for you (*to Joe*) and it appears to be confusing for you, but maybe what is important here is that Mark understands it and that it is what he needs. As he talked to me, no matter what has happened, I have been impressed how you have always tried to be there for your son.

Mary: Oh my, yes. He is our boy and we would do anything for any of our children.

Therapist: I know, and this is what he needs from you now. You really don't have to do anything so different. But just know he will be trying to do things differently with you.

CHILDREN'S SESSIONS

The children of a family form a distinct subsystem, based on their shared generational boundary. Sessions with just the children (including the abused daughter) are quite important, although they usually need to occur less frequently than marital sessions.

There are four major purposes for the children's sessions. First, these sessions reinforce the children subsystem as distinct from the parental. This can be extremely important in incestuously abusing families, where the generational boundaries are so often blurred. Second, all of the children in the family have experienced anxiety, guilt, and shame because of the sexual abuse. The sessions with the children can lessen much of this through open discussions, accurate information, and a caring, sensitive therapist. Third, some incestuously abusing families, because of their long history of denial, have engaged in the process of *mystification* (Laing, 1965), where reality is obscured or masked in order to maintain the status quo. Children, because of the limitations in their cognitive development, are particularly vulnerable to mystification, leading to impaired reality testing. The therapist must continually present "reality" to the children and use the siblings to support one another in confirming the content of their experiences. Finally, sessions with the children can be useful in improving the overall relationship between the siblings, especially among the abused and the nonabused children, which is more often than not quite strained.

Children's Session Interventions

Siblings are a hidden resource to the family therapist, partly because they are intricately bound to one another, and partly because children are quite flexible and adaptable to change. In many incest families, the children have been kept emotionally apart from one another, mostly as a way to maintain the secret. Therefore, it is important that all interventions with the children be designed to help them bond with one another and to develop normal sibling interdependency.

Interventions should be planned that will resolve the siblings' conflict with one another. The conflict resolution and communication improvement techniques described earlier in this chapter can be adapted for use with children. It is also useful for the therapist to initiate enactments whereby the children begin to look to each other as a resource in times of stress. The therapist may also wish to encourage the children to feel a sense of the "common enemy" of their parents—not in an extreme sense, but in the way most brothers and sisters unify against the "tyranny" of parental rules.

Much in-session work with the younger children should be done with toys, creative role playing, and art. For example, we have had the children write plays, centering on family themes and sibling relationships, and then perform them. Older siblings learn to use each other as a support group and to problem solve with each other. They are encouraged to work together to resolve their anger, guilt and remorse about their family and their relationship with each other. This can be accomplished through age-appropriate communication or play.

THERAPY WITH THE FAMILY'S SOCIAL NETWORKS

There are many people from the family's social network who help to maintain the incest or the factors contributing to the family's vulnerability to incest, or who have the influence to help them change. We have found it useful to include these people in the therapy process. Many therapists find it difficult to invite nonfamily members to a therapy session, but those therapists committed to Multiple Systems therapy should not view this invitation as an intrusion but as a request for help. In our experience, the schoolteacher or scoutmaster or mailman who has had "a feeling about the family for years" probably will be more than happy to "get his two cents in." And even those who may have been unconsciously supportive of the incest may be willing to help the family "make things right."

The following example illustrates how one particular offender interpreted his peer's behaviors and attitudes as support for his own sexually abusive behavior. During several sessions he related how every man at his place of work talks about younger girls' bodies and about their own children's friends in a very sexually descriptive way. Much of this offender's treatment focused on how he dehumanized his victim in order to deny the impact of the abuse of his daughter. It became apparent that his conversations with his friends reinforced this denial. On one occasion the therapist had the client bring his closest friend with him to therapy.

Client: I always thought you fantasized the same things that I did. I even thought maybe you were having sex with teenagers. The way you talked sounded just like me, so I thought you were just like me.

Friend: I did talk with you about girls' bodies, but I never really thought that was so bad. Now I see that that gave you ideas . . . I didn't mean to do that . . . it was just talk. Bar conversations always turn into sex somehow. I never fantasized, though, about teenagers. I might comment on their bodies but never went any further than that. I wouldn't want to have sex with no kid. I still don't understand how come you could with your stepdaughters.

Therapist: What is important is that you understand how your talk about sex, women, and teenagers was a sort of encouragement to Bob.

Friend: Well, I can see that now. Boy, I sure can't believe it, and I sure don't want to be doing that to nobody else.

Therapist: Then listen to what you say before you say it. Think about what it means. And don't assume you know anyone well enough that you know they won't misunderstand you. That kind of talk is hurtful and harmful no matter which way you look at it.

It was helpful for the client to clarify the difference between himself and others and between talk and abusive action. Including his friend made the differences concrete and impossible to avoid.

13

Individual Sessions

Most family therapists appreciate the role individual therapy sessions have in systemic intervention (e.g., Nichols, 1987). Individual sessions should not be viewed as a "contamination" of family-based therapy, but instead understood to be another useful modality to effect change. Individual therapy sessions are an integral part of Multiple Systems therapy, since the individual "systems" are seen as being both affected by and contributing to the sexual abuse in the family.

There are some important benefits to including individual therapy sessions in a treatment program for incestuous abuse. First, there are many topics family members will simply not talk about in front of one another, including sexual feelings, behaviors, and fantasies. Having individual sessions allows the family members to be more open regarding difficult-to-discuss aspects of their lives.

Second, people *behave* differently in the presence of a group of people, especially their families. Most incest therapists, for example, have experienced a father who is particularly hostile and dominant during family sessions, who then becomes warm and engaging during individual sessions. It is possible to access these different "parts" of people's personalities when they are separated from a particular context.

Third, there is a safety and intimacy that emerge between a therapist and a client during individual sessions that cannot be replicated in family sessions. It is important for family members, both the abused and the abusing, to have the benefits of this safe and intimate therapeutic relationship, perhaps the first one they have had in their entire lives.

Fourth, individual therapy sessions act as a metaphor for the privacy and individuation that are being encouraged during the entire therapy program. Incestuously abusing families are often so enmeshed that to have feelings and needs separate from those of the family is considered disloyal. Having individual sessions shows the family that the therapist identifies each member as a separate person, distinct in style and needs from the family as a whole.

The purpose of the individual therapy sessions is to augment the family-based program, not replace it. Some individually oriented therapists may find working one-to-one more comfortable and thus they depend more on individual rather than family treatment. We conceptualize individual therapy as a subset of our systemically oriented program, and so even when working with an individual, we are constantly integrating this with their family work. Therefore, although sometimes it cannot be avoided, at no time do we *recommend* the entire family to be seen by one therapist and the individual family members to be seen by another.

FOCUS OF INDIVIDUAL TREATMENT

The overall goal of Stage II individual therapy sessions is to challenge each family member's dysfunctional behaviors, thoughts, and feelings that contributed to the family's vulnerability to incest. There are many topics on which to focus, depending upon the specific treatment goals and crises that emerge during the course of treatment. However, there are four major issues that must be addressed throughout individual therapy. These are: (1) feelings of victimization; (2) power and control; (3) sexual problems; and (4) improvement of self-esteem.

Feelings of Victimization

One of the most common themes during Stage II individual sessions for the fathers, mothers, daughters and nonabused siblings is that each has felt victimized at some point in their lives. For all of them, these feelings of victimization can be the result of actually being the victims of sexual, physical, or emotional abuse in their own families of origin. For the daughter and other siblings, these ongoing feelings of victimization can lead to thoughts and behaviors which both contribute to their being abused and to their being abusive.

Family members in individual therapy might be viewed by the therapist as trauma survivors. The therapist can help each family member to identify the traumatic events experienced or observed in childhood, and to examine how each may have internalized these events which resulted in feeling victimized in their adult lives. The therapist can explore with the daughter how her own sexual abuse may have led to current victim-like behavior. Also, the clients can be asked to examine how their being abusive or self-abusive paradoxically maintains their current degree of victimization.

As an example, consider the father who has sexually abused his daughter despite his own childhood sexual abuse by *his* father. He claims that he despised his father for what he did, and swore he would only be the best of fathers when he grew up. And yet now, years later, he finds himself having engaged in the sexual abuse of his own child, drinking binges, fights with superiors at work, and a host of other seemingly *self*-abusive behaviors. Through insight-oriented interventions, he comes to understand that at least part of his vulnerability to abuse resides in his own lifelong feelings of being a victim, and that these patterns at least partially reflect an attempt to control his own victimization; it is difficult to be both the aggressor and the victim at the same time.

As another example, the sexually abused daughter, now in her adolescence, has become heavily involved with cocaine. She also is precociously promiscuous, and in fact has recently become pregnant at age 14. In her individual sessions it becomes apparent that she has extended being victimized by her father to victimizing herself by engaging in this series of highly self-destructive acts.

One goal of therapy must be to encourage the clients to understand the origins of their self-victimizing behavior and to control them. Although much of this work can also be done in family sessions, during the individual sessions the family members can safely explore the often forbidden realm of their own childhood victimization in their families of origin.

Power and Control

An extremely important variable which contributes to a family's vulnerability to incest is the management of power and control. For example, sexual abuse is, at least partially, the father's attempt to gain power and control over the easily dominated child when he may lack such power in his interactions with adults. The mother's distance from her daughter, and perhaps even her refusal to adequately act when the abuse is disclosed, might reflect her sense of powerlessness in the family. And the daughter is indeed most often powerless to fend off the sexual abuser, because *he is the father*, to be respected and obeyed.

An important discussion during individual sessions focuses on how each of these three family members feels powerless and/or uses power inappropriately. The therapist asks them where their values about power and control originated, and to identify how society may reinforce the *im*balance of power in a family. For example, one traditional cultural rule is: "Do what your father tells you" (a.k.a. "Honor thy father"); to *not* do so is a violation of a societal norm. It is understandable how a family already vulnerable to incestuous abuse will tolerate this misuse of power by the father simply because he *is* the father; incest is the exaggeration of the culturally accepted canon that ultimate power lies with the father.

In this regard, an important goal of individual sessions is to bring a balance of power and control among the family members. Although the parents should exercise a greater deal of control in the family, lest there be chaos, no member of the family should ever feel powerless; nor should this power ever be "abused," as it is when incest occurs. In the example given above, where the abusive father had been abused as a child the abusing father's feelings of powerlessness in his life are tied to his abusive behavior. In individual sessions, these feelings are directly confronted by the therapist, who also provides alternative ways to increase appropriate feelings of control without resorting to abuse. Also as an example, after the mother can hypothesize about the origin of her feelings of powerlessness, she is encouraged to be more confrontive and assertive with others; this is first tried in the individual sessions, using role-playing techniques, and then extended into family sessions.

Sexual Problems

During Stage II individual therapy sessions, the father, mother, and daughter are each asked to confront their sexuality and sexual problems quite directly. A myriad of sexual issues are common among the members of incestuously abusing families; from the possibility of long-standing pedophile fantasies and behaviors of the father, which were the foundation of the sexual abuse of his daughter, to the daughter's sexual acting out as a reaction to her own abuse. Individual sessions are the most appropriate place to identify and challenge any sexual problems that may be present, since this environment is less threatening than family or group sessions, and there is a better chance for a more honest response from the clients.

Sexual problems of the father. The most important issue is the father's sexual response to his daughter. There are many other contributing factors to the family's vulnerability to incest, and the majority of the incestuously abusing fathers we treat are not "true" pedophiles (those who can only become sexually aroused by children) who have generalized their fantasies to their own daughters. However, the fact remains that the father had desire for, was aroused by, and engaged in some form of sexual behavior with his child. Therefore, the *sexual* component of sexual abuse can not be ignored (Frude, 1982). Other sexual issues that must be addressed with the father in individual sessions are his cognitive distortions regarding the sexual abuse, sexual dysfunctions that might be present, and his own lack of general sexual information.

The sex-related therapeutic goals for the father in individual therapy sessions include reducing his sexual attraction to his child, controlling the urge to act on a sexual fantasy that he may have at some time for his daughter, and, if necessary, increasing his attraction to age-appropriate partners. If a specific sexual dysfunction is present, another goal is to identify the problem and begin work to ameliorate it (although most sex therapy occurs during marital sessions). A final sex-related goal for the father is to increase his general knowledge about sexuality.

Sexual problems of the mother. Although the nonabusing mother does not always have a sex-related problem, it is important during the individual sessions to review her sexual knowledge and attitudes, along with any sexual problems that she may be experiencing. The nonoffending mother often feels that if she had somehow been a better sexual partner, the abuse would not have occurred; this myth is particularly difficult to dispel if the couple had indeed experienced a sexual dysfunction prior to or during the time of the abuse. The mother needs to be reassured that this is rarely the case. At the same time, she should be encouraged to work to improve her sexual relationship with her husband for her own sake, because of the enjoyment and fulfillment that could bring for her. Of course, if she continues to maintain intense anger at her husband for the sexual abuse, sex therapy would not be appropriate.

Sexual problems of the daughter. The abused daughter often is confused about her own sexuality. Three very important issues must be explored openly during her individual therapy sessions. The first is the effect that the sexual abuse has had on her sexuality in general. Is she afraid of men and boys? Also, does she have guilt associated with her genitals? If she is older, is she afraid of dating because it might lead to sex? Does she find the thought of sexuality abhorrent, or does it lead to a phobic reaction?

The second issue is the effect the abuse has had on her own sexual behavior. Especially with the other daughters, many act promiscuously with their peers, inappropriately sexualizing many of their social relationships. This behavior needs to be confronted by the therapist, sensitively but firmly, and can be tied in to similar concerns the therapist raised when discussing how the daughter may continue to victimize herself.

The third issue is that the daughter may have responded sexually during abusive episodes with her father. It is common for girls to become aroused, and even orgasmic during these encounters, but then to feel tremendous guilt and shame later. The therapist will need to teach the daughter about the sexual arousal cycle and that it is normal to respond sexually to situations that are not necessarily of one's choosing. The therapist may also have to reassure the daughter that if she indeed enjoyed the sexual episodes with her father, this does not make her responsible for them, and that hers was a common feeling.

The goal of the daughter's individual therapy sessions with regard to sexuality is to help her return to an appropriate sexual-developmental period. The therapist works with her to reduce her guilt about sex, but at the same time discourages her from behaving promiscuously.

Improvement of Self-Esteem

Even after the interventions made during Stage I, which were designed to make the family feel better about itself, the self-esteem of the father, mother, and daughter are usually still impaired during Stage II. It is not uncommon for all three to state that they do not like themselves, or that they cannot look in a mirror without feeling revulsion. As Stage II progresses, happily their self-esteem usually improves. The cessation of the abuse, their understanding of the origins of the incestuous behavior, the Apology Session, the improved family communication, the lessening of family rigidity and increasing of personal autonomy—these all eventually contribute to improved self-esteem of everyone in the family. However, individual therapy sessions should also be used to reinforce these improvements via the relationship with the therapist.

INDIVIDUAL THERAPY INTERVENTIONS

All therapists have their own clinical orientation and corresponding interventions. We encourage therapists in our program to use their own style when working to meet the goals of the individual therapy sessions.

TABLE 13.1
Individual Therapy Interventions

I. Identification of Transgenerational Patterns
   A. Genograms
   B. Structural Session
   C. Improve relationships with family of origin

II. "Parts" Intervention

III. Interventions to Reduce Sexual Attraction to Daughter
   A. Stimulus satiation
   B. Covert desensitization
   C. Cognitive distortion elimination
   D. Sex education

There are some common interventions, however, that have been developed over the years which have proven quite effective when working with the fathers, mothers, and daughters in incestuously abusing families. A list of standard individually oriented interventions appears in Table 13.1.

Identification of Transgenerational Patterns

The purpose of these fairly straightforward interventions is to help the father and mother understand the relationship between their own childhood abuse or neglect and either their current abusive behavior or their *reaction* to their spouse's abusive behavior. These also help the offender and mother to develop and communicate empathy for the victim's experience.

Genograms. The client might spend a few sessions constructing a genogram (cf. McGoldrick & Gerson, 1985) of his or her family of origin. The therapist asks the client to outline abuse or neglect that occurred throughout the family's history and feelings associated with it. These are then graphically associated with his or her current family situation, and the developmental nature of abuse becomes more apparent.

Structural Session. Another useful intervention is to have a modified Structural Session with the father or mother as part of an individual session. The same format that was described before (see Chapter 8) can be used, but this time the family whose structure is analyzed is the client's family of origin. Briefly, the five structures common in incestuously abusing families is drawn on the blackboard. The client is then asked to identify the one who was present when he or she was growing up, and what feelings accompanied being in that particular structure. The client is then asked to make a connection between the family-of-origin's structure and the current family's structure. The client eventually comes to appreciate that transgenerational patterns do exist in families, and these patterns do contribute to a family's vulnerability to incest.

Relationship with Family of Origin. The client's current relationship with his or her family of origin should also be explored. It is quite common for patterns that occurred in childhood to continue through the years, and for the individual family member to maintain the sense of victimization, or neglect, or the need for affection that is still present. Individual session interventions can be used to help the client break from those feelings. Gestalt-style techniques, where the client talks to his or her parent in an "empty chair," or writes an unmailed letter expressing what it was like to be an abused child, can have a powerful and important effect on the client.

The therapist should be cautioned that many offending fathers deny that their families of origin had anything to do with their own abusing behavior. In fact, it is quite common for a father to insist that his was the ideal family, in spite of clear evidence to the contrary. The therapist will have to insist that to never be allowed to go outside and play, or to have an inordinate amount of work to do in the family, or to have to sleep with Aunt Mary because she was afraid to be alone—any or all of these kinds of experiences can be seen as abusive.

Case example of a transgenerational intervention. This example is taken from a mother's individual treatment. In this part of Stage II she is recognizing the transgenerational patterns of her family that have contributed to her marrying an abusive man and then not consequently protecting her children.

Through a genogram and extensive questioning and discussion, the mother recognizes three generations of neglect and messages that produced a woman who is not aware of her competent, nurturing, assertive, and intelligent parts.

Therapist: What do you know about your grandparents on your mother's side? Would your mother have said they were positive people?

Mother: My grandmother was wonderful to me. She was everything you would want in a grandmother. And now that you ask, I think my mother was always jealous of that. It almost seemed that my grandmother loved me more than she loved her own daughter. She never criticized me, and yet I never remember a loving word pass between her and my mother. I guess my mother could not have felt very good about herself either. But my mom was positive with me. She always said that she did not want to be as negative with me as her mother was with her.

Therapist: So she was positive with you, made you feel like you could do a lot of things right?

Mother: Don't get carried away. I didn't say that. She made me feel like I couldn't do anything right unless she was with me or gave me her opinion. She was not negative, but it was like she could not survive without us being together and me needing her help and opinion on everything.

Therapist: So your way of being a good daughter and loyal—we all try to be loyal to our parents—was to need her and be very dependent on her?

Mother: Yeah, I think so? Why would she be like that after having a mother who was always on her case and so negative.

Therapist: Certainly I don't know for sure. Maybe we can figure out a way for you to talk with her about that sometime. But a guess might be that her mother never helped her create a positive sense of "self," so she turned to you to help her establish it. She could have a sense of self as she formed you and stayed involved in every aspect of your life. It is like your sense of "self" would become her sense of "self," unfortunately that left you with none, and certainly none to pass on to your children.

Mother: That sure makes sense. I never think I can do anything without input from someone else. It is like I have no ideas or opinions of my own. Now I am beginning to understand where that came from.

Therapist: And does it make some sense why you pick someone like Steve for a husband?

Mother: Absolutely. He wants to give me all his ideas and opinions and run my life, too, just like my parents did. I married my parents.

Therapist: A lot of us do.

Mother: But then he also gets angry at me for not having any backbone or making any decisions. It gets confusing. How can I win?

Therapist: I know. He has different parts that want different things at different times, just like you. He is working at that, too, so you both will be able to be less confused. Your mom had different things she wanted, too. She did not intentionally hurt you, do you think?

Mother: No. Neither did my dad. He was just not very interested in kids, period. He worked so hard, and I am not sure he had much use for girl-children.

Therapist: So what kind of message do you think you internalized from him?

Mother: I love you, but I don't know what to do with you, so I'll ignore you and let your mother worry about it. I'll be a good provider and the rest is none of your affair.

Therapist: Again, sort of like how you interact with your husband.

Mother: I guess you're right. It sure seems that way.

The following is a segment of one her husband Steve's sessions regarding his overresponsible, intrusive, and controlling behavior and how this behavior was conceived.

Therapist: You were telling me about being the little man in your family.

Father: My father was always gone—either working or out with the guys. So my mother had to count on me alot. She had no choice. She did a fantastic job of raising all of us kids, basically alone. I can't blame her for a thing.

Therapist: Steve, talking about your family and trying to discover patterns that are being repeated in your family now is not blaming anyone. It is helping you and your kids. We need to know you better. One of the ways to know you better is to try to understand how you are replicating your role in your family. So what did it mean that you were the responsible son, like in our drawings you were above the line most of the time. When were you a kid?

Father: I never was a kid. I had to help my mom, raise my brothers and sisters, and make the decisions around the house for as long as I remember.

Therapist: From some of the things you have told me, it sounds like even now.

Father: They really have no one else sometimes.

Therapist: You had alot of control for such a small kid. Did you have any fun?

Father: You are right. I had a lot of power and no fun. Being a kid was not fun. It was a drag. But there were no other choices.

Therapist: You are right. As a kid you did not have any choices. Kids do what they are told. You know that from this sexual abuse experience with Tina. So you could not really tell your mom and dad that it wasn't fair and you wanted to be a kid. (*Father starts to get a little teary)* It wasn't fair and you couldn't fight back. It was a little like being a victim yourself.

Father: Tina couldn't fight back either.

Therapist: Right.

Father: But how could all that back then make me sexually abuse her now?

Therapist: It did not make you abuse her. It just contributed to it, remember?

Father: Yeah, but how?

Therapist: Well, it made you form some opinions about how you should act in a family and how a family should act around you.

Father: Like I should always be in control. Everyone should always listen to me and respect me. Nobody's opinion matters but mine. I can do whatever I want.

Therapist: Yes, keep going and any other messages? Anything about women and wives.

Father: They need my opinion and they cannot do things by themselves. They need me for everything. That sometimes is a pain in the rearend.

Therapist: You can't always be perfect, can you?

Father: No I really can't.

Therapist: But your family wanted you to be, and you think your wife wants you to be, and then when you aren't, you get really critical of yourself and start to feel bad. It becomes a pretty vicious cycle. And it isn't your parents' fault Steve, but a hell of a lot of it started back then.

The Internalized Parts Model of Intervention

It is not helpful to view a person in terms of a monolithic model of personality. In other words, it is a revictimization of the person to see him or her as having only one type of personality and having to change the entire self to be asymptomatic. It is more productive to help people understand themselves in terms of multiple characteristics or "parts" (Schwartz, 1987). Many therapeutic models use a parts conceptualization when viewing human behaviors, for example, Transactional Analysis, Gestalt, or Rational-Emotive Therapy.

We have found the model developed by Richard Schwartz to be extremely helpful when working with sexually abusive families because it is based on an internalized family therapy construct: we have parts of our personalities that get expressed through our feelings and behaviors.

In this way a family therapist can take what he or she knows about interactions, transgenerational patterns, communication, family structure, resistance, and other interactional sequences and apply it to the internalized "parts" of ourselves. The purpose of the "parts" treatment model is to: (1) allow the individual to understand how a "good" person/self can do "bad" things, such as sexual abuse, or ignore the requests for help from a daughter; (2) give the client a powerful metaphor and skills upon which change can occur; and (3) increase the client's ability to improve their self-esteem.

The client is told that people have many parts to their personalities and that each individual also has a core "self" that is highly functional, wise, and centered. All of these parts and self do not express themselves at any given time, and often when they do express themselves, it is in an extreme fashion that can appear to be quite negative. For example, the father who has a "part" that is scared of many things in his life may drink too much, but he also has a "part" that needs to be in control, so he will join these parts together and then abuse a child. This same father can also love his family and want to be intimate (an intimate part), can work hard and be responsible, and can feel guilt for what he has done and want to change. Or the mother who has an extreme "denial part" that denies her daughter's cries for help, because of her own powerlessness or even selfishness, also has "parts" that are loving, nurturing, and caring.

Again, like Family Therapy, this model is based on strengths, not deficits. Every "part" contains positive intent to either help us get out of pain or protect us in some way. But just like well-intentioned family members, many of the methods we internally choose to solve our problems become extremely dysfunctional, symptomatic, and even harmful. "I want to gain control over what seems to be out of control in my life; I will control my daughter and family through abusive behavior." This is an extreme, out of control part talking.

The clients appreciate this seemingly simple metaphor because it taps into a reality about themselves that they honestly experience. It also provides them with a positive remedy: Make the "out of control/extreme parts" less extreme and have the "centered self" more available to lead the feelings and behaviors; the abusive and symptomatic feelings and behaviors become manageable within the client's realm of experience.

This intervention provides the therapist with an array of possible exercises during individual, marital, and family sessions. The family members can view not only themselves but each other in a way that is neither all good nor all bad. For example, the victim might be asked, through imagery or an empty chair technique, to have her "self" ask the "sad child" what it needs in order to feel nurtured and cared for without getting revictimized. Or the father's "self" might tell the "part" that controls others through violence or sexual actions that this type of behavior will no longer be tolerated, and together they ("self" and "part") must find a more acceptable way to have control and also learn to allow others in the family and the world to have control. Just like in family therapy, the "self" might ask the "controlling part," "What are the negative consequences if you no longer abuse others in an attempt to gain control?"

Case example using the internalized parts model. Dale is the father of two natural children and two stepchildren by his second marriage. He sexually abused one of his natural children and both stepchildren. In his individual work he has identified several parts that have extreme behaviors and have become dysfunctional. In this segment of a session he is discussing the sequence that has become problematic and some alternatives that are perhaps more functional.

Therapist: You were talking about how your "critic" part eggs on your "power-house" part by saying what kind of things?

Father: The critic says, "What kind of man are you? You let all those people walk all over you at work and then you come home to a household of women who, if you let them, would spend all your money and run the house. Where in your life do you have control?"

Therapist: Do you want to change chairs and pretend to be the powerhouse responding?

Father: Sure. (*He changes chairs and as the powerhouse responds*) I can control the house or work, for that matter, whenever I want. I can always quit, then I'll be in control. The family knows I am boss, both families.

Therapist: You know what, Dale, usually whenever two or more parts of anyone talk to each other, they escalate, just like in a family. It is better that the parts either talk to me or to your "self" and someone mediates to help them maintain a middle ground.

Father: (*speaking from a "self" position*) The problem is whenever you try to control, you usually bring in the angry/aggressive/abusive part of our being. Then when anger, control, and critic are there, we sort of merge and become victim. Something always happens extreme, like quit a job, hit a wife, abuse a kid . . . we get power for a moment, but then we are victims again. It hasn't worked.

Therapist: Dale, with whomever has the loudest voice that influences you to be abusive to others and yourself, maybe you could negotiate another way to express itself and get its needs met.

At this point, because he is familiar with the techniques utilized by the therapist, Dale closes his eyes and images a negotiation between the "self" and the three parts. In his mind it resembles group therapy.

Father: Well, the control part does not want me to feel pushed around. The angry/aggressive part does not want me to be helpless. The critical part says that he can always find something to criticize me about. The negotiation is to figure out how I can not be pushed around, not be helpless, and not hurt me or anyone else.
Therapist: Maybe the critical part can help decide what is hurtful to others and to yourself. Is he very abusive to others if no other parts are influencing him?
Father: No, that is probably a good idea. Maybe he can be helpful in that way and not feel left out.
Therapist: Has the self learned enough, like from group maybe, to work with the parts around assertiveness?
Father: Yeah, when I imagine them in the room I sort of make them sitting in a group.
Therapist: Why don't you image a group and have the self teach them about assertiveness, like in the offender's group, and help them see how that can meet their goals, as well as the goal of no longer victimizing anyone—including Dale.

In another example of a parts session, an adolescent victim of incest helps her very sad child part let go of her fantasies regarding her mother.

Therapist: Liz, what does the "sad child" want? Why does she keep hounding you, making you feel like you will always be sad?
Liz: She just keeps hoping that my mom will really love me and stop being so angry about everything that has happened. She gets so sad because she wants to be close with my mom.
Therapist: (*implying a centered self*) Is there anything that you can do or say to her that might help her sadness?
Liz: Like what?
Therapist: Almost all the clients I know, victim or not, have a very sad child inside of them. No one ever gets from their parents everything they would like. We are all sad about something that is miss-

ing. It seems to help my sad child when I try to take care of her in different ways and also help her understand my own mother's limitations and what she is capable of giving me, rather than focusing on what she is not capable of giving me. Does that make any sense? (*Liz nods yes*) You have an image of what this sad child looks like and feels like, right? Let me talk with her now, you be her for a moment.

Liz concentrates with her eyes closed for a moment and then opens them, looking a little teary.

Therapist: I know it is sad to feel like your mother will never love you in the way you want her to. What do you know that you can have with your mother that is positive? Are there any times you feel close and loved by her?

Liz: When my overresponsible part is taking care of her, then she loves me.

Therapist: But that makes you sad, too, doesn't it?

Liz: Yes.

Therapist: Is there any time you can be a child and feel loved by her?

Liz: When I am sick and when she sits with me before I go to bed. But I am getting too old for that.

Therapist: You aren't—other parts are. But we all always have a part that wants to be taken care of when we are sick or even at bedtime. Unfortunately, those moments are not as frequent as would feel good. Your mom is limited because of her own life and her own parts. She will probably never be able to give you everything you want or deserve. (*Liz is crying.*) But you can get some of that caretaking from yourself and some things from your mom, and we will figure out what.

The therapist asks Liz to change chairs, close her eyes, and bring her "self" to the room.

Therapist: Liz, how can your mother take care of that sad little girl without her getting sick all of the time? What can you do to help? She already warned us that bringing in the overresponsible part, or any others for that matter, isn't fair. I'll let you know if I think some other part of you is sneaking in here in response to me.

Liz: Maybe I can let the little girl have my mother read to her at night or at least sit on her bed and talk with her. It will feel real immature, but it sounds like you are saying it is OK. I guess my friends never have to know. It sure would be better to have my mom there instead of Marty (the offender).

Therapist: Do you think your mom would think it was strange?

Liz: Yeah.

Therapist: Maybe that is why you get sick alot. Sick isn't as strange as just wanting your mother.

Liz: It feels real.

Therapist: I am sure it is real. You really want her to be with you. How can I help?

Liz: Maybe you can help me talk with her?

During a mother-daughter session, the therapist, using this model, will help the sad child talk with the nurturing mother. She will also try to have both the daughter's "self" and the mother's "self" metacommunicate about their parts—which parts activate each other and end up not being helpful and which parts can work together.

Interventions to Reduce Sexual Attraction to Daughter

There are a number of interventions that should be used to reduce the sexual attraction an incestuously abusing father might have for his daughter. However, before these are illustrated, a few words of caution are in order. First, even if an incestuously abusing father has pervasive pedophile fantasies and behaviors, it is unlikely that he will admit to them, even in Stage II of therapy. Short of administering an extended psychophysiological assessment, which also has significant limitations (Langevin & Lang, 1985), the best approach is to assume at least that he can be aroused by *his* daughter sexually and that this must be reduced. If there is evidence that he has molested other children, and the current facility is not equipped to conduct treatment of this type of disorder, the offender's individual therapy may have to be augmented at a treatment facility that specializes in treating pedophilia.

The use of behavioral treatment approaches to reduce the sexual arousal to his daughter is an important component of the father's individual therapy program. Joseph LoPiccolo has developed an effective program for the treatment of sexual deviants in general (LoPiccolo, 1985). We have adopted interventions of his program in our individual treatment of incestuously abusing fathers: *stimulus satiation, covert desensitization,* and *cognitive distortion elimination.*

Stimulus satiation. First described by Marshall and Barbaree (1978), stimulus satiation is a behavioral procedure where the father's arousal for his daughter is reduced through continued exposure to the fantasy of having sex with her *after* he has become sexually satiated. For example, he might be first assigned to masturbate at home, using an age-appropriate, nonfamily member as a sexual fantasy. An erotic magazine such as *Playboy* or *Penthouse* might be used to facilitate arousal. After he has ejaculated, he then switches to his deviant sexual fantasy, in this case having sex with his own daughter, and continues to masturbate vigorously for the next hour. Although some men can continue to maintain their arousal and erection for a while after the "switch," almost all remain flaccid and unaroused. It is useful to have the father verbalize his fantasies into a tape recorder during his daily sessions, to ensure that he is doing the assignment properly (LoPiccolo, 1985).

Stimulus satiation appears to work by making the fantasy, which previously was exciting and sexually arousing, boring and even painful. Not only does the fantasy appear to extinguish, but itself becomes an aversive stimulus. Many incest fathers, however, are quite resistant to this intervention, claiming that to "bring back that old fantasy" is painful, and they would just as soon forget it. With fathers for whom incestuous or pedophile fantasies were quite powerful, such as those who abused more than one child or appeared to have this as their primary sexual fantasy, this technique can effect meaningful, first-order change. In these cases the therapist should prepare the father for this intervention during Stage I of therapy, work with him to see the ultimate benefit of its use, and finally ensure that the intervention is made.

Covert desensitization. Another useful behavioral technique to reduce the father's sexual arousal to his daughter is covert desensitization (LoPiccolo, 1985; Marshall et al., 1983). Covert desensitization is a classical conditioning technique in which the previously arousing stimulus (i.e., having sex with his daughter) is continuously paired with an aversive stimulus. For example, the father is asked during the session to relax, close his eyes, and imagine the beginning of a typical incestuous episode. When it appears that slight arousal may be occurring, the therapist instructs him to switch to visualizing and verbalizing an extremely negative consequence, such as his wife walking in, screaming, calling the police, the police coming and arresting him, his being taken off to jail where he is raped by other prisoners, and so forth.

A variation of this technique can be used by therapists trained in hypnosis. In this case, the client is inducted into a light-to-medium hypnotic trance. After that the therapist describes the beginning of a typical incestuous episode, and then changes to *extremely* negative consequences with very powerful negative imagery. We have included scenes designed to sicken the father, such as having to scoop up his daughter's bile that she vomited in reaction to being forced to having sex with him. The therapist can also project images of his daughter in the future, where she has severe psychological problems, perhaps being involuntarily committed to a mental hospital for the rest of her life. These negative images can be made quite compelling through hypnosis and can prove effective.

Cognitive distortion elimination. Another important intervention for the father in his individual therapy sessions is for the therapist to confront commonly held cognitive distortions about having sex with his children. Abel and his associates have listed a number of commonly held beliefs held by pedophiles (cited in LoPiccolo, 1985), which we have adapted to incestuously abusing fathers. These include:

1. My daughter can make up her own mind as to whether she will have sex with me.
2. If my daughter doesn't physically resist me, it means she wants to have sex with me.
3. If my child is flirtatious with me, it means she wants to have sex with me.
4. Sex with my daughter did no emotional harm; in fact it was good for her.
5. If my daughter allows me to see her undressed or looks at me while I'm undressed, it means she wants to have sex with me.
6. If my wife doesn't have sex with me, it's justifiable to have sex with my daughter.
7. It's better to have sex with my daughter than to have an extramarital affair.
8. I had sex with my daughter to teach her about sex in a positive, caring, emotional context, and to prevent her from having sexual problems as an adult.
9. I wasn't really sexually involved with my daughter; I just love her and was physically affectionate with her.
10. If I tell my daughter to do something sexual and she does it, it means that she wanted to do it with me and that she enjoyed it.
11. I am not a child molester because I only had sex with my own daughter.

Many of these will be recognized as types of denial that are the focus of much of Stage I therapy. During Stage II, the therapist confronts each of these aggressively and continuously (as will be shown in the next chapter, these beliefs are also confronted during the father's group therapy). It is useful for the therapist to explore what might underlie the need to hold these cognitive distortions; for example, they might provide a rationalization to allow him to continue the abuse; an expression of fear or anger at women; or perhaps even an indication of a more serious thought disorder or psychopathology (LoPiccolo, 1985).

Sex education. It is not surprising that a majority of incestuously abusing families lack a basic knowledge of human sexuality. This is as true for the parents as it is for the daughters. Individual therapy sessions can be used to assess their general knowledge about sex and to provide basic sex education. There are many excellent texts available, both at the college reading level and a more elementary level (e.g., Denney & Quadagno, 1988), which can be loaned to clients so that they can read assigned chapters. The therapist can then discuss each chapter in a tutorial fashion. A broader understanding of all aspects of human sexuality will help family members to place their own sexual problems in perspective, and provide them with a wider range of sexual choices in the future.

Other Interventions

Because the Multiple Systems treatment model is action oriented, much of the time spent in individual sessions focuses on practicing new interactions and behaviors. We believe that self-esteem improves the more positive experiences one has in his or her world. Many of the interventions and tasks are then centered around having the client (1) identify a problematic interaction or relationship; (2) identify the problematic components; (3) design improved behaviors; (4) practice those behaviors; (5) implement the new behaviors in the real relationship or context; and (6) process outcome in therapy.

This sounds simple but it is not, and we are constantly aware of the client's natural resistance and ambivalence to change. Because of this, we are continually helping the client recognize the risks and negative consequences of change involved in their new behaviors, thus helping them find a comfortable pace for implementing change.

THE THERAPEUTIC RELATIONSHIP

All experienced therapists understand the importance of the therapeutic relationship itself for invoking change. We believe that the relationship that develops with the therapist is particularly important for members of incest families. We have found that much of what occurs during this relationship involves the "parenting" of these individuals by the therapist. In fact, they often describe the relationship with the therapist as the type they wished they could have had with their own parent.

Therapeutic "parenting" of the clients during their individual sessions is analogous to the parenting that occurs in functional or "healthy" families. First, the therapist provides the "unconditional positive regard" that parents usually provide in functional families. For example, the message, "I love you, but not necessarily what you did," is typically given by the therapist. Second, the therapist offers structure for the client within which he or she may try new behaviors in relative safety. Most functional families allow their children the freedom to explore new options within certain parameters. Third, the therapist eventually encourages the clients to achieve independence from their relationship with the therapist. Again, healthy families also encourage autonomy and self-growth as their children mature.

14

Groups

Group therapy is an integral part of our treatment program for incestuous abuse. While other excellent programs exist which use group treatment as the primary modality (e.g., Giaretto, 1982), we integrate therapy groups within the context of the Multiple Systems model. As such, we view the use of groups as important an element of the program as the family or individual sessions. This is because many specific vulnerability factors, especially those under the socioenvironmental rubric, can be best reduced through the nonfamily social interactions a group can provide.

PURPOSE OF GROUPS

Group therapy is often the most appropriate modality to address certain social, psychological, and sexual aspects of incestuous abuse and/or victimization. Socially, clients learn to interact with one another, which models more effective family interactions for them all. Also, the clients begin to identify how they act within the group, which will then be generalized to how they act within their families and society. Psychologically, the clients confront their own levels of denial through the denial of the other group members. They also learn eventually to better understand the universality of their feelings, motivations, and fears surrounding family relations and abuse. Sexually, they discuss openly previously unspeakable issues such as sexual attractions, preferences, practices, and fantasies. These are usually far more easy to talk about with other group members than with family members.

Group therapy can provide new information for the members of the group, can repeat and reinforce information gleaned during family and individual sessions, and can provide another context in which to practice new patterns of behavior learned during other Stage II therapy sessions. Group therapy provides this learning in a relatively "safe" environment; that is, one where the client may be challenged but not threatened, motivated but not cajoled, dealt with bluntly and honestly but not meanheartedly.

Many therapists working alone, or some smaller programs, may not have the luxury of being able to provide group therapy. In this case, the therapist may wish to contact other local therapists in a similar situation and "pool" clients to form the appropriate groups. Also, many community mental health centers are willing to start groups based on the recommendations of outside therapists.

In our opinion, if a program has only the resources to do one group, it should be an offending fathers' group, since they typically benefit most from the intensity of this modality. Next in order would be a victims' group, and then a mothers' group. Obviously, if possible, couple groups and sibling groups would enhance a program greatly. With limited resources another possibility would be to stagger the groups; for example, running an offending fathers' group for a 12-week period, then a victims' group for the next 12 weeks, then returning to an offending fathers' group.

GROUP SESSIONS

Group therapy occurs in Stage II of the program. The only exception is an Orientation Group, which occurs during Stage I and is designed to "Create the Context for Change" within a group later in therapy (see below). Being a Stage II intervention, group therapy is seen as directly altering the behavior and expanding the alternatives for the clients. As such, group therapy is directive, confrontational, educational, and change-oriented.

Individuals are usually placed in groups at the beginning of Stage II, right after the Apology Session. The client is assessed for appropriateness by his or her therapist and the group therapist. If a therapist finds that a person who is in Stage I of treatment is denying the facts of the abuse, and that he or she might benefit from the confrontational style of a group, then the therapist may elect to place this individual in a Stage II group. If there are individuals in the group who are still denying the abuse, the group must consist of a few individuals who once denied and now admit to the facts of the sexual abuse. This is because the "admitters" tend to be articulate and persuasive, and are usually very effective in helping the "deniers" confront the facts.

Orientation Group

We have found it useful to place individual offending and nonoffending parents (although not necessarily from the same family) in an Orientation Group (Giarretto, 1982) during Stage I of therapy. This group meets for between four and six sessions, and its purpose is to: introduce the social process of groups; evaluate the clients' ability to use groups effectively; provide a common language about abuse which will transfer to the family therapy; establish the universality of experiences surrounding sexual abuse; and begin to reduce denial.

There are a number of standard interventions used in the Orientation Group. At the beginning each member gives the group a brief summary of his or her case, including the status of living arrangements and legal system involvement. This is similar to the "coming public" which occurs at Alcoholics Anonymous meetings. Next the therapist gives an overview of the purpose of groups and asks the members to list those things they would like to get out of a group. The therapist then makes some predictions regarding the group's process—for example, that most do not wish to be there, that some members will lie, and that some may fight the process the entire way. Each member is asked to identify some of the possible negative consequences of his or her being in the group. Finally, dialogues are encouraged between the offending and nonoffending parents. The Orientation Group tends to be less structured than the regular groups, which allows for more social interaction and increases the comfort level to the group process in general.

Structure of Groups

There are three elements that differentiate these types of groups from more traditional psychotherapy groups. First, these are closed-membership groups, meaning that once the group has begun no new clients will be added. They also are time-limited groups, continuing no more than 12 sessions. Finally, the groups are highly structured, with the sessions organized around 10 major themes. We have found it important to operate the groups in this manner to prevent the reification of the clients' abusing role; for example, we would not want to encourage the adolescents to identify themselves as "victims" forever (an unfortunate outcome of some long-term group programs), but instead to see themselves as "victims who are becoming nonvictims."

Clients are not allowed to miss more than three sessions under any circumstances. Also, socializing outside of the group is not encouraged. The groups often include a "lay leader" who is a client who recently "graduated" from a previous and similar group. The lay leader acts as a co-therapist with the clinician and can usually be more direct and persuasive than the therapist him- or herself.

Organizing Themes

Group sessions are centered around organizing themes which provide a conceptual guideline for the therapist upon which to develop structured exercises. Therapists have great latitude when planning group activities, as long as these particular organizing themes are adequately addressed. The themes have evolved over the years and focus on what we consider essential issues for incestuously abusing families.

The 10 themes set out in Table 14.1 are used for fathers', victims', and mothers' groups. The most commonly used order is presented, but the therapist may wish to deviate if a particular theme emerges conveniently from another. Usually one theme is covered during one session, but quite often another session is required to complete the topic. Also, previous themes are incorporated when new ones are presented, so that previously learned material can be assimilated into the next topic. For example, the issue of "fear" which is explored as the first theme will

TABLE 14.1
Organizing Themes for Group Therapy

1. Fear and Secrecy
2. Denial
3. Victimization
4. Family of Origin
5. Family Structure
6. Sex Roles
7. Communication
8. Assertiveness
9. Sexual Problems
10. Cognitive Distortions

again be encountered when the family is discussed (Themes 4 and 5), such as, "What might you be afraid of in your family? What do you think others are afraid of?"

Theme 1: Fear and secrecy. The members are first asked to discuss their fears about the group itself. They are encouraged to share their fears of what would happen if they were honest and to disclose things about themselves. The therapist positively connotes the intention behind secrecy, and then asks each to discuss the negative consequences of being truthful and honest in the group. A common negative consequence is that each time an individual has been truthful something "bad" has resulted; in fact, at least one group member will usually state that openness and honesty led to their family being broken up, trouble with the law, and so on. This should be noted and explored later during discussions about denial, since this perceived negative consequence is clearly a denial of responsibility. Denial might be reframed as a response to fear.

Group members should discuss the status of any legal involvement and potential incarceration, and share their fears about its outcome. Other common fears that may emerge relate to the permanent separation of their family, of the loss of jobs and community status because their families were involved with incest, and, particularly for the victims' and mothers' groups, the fear that the sexual abuse will continue in spite of therapy.

A rule is established that members will confront each other when they see secrecy emerging in the group. They are also instructed that when a member takes a risk in the group and discusses something that he or she is afraid of, that person will discuss it immediately with the group or the therapist. This prevents that individual from harboring fears or anger that may reinforce the negative consequences of being truthful.

In this offender's group, the therapist is helping the members understand and discuss the difference between secrecy and privacy. A similar discussion might be found in a mothers' or victims' group.

Therapist: One of the things that gets real confusing within ourselves, in our families, and even in group is the difference between *secrecy* and *privacy*. Do you have any ideas of how to tell the difference between the two?

Client: Sometimes the only way to have any privacy is to keep a secret.

Therapist: I can see how you can feel that way. Probably for a lot of you that's true. We have already talked about how your secrecy has protected you in the past. But can you have privacy without secrecy? Maybe the problem falls in the area of motivation or the purpose of the privacy. If you're being secretive or asking someone else to be secretive as a way to protect yourself from trouble, then that's inappropriate. So, for example, you sexually abused someone and then threatened them if they told, or somehow forced them not to tell anyone about what you did. That isn't *privacy.* However, if you thought something or wrote something in a journal, that would be privacy. Does that make any sense?

Client: So if it doesn't hurt anyone, then it can be kept a secret?

Therapist: Well, generally yes. But many of you didn't think it was hurting anyone when you sexually abused them. That might be another problem, if you can't adequately tell what "hurt" is.

Client: We can always ask the person if it's bad.

Another Client: Or ask the therapist.

Therapist: I'm not sure anyone can always answer what is hurtful for another person. And a lot of times if you ask a person if this is going to be bad for them, they don't even know or are afraid to be honest. Just like we said, kids are often afraid to say no to adults. Maybe all of your therapy is a way to help you decide what are hurtful behaviors. But somehow you can't have a secret if it is going to be hurtful, and somehow you will have to eventually figure out honestly what is hurtful and what is not.

Theme 2: Denial. The topic of denial is didactically presented by the therapist. First, the therapist positively connotes the intent behind denial, normalizes it, and even suggests it to be a positive, healthy response to an acute crisis. The therapist makes it clear, however, that a "natural" defense can become lethal, then gives examples of how the denial surrounding sexual abuse can be detrimental to the family. The four types of denial are then submitted to the group for their consideration, along with examples of each (see Chapter 7). Finally, the group members are asked to give personal examples of each of the four types of denial. The therapist obtains permission from the group members to confront each other when they see other members engaging in denial. For example:

Client: What pisses me off is that I'm in the same group as you guys and what I did is not half as bad as what you did. What some of you did is sickening!

Therapist: Who'd like to respond to that. Jack, you used to feel that way. Can you share what you learned?

Client (a lay leader): In a way, what any of us did is no different. We all did "sickening" things, and to your daughter it's just as bad as what I did to my stepdaughter, because it's the worst thing that has happened to *her*.

Another Client: Rape is as bad as touching? Come off it.

Therapist: In one way, absolutely not. Rape is much worse because it is violent. But in another way, it's almost as bad. If touching is the worst thing that has happened to *me,* then to me it can be devastating.

Theme 3: Victimization. It is quite common for all members of families who have engaged in incestuous abuse to feel like victims, including the offending fathers. In fact, since so many abusing fathers were themselves victims of at least emotional neglect or abuse, these feelings are based in reality. During this session the therapist encourages all the members to discuss how they have felt like victims, how they victimize themselves, and what they learned about being a victim from their families of origin and procreation. The Transactional Analysis notion that each person plays the triangular roles of perpetrator, victim, and rescuer at various times in his or her life is presented to the group, and each member explains how he or she had acted in those roles and what it felt like.

Once the members of the group can identify when and how they are victims, the therapist gives them tasks to practice that will release them from their victim roles. For example:

Therapist: (to a mother's group) During the next two weeks, I want you all to keep a journal. In this journal, I want you to identify all the times you were victimized.

Client: Were, or *felt* like we were?

Therapist: Both. Every time you felt like a victim, I want you to briefly describe the situation—where you were, who was involved, how were you involved in setting it up, what you did or did not do during or after the interaction, and finally, what you would have done different ideally. Over the next few weeks, we will be talking about how these things get set up within us that then make us respond like victims. Then we'll practice, inside and outside the group, new ways to keep yourselves from getting victimized.

Theme 4: Family of origin. This theme is used for the fathers' and the mothers' groups. The members explore the various roles they had in their families of origin. For example, were they expected to be the strong one? The savior? Were they scapegoated? Here the therapist can build upon the previous themes of fear and of victimization. The client states how he or she felt in those roles, and what he or she liked and didn't like about those roles. The therapist connects the individual's present family patterns and the family's current sexual abuse with each member's story.

During this session the members are asked to tell the group about their current relationship with their families of origin, the healthy aspects of their relationship with them, and the problems they are presently having, particularly with regard to sexual abuse. If appropriate, the therapist may teach the group some related family systems concepts, such as triangulation, and ask group members to identify when this occurs in their families of origin.

The therapist must be careful not to let this session turn into a blaming exercise. The reality should be created that the members are each capable of different relationships with their families of origin, that there is a middle ground between being enmeshed with them and totally disengaging from them. The therapist should help the group members develop strategies to eventually have better relationships with their families of origin. For example:

Therapist: (to a mothers' group) Sally has identified that when her mother calls her on the phone she finds herself lying about her relationship with Dave (*the offender*), telling her mother she is getting divorced when in fact she isn't. She says that's just what it was like when she was growing up. She told her mother what she wanted to hear in order to get approval.

Jane: That sounds just like me. Then my parents found out the truth anyway. It was always worse, but I was always afraid.

Sally: We are all still like kids.

Therapist: And yet you expect yourselves to do everything right as mothers, when you're still confused about how to be with your own parents.

Sally: I never feel like an adult with my parents. And now after all this incest stuff no one thinks I can do anything right. I barely trust my own judgment.

Therapist: Maybe you have to start with something small. Can anyone think of a small decision you could make and then tell your mother about?

Sally: I have an example maybe, something I'm trying to figure out now.

This Sunday is Mother's Day. Now my ma knows that I'm separated and not sure whether I want a divorce. She really wants me to get a divorce. I don't want to spend the whole day with my family. I'd like to see my ma a little bit, then I'd like to be with my kids and my husband. We've never had a good Mother's Day, and I'd like to see if after this therapy we could pull it off. I feel like lying to my ma and making up some excuse about why we have to leave because she'll be real mad if I pick my husband over her again.

Therapist: There is that theme again. Having to choose between people you love. Is there a way you can do both without lying?

Sally: Not without my ma being mad.

Therapist: How about not worrying about whether or not she gets mad but just not letting it escalate. Does anyone think it is possible?

Jane: I've done it. Your mom will probably get mad. But just tell her that you know why she's mad. You know she loves you and that's why she's mad, but that you have to try it.

Paula: Let her know that you are not choosing anybody over anybody. Its just that you want to see both of them so you can figure this whole thing out.

Therapist: Maybe you can agree to disagree on this one?

Sally: I'm not sure it could work.

Therapist: Let's role play it. First you be your mother and then I'll be you. . . .

Theme 5: Family structure. It can be extremely useful to have the group members do a brief Structural Session (see Chapter 8) and for the members to discuss similarities and differences in their current families. Each person draws a structural diagram of his or her family on a blackboard the way he or she saw it during that Stage I intervention, and how he or she sees it now. This session can be particularly revealing for group members, as they try to make sense out of their own situations, to answer the question: "How did this happen to my family?" Consider the following example from a victims' group:

Therapist: You have all seen these pictures in your other sessions. I thought we'd bring them out today and talk about our roles in the family. June is going to be the leader for today, so she'll be leading the discussion.

June: First, let's just go around and tell which of the different family pictures *we* felt like most of the time in our families, and what roles we had. Like we were the moms or the little kids. (*They take turns and discuss the similarities and differences in their structures, adding and changing from one another's stories.*) What kind of stuff is still happening that makes you feel like a different age than you are?

Therapist: Good question, June. You prepared great for this topic.

April: My mom still asks me to stop doing whatever I'm doing to watch the younger kids.

Therapist: How old does that make you feel?

April (who is 16): About 30.

Jennifer (who is 15): My dad doesn't let me talk on the phone after school with any friends, and I can never call boys. I feel about 10.

Cindy: I have to be the middle person between my mom and my grandma because they are never speaking. So my mom's always saying things like, "You ask her if you want such and such from her," or, "Go see if your grandma has this at her house," or, "Who do you think is right, me or her?"

Theme 6: Sex roles. A pervasive theme throughout the client's family and individual sessions is that a rigid adherence to culturally stereotyped gender roles is a powerful contributor to many families' vulnerability to incest. Since it is rare for only the father to hold to the male-in-charge sex role, it is important for the victims' and the mothers' groups to focus on the problems associated with holding firmly to rigid sex roles in their families.

Group members are asked to make a list of the "purpose" of men and women; for instance, some say men's purpose is to provide for the family, and women's purpose is to take care of children. From these lists, the therapist helps the group confront sex-role stereotypes and suggests how these belief systems might lead to abuse. Sex roles should also be tied in with the issue of power and control, which probably was first addressed during the previous "Structural Session" theme.

The following are examples of sex roles generated in an offenders' group. After the list is put together, the therapist, through a didactic presentation or group discussion, attempts to dispel some of the more erroneous beliefs.

The role of women:

1. To take care of the family
2. To cook
3. To clean
4. To take care of the kids

5. To be a sexual partner
6. To help provide money in a crisis
7. To be loyal
8. To keep the family together
9. To stand by their man
10. To be understanding
11. To take care of themselves—to stay looking good

The role of men:

1. To provide money
2. To take care of the house
3. To fix things
4. To protect the family
5. To help out with the kids
6. To worry about the bigger matters outside the family
7. To provide for the future
8. To be a good sexual partner
9. To set and implement the rules in the family

Based on these notions, the therapist might offer a number of questions that address some of these stereotypes and the effect that acceptance of them might have on their families:

1. Do you feel as if you have failed if a woman does your job?
2. What feeling do you have when you see a woman in your role—sad, angry, frustrated, scared, helpless?
3. What are some of the things you do to regain what you think is your rightful position?
4. Do you punish women if they are as good as you in your role? If so, how do you punish them? overtly and covertly?
5. What would it take for you to feel more comfortable with equality between men and women?
6. Is there anything to gain by having more equal roles between men and women?

Theme 7: Communication. Although communication exercises are an integral part of the clients' family sessions, it is helpful for group members to practice newly learned communication skills with each other. This is because there is usually less emotionalism attached to talking with group members than with family members, and therefore clients can focus on the *skill* rather than the *content*. Basic communication exercises, such as talking in "I" statements rather than "you" statements, paraphrasing, and empathic listening skills can be practiced. Also, conflict resolution is addressed, with the group members encouraged by the therapist to "finish a problem" rather than to let it go unresolved. Finally, the group members are assigned by the therapist to practice the same skills at home with their families during the next week, and then to report back to the group at the following session.

Theme 8: Assertiveness. Since almost all incestuous family members experience assertiveness difficulties (even the offending fathers!), an assertiveness training component is included as a group theme. The therapist gives a short lecture on the differences among aggressiveness, passivity, and assertiveness, and argues that the latter is ultimately the most productive in terms of the clients' getting what they want. The group members are then asked to identify examples during the previous week when they used aggressiveness, passivity, and assertiveness, and then to discuss which worked best under what condition. The therapist finally has the group members role play a few of the aggressive or passive responses and then to replace them instead with an assertive response. For example:

Therapist: I want to spend a little time giving you a short talk about assertiveness. Let's define the terms aggressive, passive, and assertive. Aggressive means to attack, to say something in a manner that is not very productive. You get your point across, but you send many other messages with it. Being aggressive usually makes people angry, defensive, vindictive, or extremely passive or passive aggressive. Passive means that you say yes when you mean no, or you say no when you mean yes. Passive-aggressive means that you look passive while finding a way to be aggressive. You certainly all know people who were passive with you and times when you were passive. Assertiveness is to self-confidently declare an opinion or a belief without being hurtful, which results in you getting what you want. Here are five quick rules on how to make an assertive statement. They might sound a little contrived, but they work!

Rules:

1. Use the word "I" instead of the word "you."
2. *State* what it is that you *want*. Those are the key words: You "state" (not "demand") and "want" (not "must have").

3. State some kind of feeling when asking for what you want.
4. Be direct, clear, and concise.
5. Make sure that by the end of the statement you have said something positive about the person you are talking to, the situation you are talking about, or the relationship you are in.

Theme 9: Sexual problems. For clients to discuss their sexual experiences and problems in a group setting is important but often quite difficult. Usually the therapist begins by asking group members to share what messages about sex they remember from their families of origin. For instance, Was sex openly discussed? Were there open displays of physical expression or was touch inhibited? They also talk about their first sexual experiences and what effect, either positive or negative, these had on their future sexual functioning. The group members are then asked by the therapist to talk about current sexual problems they are having, including specific sexual dysfunctions; the therapist assures the members that to have a sexual dysfunction is normal but notes when a problem exists, so that the member's family therapist can be informed.

Members are finally asked what their ideal sex life would be. Would they have sex six times a day? Would it include multiple partners, or sexually variant behavior? What are their limits of sexual normality? The group as a whole discusses each person's range of sexual fantasy, behavior, and expectations in light of sexual abuse or victimization. For example, adolescent victims may confront a sexually active group member in terms of her being continually victimized sexually, this time by male friends rather than her father.

Theme 10: Cognitive distortions. Following from the previous sexual themes, the group finally focuses on distortions in perceptions about sexual abuse (see Chapter 6). The most common distortions are presented by the therapist, and then the group members are asked to identify which ones they have engaged in, or the ones their offending husbands or abusing fathers may have accepted. Consider the following dialogue:

Therapist: (after presenting the list of common distortions the group members came in with to the fathers' group) Now most of us have accepted a couple of these at various times in our lives. For instance, Joe, which of these strikes out and hits you as one you've believed?

Joe: (hesitating) Well, I talked about this one with my therapist . . . that one about *(reading)* "If a daughter doesn't physically resist me, it means she wants to have sex with me." I guess all guys kinda grow up to believe that when a girl says no she really means yes, and that if she goes along with you and doesn't try and stop you this means she really wants to.

Bob: Yeah, you gotta admit it's hard sometimes for a guy to know. I mean, we're expected to make the moves, and they're expected to say yes or no. Only they never say yes, they just only don't resist.

Therapist: You mean, that's what you learned growing up, as teenagers, about other teenage girls?

Bob: Right. That's what it feels like, anyway.

Therapist: Then why is this a "cognitive distortion"?

Joe: (*after a pause*) 'Cause it's on the list (*laughter*)?

Therapist: I think you all know what I mean . . .

Joe: Sure . . . 'cause we're not talking about girls our own age, we're talking about our daughters?

Therapist: Right. Very important point. But something else, something that makes it a "distortion."

Bob: Sure, I know. Just because someone doesn't try to stop something doesn't mean they want to do it. Like when we did that stuff about passive and aggressive, it came out that we've all sat back and let things happen we didn't want.

Therapist: Exactly. And don't you think kids can be pretty passive sometimes, especially with their fathers?

James: I don't know, mine are pretty "aggressive" (*laughter*).

Joe: But I get the point. It's pretty stupid to think if I gave a robber my wallet when he had a knife in my back that I *wanted* to give him my wallet.

SPECIFIC GROUP ISSUES

Fathers' Groups

Denial. There are a number of concerns for the therapist running an offending fathers' group. First, denial in some form will typically continue to sneak into the sessions. The therapist should be prepared to directly challenge the denial; more important, however, the group itself should be mobilized to defend against denial by its members. This is best accomplished during the first sessions, when the therapist predicts this will occur, and to ask the group for the promise of help when it does. There will usually be at least one "ex-denier" who can be counted on to assist the therapist; also, if the group has one, the lay leader can often challenge denial more effectively than the therapist himself.

Commonness of the problem. An offending fathers' group can give its members the feeling that everyone abuses their daughters at some time. The therapist should not let the group suggest that the universality of abuse (or at least its frequency of occurrence) in some way *justifies* it. The theme should be consistent: It would be wrong even if every father in the world were to do it. The group usually has no problem accepting this; the therapist must simply be aware when a justification is being made and that it needs to be challenged.

One-upsmanship. An interesting but problematic phenomenon occurs in many fathers' groups. The fathers will sometimes form hierarchies of acceptability with regard their sexual abuse: "Well, he penetrated his daughter; I only fondled mine," or "He did it with his daughter; at least mine was just a stepdaughter." In addition to sounding foolish, this type of interaction suggests on ongoing denial of impact that must be challenged. The therapist is well advised to predict during the first group session that this sometimes will occur but that it will not be tolerated.

Pedophile fantasies and behaviors. During the "sexual problems" theme session, the therapist may be tempted to remain in "safer" territory, such as early childhood memories and first sexual experiences. However, it is essential that the group talk about each one of its members' fantasies surrounding young children *in general.* Although most will insist that they have no pedophile tendencies, the burden of proof should be placed upon them. Oftentimes a group that has grown to trust one another can provide the only forum where a member will feel safe enough to admit to generalized pedophile fantasies and behaviors.

Awareness of odd behavior. Although it should go without saying, a therapist must be aware of changes in the group's behavior that may signal acting-out problems are emerging. For example, one group seemed quite uncomfortable during a particular session. When confronted for the third time, one of the members finally admitted that another father had brought a "kiddie-porn" magazine with him, and they had all looked at it with interest in the waiting room prior to the session. The therapist should not lose track of the fact that he or she is dealing with a "special population," and changes in their group behavior may be serious.

Mothers' Groups

Anger. The major organizing theme around mothers' groups is anger. This anger is often diffuse, but can be directed at the women's husbands, their daughters, therapists, or each other. The theme of anger will usually continue throughout the group therapy. The therapist can make a couple of interventions around the issue of anger. Anger can be described as a common way mothers deal with their *fears* during the first thematic session of "fears." Also, the therapist might add a session on how anger can be appropriate and put to constructive use.

Another intervention, suggested by Evan Coppersmith-Black (personal communication, 1985) has the therapist making the following assignment: During the upcoming week, the group members are to write down exactly how they feel each time they are angry; but they are to do this on construction paper that is colored to match the *type* of anger they are experiencing. For example, red might be *rage* anger, blue might be *depressed* anger, purple might be *confused* anger. They then bring these back the next week, discuss each with the group, and then put their papers in a box, which might be ritualistically buried at a later time.

Pressure from the group. One of the pluses to group therapy is the ability of the group to "pressure" its members to make useful changes. However, the therapist must be cognizant that many of these mothers have a life history of being coerced or pressured, and that their family and individual therapy are probably focusing on their becoming more independent of thought and action. In other words, it is important that other group members do not successfully overpower a mother into making a decision that she does not wish to make. The common issue around which this occurs is divorce: Those who choose *to* divorce attempt to influence those who have chosen *not to* divorce. The therapist should predict this might occur during the course of the group and make a rule that members will not intimidate or coerce other members into making decisions.

Victims' Groups

Control. The victims' group follows a similar sequence of theme sessions as the mothers' and fathers' groups, with a few exceptions. After the second session, the victims' group members are told to come back the following week with lists of what they would like to discuss in the group. The group then picks one girl to be the leader of each one of the topics, which usually correspond to the 10 organizing themes presented earlier. The group leader is responsible for the theme being adequately discussed, and for dealing with those other girls who may become upset during that discussion. The purpose is for the girls to have a major element of *control* in their therapy, which is isomorphic to their obtaining control within their families and in their lives. The therapist, whenever possible, accentuates that power should be gained through assertion, not victimization.

Individuation and privacy. Another overriding theme is that of the victims' normal separation and individuation from their families. Incestuously abused daughters often live within extremely enmeshed family structures; this is a major family vulnerability factor. In addition to the relationships the girls develop with other group members, they also encourage each other to engage in appropriate outside-the-family activities and establish responsible peer relationships.

Younger children. For younger girls, the groups are shorter, more social, and more play-oriented. Through the use of play, games, and drawings many of the themes can be addressed. For example, a problem may be posed to the children: What should a little girl do when someone tells her to keep a secret that she knows is bad? The children might then put on a little play where they act out each of their "solutions" to the problem. The sexual abuse is usually dealt with in these more metaphoric ways than is the case with the older children or the adult groups.

SECTION III

15

Stage III: Consolidation

Whereas there is a distinct line of demarcation between Stage I and Stage II of the therapy program, no such line exists between Stages II and III. Stage III is called "Consolidation" because the family at this juncture is expected to integrate all the changes they have made during the course of treatment with their own style and personality. The family now *consolidates* what they have learned into what they would like to be.

The therapist can recognize when the family has entered the Consolidation stage because meetings with the family feel more like reporting sessions than therapy sessions. In response to the question, "What's been going on this week?" the family tells the therapist about issues and crises that have arisen *and how they have solved them*. The therapist then reinforces them for their abilities, reminds them how they might have mishandled that particular situation in the past, and asks them how they might handle similar situations in the future.

For most incestuously abusing families, the journey through the therapeutic stages is really the journey from dependence to independence. It is not unlike moving from childhood through adolescence through adulthood. At first the family, like the child, needs the therapist for practical reasons (such as to help them deal with the legal and protective service systems) and to prepare them for change (e.g., they cannot see their own resistances or what needs to be changed). Next, the family is aware of what needs to be changed but does not know how to do it; the family needs the therapist to suggest new behaviors and to inspire the family to implement them. Finally, the family members make their own life decisions and select appropriate behavior, with advice given from the therapist only when solicited. At this stage the therapist, like the parent of adult children, is most like a counsel and friend.

The differences among the three stages of therapy are best illustrated in how information is exchanged with the therapist in each stage. In Stage I, the client is unlikely to provide the therapist directly with much information. Instead, the therapist must constantly probe, cajole, and "be strategic" in getting the facts about their lives. In Stage II, the family members offer the therapist information about their lives, both the good and the bad, but the actions that are taken upon that information are performed under the direction of the therapist. In Stage III, the family members first provide the therapist with information about their family and individual lives and then tell the therapist what action they took. At this point, there is little need for any more direct therapeutic intervention.

In Stage I, the family had contact with a therapist two or three times a week, in family, individual, and group sessions. By Stage II, the family has only one or two therapeutic contacts each week. Stage III is characterized by decreasing numbers of contacts, usually once every two to three weeks or longer for approximately three months. Once the family has formally completed the program, a follow-up session is scheduled after six months, and telephone follow-ups are made every six months after that. The major purpose is for the therapist to become one of the family's individual and joint "coping mechanisms"; that is, when crises arise, the family members know that an appropriate response is to call their therapist who can help them solve that particular crisis.

STAGE III INTERVENTIONS

Stage III interventions are characterized by therapeutic rituals and enactments whose purpose it is to reinforce both the changes the family has made and their ability to creatively solve new problems as they appear (see Table 15.1). This is done in both individual and family sessions.

Crystal Ball

The purpose of this technique is to encourage the family to anticipate problems that may emerge in the future and to think about how they

TABLE 15.1
Stage III: Consolidation Interventions

1. Crystal Ball
2. "What Could Make This Family Incestuous Again?"
3. Old Sequences, Old Behaviors
4. Normal Family Activities with Therapist
5. Final Apology Session
6. Sessions in the Bank

will solve them. The therapist takes out a "crystal ball" (available at magic shops; a small fishbowl turned upside-down will also do nicely), place it on the table, and, depending upon his or her style of "patter," says something like the following:

Therapist: Let's look into my crystal ball and see your future. When we look into it we'll all see something different. No two people ever see the future the same way. So what I want you each to do is look into the ball and tell me about your future and the future of the members of your family. So, for example, just kind of reflect on the normal course of action for all people, like going to school, getting new jobs, leaving home, marriages, births, and deaths. Then see what your family is in store for, and perhaps everybody's reactions. What will be the positive reactions and what will be the negative reactions to some of these life-cycle events? In what areas will there be problems and what areas will you sail through? Like John and Jill, what will be easy and what will be hard for the marriage when the kids leave home? Sally, how will you handle leaving home? Any fantasies about work and men? What kind of adolescent will John Jr. be, and how will you handle him?

"What Could Make This Family Incestuous Again?"

This question leads off a session where the family is asked to explore the possible sequences that might lead to a return to incestuous abuse. The family will typically protest this question, insisting that there is *nothing* that could make incest occur again. The therapist must be strategic in getting the family to do this exercise without inferring that he or she does not trust the family or thinks that they are still incestuous. The following illustrates this intervention:

Therapist: I know that what we are going to talk about in this session and maybe in the next few sessions is going to make you totally nutsy. Every time I do this with a family or an individual they always fight me and get irritated with me. (*The family snickers.*) Why are you laughing?

Father: I can see how people can get irritated with you. I have a few times over the past two years.

Therapist: I know, that's how you can tell we like each other—we get irritated with each other. Anyway, I'm prepared to fight you on this one.

Daughter: Get on with it already.

Therapist: Is there anything that could happen in this family, or what would this family have to look like, to have incest happen again?

Mother: It could never happen again.

Daughter: I would never let it happen. If he got close to me, I'd stop him right away . . . you know that!

Younger Daughter: My mom wouldn't let it happen, I would tell her!

Therapist: You know what? I'm sure about everything you're saying. But you know what is even more convincing for me is to have you talk about it. You see, if you can identify the areas that your family would have to be weak in again, then I know you really know what has changed and what would have to change back. Does that make any sense?

Father: Oh, you mean like for me to sexually abuse the kids again I'd have to start hating myself again. Or I'd have to stop talking to my wife? I'd have to cross the line and turn to the girls to be my pals, my girlfriends? That kind of stuff?

Therapist: Right. Those are a few of things that if they were to sneak back in would certainly make you extremely vulnerable to the sexual abuse. What else?

Mother: I know what would make me vulnerable. If I let my critical "part," my victim "part," or my overprotective controlling part get too big, and then I don't listen to my "self" . . .

Daughter: If I started feeling like I had to take care of my mother and try to save their marriage. If I stopped caring about what happens to me and let my wild part just do whatever it wanted to.

Therapist: Whoo! Slow down. For a group of people who first says nothing, now you're going so fast I can't keep up. Let's talk about this for a while. Don't think if you get it all done today that this is the end. I won't let you go that fast. I like you guys, too much. I mean, I'm going to miss you!

Old Sequences, Old Behaviors

An important Consolidation exercise is for the therapist to have the family engage in some "old," interactional sequences and behaviors that were identified as contributing to the family's vulnerability to incest. For example, the family may be asked, during the session, to have a fight the way they used to; or for the father to talk to the mother as he did before therapy, with the children responding in their old manner; or for the daughter to withdraw from the family the way she used to. Then the therapist asks the family to do what it needs to stop that particular dysfunctional sequence. The purpose of this is twofold. First, it dramatically demonstrates how far the family has come from those problem behaviors, which now seem distant and awkward to carry out. Second, it reinforces their ability to identify those sequences and behaviors and alter them before they can again become problematic. Here is an example of this intervention:

Therapist: We talked about doing this pretend thing in each of your individual sessions. We decided to do it together as a group in a family session. Everyone remember how they used to be in relation to themselves and to each other. Sally (*a seven-year-old victim*), do you understand what we're talking about?

Sally: Yeah, we're going to act, like in a play, and we're going to act like we used to act with each other when we were all unhappy and there were all the problems between all of us.

Therapist: Right. Now, we are going to put on a little play. A play that would show people in the audience how a family acts when there is sexual abuse. You are not going to abuse each other, but you are going to fight the old way, not resolve problems like in the old way, cross the lines all over the place. Be the Smith family of two years ago. Go ahead, the scene is your home in your kitchen. (*They take a few minutes to "set up."*)

Mother: (*as she starts to leave the room, turns to her daughter*) He never understands me. I don't know what I do to upset him so much. I just can't think of everything. Oh, honey, I didn't know you were there. Did you hear the whole thing?

Youngest Daughter. No, Mommy (*turning to the therapist, says out of her play-acting role, "I always used to lie"*), I didn't hear much. Don't worry, Daddy's just tired, he's not that angry.

Mother: Weren't you going out to play with your friends next door?

Youngest Daughter: Yes, but I think I'll stay home, I don't feel like going out much. (*Daughter pretends to walk into next room where father is.*) Hey, Dad, what do you want me and Lisa to make for dinner?

Father: Why? Is your mother going to one of her classes again tonight? She'll be the best word processor in the world at this rate. I don't care, make whatever you want. I'm not hungry. I have too much to do around here.

Oldest Daughter: What do you have to do around here? Ever since you lost your job you haven't done anything.

Father: I told you, I didn't lose my job.

Daughter: I don't know what you call it, but we don't have anything more done around here, that's for sure.

Father: Don't talk back to me! Your mother is filling you with ideas.

Daughter: No she isn't, she never ever feels safe enough to complain about you. She's stupid when it comes to you.

Father: Don't talk that way about your mother (*pretends to grab for a beer, and they all laugh*).

Therapist: Was it scary? It was so real.

Mother: That was really us. We did it for a lot of years, so we can do it good.

Therapist: Any difference?

Father: This time I knew it was wrong, and I even had an idea in my head what I should be doing different.

Therapist: Great! How about the rest of you?

Youngest Daughter: It was fun, but I was glad we were just playing. It wasn't fun before, hearing everyone but me fight.

Oldest Daughter: It was hard for me to be so hateful. And what is weird is that a few years ago that's how I felt all the time.

Mother: I really didn't like that part of me. It felt so crazy and confused. I don't feel confused much anymore. That's a real relief.

Normal Family Activities with Therapist

During Stage III some therapists find it useful to engage in activities with the family that accentuate their "normality." For about two years the family's experience with the therapist has focused on their pathology. This has happened both directly through the therapy process, but also indirectly by virtue of the relationship, which is based only in a clinic, with directives being given, with a bill being paid. In Stage III, some therapists go out to dinner with the family, go bowling with them, share family pictures with them, and other "normal" activities one might do with a family that is *liked*. Although some therapists may be uncomfortable with this, we have found it extremely useful in consolidating the message that we now see them as the type of family we can appreciate, have fun with, and act *normally* with.

Final Apology Session

Although this session is "billed" to the family as the final Apology Session, in reality it is the summary of therapy. The therapist asks each member to discuss how he or she has changed, how the others in the family have changed, and, most important, how the family as a whole has changed. The abusing father does apologize once more, but this time it is usually more in terms of *feelings*. The apology occurs in tandem with his summary and allows him to put the entire process in a perspective that is meaningful to him. Here is an example:

Mother: Larry, how do you think Mom and Dad have changed? I mean how do you think we've changed as people?

Larry (older son, not a victim of sexual abuse but a child who had been hospitalized for elective mutism for 10 months): Well, I don't know. I guess you used to be a "mouse that roared." You never did or said anything and always sort of snuck around with your tail between your legs until you had it, and then you'd go crazy but no one ever listened to you. It was like you never cared what we did: "You want to stay out till 12 and you are only 11 years old, go ahead."

Seth (younger son, also not abused): I have to be in by eight. That's not fair.

Larry: Yes, it is . . . that's how she has changed.

Shauna (incest victim): You know you have a family to watch now.

Larry: Yeah, you want to take care of us.

Father: You mean, you think your mom and I have grown up, in a way?

Larry: Mom has grown up, you have matured. There is a difference.

Father: (*said with pride*) Stand back, this is my professor talking!

Shauna: Mom used to act like a scared kid. You never acted like a scared kid, you were an old bully.

Larry: Right, it's like you don't have to flex your muscles so much anymore. You have matured, cooled out. It used to be, "This is what I said; I said it so that is how it goes."

Shauna: Now it's, "Maybe this is how it goes, but let's talk about it." Believe it or not, I think you've gotten more easygoing.

Seth: He hasn't gotten so easygoing with me. I still have to follow a lot of rules!

Father: I'm still your father, and you are not so old that you don't need both your mom and me. Maybe what your brother and sister are talking about is that I'm not so strict like I used to be.

Larry: I'm not sure you even thought you could be happy.

Shauna: We certainly never thought we could be happy. You never let us believe that there was anything in our lives that we could have control over.

Father: I never really thought I had control over anything in my life. I pretended a lot and I tried to control everything, but I never really felt like I was in control of anything.

Larry: Maybe that's how you changed, how we all changed. You don't act like you have to be in control, and when you are being a parent it's like a real parent. It's like you started to care for real. It is like we all started to care for real.

Shauna: It's like I have a family for the first time.

Sessions in the Bank

There is usually a six-month follow-up, along with scheduled telephone follow-ups, after therapy has officially concluded. As added insurance, the family during their last session is given the opportunity to ensure that the therapist becomes one of the "coping mechanisms" to prevent the possibility of abuse in the future. The family members are told that they are going to have two sessions "in the bank," one that they pay for now, one that is "on the house." They can redeem these sessions any time they choose in the future. The purpose of this is to normalize their needing a little help in the future, and to reframe requesting this help from "We are failures, we need to come back" to "We are taking advantage of our savings account, using what is owed us." Some families never do use these saved sessions, but knowing they are there when they are needed can be comforting.

The family and therapist have become extremely intimate over the course of time. It is important that in the final sessions they summarize their feelings and experiences with one another.

Therapist: It's really hard, saying good-bye after all this time. I feel like I have so much to say to you, and yet I don't know where to start. You have all said to me in different ways that I have become a member of your family. Some of you say that sometimes it's as if I'm sitting in the living room with you. Dave, you said I sit on your shoulder. There are things about each of you that I value, appreciate, and have learned from that hopefully will help me have a better life, too. I just want to share a little of that with you.

Joan (*the mother*), I have learned from you that a woman can really change. You have learned to be strong to protect yourself and your kids. You have grown to include the outside world and handle it terrifically well. And yet you have stayed loving and soft and very available. Your competent, independent side is not a "bitch," and your loving side is not a "door mat." I have learned more about those parts of my self by watching you grow.

Dave (*the father*), through you I have learned not to give up on myself or others. I wanted to give up on you so many times. You scared me and repulsed me, but somehow you kept me convinced that your heart was real and that you wanted to get in contact with it again. As many times as you tried to push me away you always were ready to reach back out. I guess you taught me something about real strength. You became a truly strong human being when you could admit that you were a mere mortal. You reconvinced me that being vulnerable is the real test of strength.

Maggie (*one of the victims, 14 years old*), you have taught me that a child can love and hate a parent at the same time and that it does not have to be devastating. My kids will be glad that I have learned that from you. You are truly a compassionate human being and I see through you that one can be that way without having to protect people or to take care of them beyond your years. You are an individual now, and you know that is OK. I see that kids can really be their own persons with their own ideas and be part of a family at the same time. You are your own person, a wonderful one at that.

Seth (*12-year-old nonvictim*), you have taught me about flexibility. You have real "stick-with-itness." You hated therapy, but you came. And a lot of the time you were one of the most helpful participants. You have a very keen eye for human beings and how they communicate. Maybe you should be a therapist. You helped me learn to stick with it. When I was worried that things were not going to get better, I always could think of you and know that you hated being here but you came. I see that your commitment and loyalty are a great part of your personality and have helped and will help you always.

Finally, Annie (*8-year-old victim*), you have helped me see how important laughing and having fun is to a family and to feeling better. I have learned that play can help someone talk about their feelings, communicate, get closer to each other, and learn to trust again. Watching you with your parents and seeing how honest you are and how you tell them what is on your mind now makes me

> realize how important that is. I can see that you will always be able to do that. You will be able to play and have fun and yet be honest and stand up for yourself whenever it is necessary. Those are wonderful qualities and I am going to try to be more like you.
>
> So you will all always be with me. And that is why I want to hear from you, and will be calling you, and want you to come in and let me help whenever things get tough in the future. Because in some strange way, we are part of each other and we will always want to know how those parts of us are doing.

Change is an evolutionary process, and the clients need to know it is normal and expected that they will keep "changing their changes."

16

Special Issues

In this book we have presented the Multiple Systems model for the treatment of incestuously abusing families. Although this model was designed primarily to treat ongoing sexual abuse between parents and their children, we will briefly discuss in this chapter how many of its components can be applied when treating adult survivors of incest and extrafamilial sexual involvement.

ADULT SURVIVORS OF INCEST

It may be psychotherapy's psychoanalytic origins, or it may be our own fascination with the morbid or prurient, but therapists have a strong tendency when working with an adult incest survivor—who may be in therapy with any variety of presenting problems—to focus therapy on the client's childhood sexual abuse. It is very important for adult survivors to confront their own childhood abuse openly and understand the impact it may have on their current life. However, the abuse was not the only event in the adult survivor's life, and all of her existent adulthood behaviors are not a function of that abuse. Each of the client's systems must be taken into account when developing a treatment plan lest she be forced to remain in the role of the victim, this time not of her father but of the institution of therapy.

What makes the use of the Multiple Systems framework unique in counseling adult incest survivors is the emphasis on understanding, confronting, and changing family patterns. Therapy addresses both her family of origin, where the abuse took place, and her current family, where the results of the abuse manifest themselves. The therapy should also examine the societal, cultural, and political factors that contribute to the adult's childhood experience and her current adult functioning. The treatment program, like that for ongoing incest, includes individual, couple, family, and family-of-origin sessions which are all provided by one therapist. If group therapy is offered, it may be conducted by a different therapist, but who is in continuous consultation with the primary therapist.

Many adult survivors of childhood sexual trauma are often misdiagnosed and therefore wrongly treated. We see much of their adult dysfunctional behavior as a learned response to childhood sexual abuse. In other words, if as a child, one is trying to control or fend off abusive behavior, one's interactional experiences will be quite different from those inherent in normal childhood development. The thoughts, feelings, and behaviors that helped abused children survive in childhood become their symptomatic behaviors in adulthood. For example, the child's attempt to control the abuse by initiating the contact perhaps becomes promiscuity during the teen or adult years. The act of pretending not to be in the room during childhood abuse evolves into dissociative symptoms in adult life. The therapy must identify these patterns, interpret them, and then help the survivor learn new ways to think, feel, behave, and cope, and this is no easy task. What follows is a brief outline of some of the applications of this model.

Interventions

Therapy for adult survivors occurs in the same three stages as it does for ongoing family sexual abuse. The client is usually seen individually and with her present family during Stage I "Creating a Context for Change." Four themes are offered for her consideration by the therapist during this stage:

Victimization. Fairly early the client is asked to ponder her own victimization. She will be asked to describe the details of her own abuse, how she coped during the time of the abuse, how she believes it affected her as she grew up, and how it continues to impact her life. For example, does she become involved romantically with men who are controlling or who abuse her? Or does *she* abuse others, alienate them, and then feel hurt and alone? The therapist is at this juncture quite supportive and empathic of the experiences she had and her feelings about them. This exploration can go on for many weeks or even months, and should include her spouse (if she is married), when she can comfortably share her feelings and experiences with him.

Negative consequences of change. After a number of sessions where the client focuses on the results of her own victimization, she is then asked to deliver a list of all of the possible ramifications of giving up her victim role, again understanding the natural resistance to change. The client will typically protest that there are no negative consequences in relinquishing being an incest victim, but with some encouragement and example giving the therapist will usually be able to elicit some meaningful illustrations. Some common negative consequences include: the loss of power ("You can't talk to me like that; I've had enough abuse in my life"); the loss of an "excuse" for her current failings in life ("Well, I couldn't be expected to have a normal relationship after what I went through, could I?"); and loss of "victim identity" which is supported in the contemporary culture ("I am an incest survivor!"). The client may be reminded of the negative consequences of giving up her victim role during periods in treatment when she becomes resistant to change.

Structural Session. After the negative consequences are examined, the client goes through a version of the Structural Session (see Chapter 8). She is presented with the diagrams of the six family structures common in incest families (Figures 6.4 to 6.9) and asked to describe which were similar to her family of origin and under what conditions. She then does the same for her current family. Similarities and differences are discussed, and the theme, "family patterns repeat themselves," can then be developed by the therapist. These sessions can be held with the client alone or with her partner, depending upon her feelings and the judgment of the therapist.

Parts. This metaphor, described in Chapter 13, suggests to the client that she has many "parts" to her personality, some functional and some not functional. For example, she may have a "part" which is strong, secure, and knows what is best for her. At the same time, she may have a competing "part" which is insecure, frightened, and subject to abuse by those around her. Each of these "parts" serves her overall personality in some way, and a positive intent can be connoted by the therapist for each. This metaphor is useful to help the client understand that a "good" (i.e., strong, secure) person can sometimes act "bad" (i.e., weak, tolerant of abuse). It also provides an understandable blueprint for change: work to make the self facilitate functional interactions between her "parts."

In Stage II of the adult survivor's therapy, she is expected to change her own behaviors that contribute to her problems, and to work with the therapist to transfigure the systems that continue to have a negative impact on her life. Besides individual and couple sessions with the therapist, sessions with her family of origin are encouraged, and group therapy is usually provided.

Hypnosis/Imaging. One way to challenge old patterns and begin to develop new alternatives is through the use of hypnosis, or imaging. We use regressive techniques in reenacting the abuse with new outcomes. Also effective is the use of imaging new patterns/behaviors from a position of strength and power. Obviously, a clinician needs to be well trained in these types of interventions.

Family-of-origin sessions. One of the most difficult therapy experiences must be when an adult survivor of incest meets with and/or confronts her abusing parents. Most clients would shudder at the thought, and many therapists would never consider having such an emotionally charged and potentially volatile session. However, we have found these sessions to be one of the most valuable components of therapy, and, if planned properly, more healing than divisive. There are, of course, some families in which these sessions would be impossible: for example, where the parents are both dead, or living in another region, or refuse to participate at all. Nevertheless, it is usually possible to get *some* member of her family to a session. And with persistence on the part of the therapist, even those living in another region of the country can be convinced to travel in for at least one appointment.

Some might argue that to place the adult survivor of incest in a situation where she must face her abusive parent could lead to renewed victimization. In our opinion, just the opposite is true. Most adult survivors of incest, even in adulthood, continue to feel helpless within their families of origin. This is one reason many have chosen to remove themselves entirely from that family, even though a part of them wishes to maintain some relationship with the parents. The adult daughter should confront her family of origin as a way to become empowered. The therapist can begin this process by simply *assuming* that she will indeed meet with her parents at some time when she is ready; this effectively offers the message, "You are strong, you don't need protecting, *you are not a victim.*"

The same format and preparation is used for the family-of-origin sessions as was described in Chapter 12. What is most important is that: (1) the client knows what her goals of the session are; for example, to confront her own past abuse with her abuser, to question the family about her childhood, and/or to attempt to begin the makings of a new parent/adult-child relationship to terminate her co-dependency in relationships; (2) the client is well prepared for any contingency that could occur; for example, What if the parents deny abuse took place? What if they reject her emotionally? What if they *blame* her?; and (3) the therapist provides a reality base for the client; that is, after the session, the therapist can confirm the client's perception that what occurs in this family is *not* normal or functional.

This dialogue is taken from a session in which the therapist and client are processing the interaction that took place earlier in the hour between the mother and daughter. The therapist is trying to help the client see her mother's limitations and to let go of her fantasy that she will finally get what she needs from her mother.

Denise: Did you see it? She just couldn't hear me. She spent the whole time trying to tell me how to get over this, and how bad her life had been, and how she had to move on, and so should I, or how I am overexaggerating. Did you see it, or am I crazy?

Therapist: Yes, I saw it. I saw a woman in a lot of pain who did not want to feel any of it and so wants you not to remind her.

Denise: How can I make her see me?

Therapist: I don't think you can. It was unbelievably painful for me to watch it. She didn't hear your pain, nor did she want to. Denise, you will *never* get from your mother what it is you want. I'm not sure she is even capable of giving it to you. (*Denise starts to cry.*) It hurts, and I feel bad that you have to face this, but perhaps if you let go of the dream, you can create a more realistic life with her now. And maybe you can have something with her. I do think she is capable of giving you some things—just not the "mothering" that you want. I'm afraid she just may not have it in her . . .

Denise: So I'm not crazy, and *I* didn't do anything that makes her not hear or love me?

Therapist: No, God, no. You were wonderful. You were much more patient than I could have been. Yet you were direct and didn't act like a victim. You are not crazy. It isn't you, now, it's her pain, her history, her guilt. You didn't keep her away tonight. She just couldn't stand the pain of being too close.

Denise: But I'm so angry. How can I not be so angry?

Therapist: Over the next couple of sessions we'll talk about how to present your anger to her in a way that will be helpful to you. Who knows if she will hear it or what will happen, but I'll help you tell her, and we'll stick it out. She wants some type of relationship with you. She just can't give you exactly what you want.

EXTRAFAMILIAL SEXUAL ABUSE

We refer here to sexual abuse of a child who is not living with the offender, but where the child knows, trusts, and has some emotional bond with him. This can include a relative, teacher, boy scout leader, or minister; what is important is that he is a caregiver to the child for a period of time.

We have included extrafamilial sexual abuse in this brief discussion for two reasons. First, we have found that these cases are more similar to intrafamily child sexual abuse than sexual abuse committed by strangers. There is an emotional bond that is present which gives the offender the opportunity to have access to the child and which evokes the trust of the child. In fact, one reason the child may acquiesce is that he or she loves and trusts this individual.

The second reason we have included extrafamilial sexual abuse in this discussion is that our Multiple Systems therapy is appropriate for many of these cases. Many of the same vulnerability factors apply, and these can often be changed with a theapy program that impacts upon the many systems contributing to the maintenance of the abuse. Examples of some of these common vulnerabilities include: (a) an intense relationship combined with social isolation and opportunity (e.g., the youth camp leader who is alone with the children for long periods of time without any external supervision or controls); (b) the great deal of power and control the abuser has over the child; (c) incongruent hierarchies which place the adult in the same structural generation as the child; (d) the abuser's own abuse and/or neglect when he was a child; (e) his own lack of social skills and abilities with age-appropriate sexual partners; (f) his being ineffective in obtaining his own emotional needs with adults; and (g) his own sexual problems, which may include primary pedophilia.

Interventions

The same Multiple Systems therapy program detailed in this book can be applied to treat extrafamilial sexual abuse. Treatment is offered to both the offender and his family, and to the child and her family. The same therapist may see both sets of clients, if possible, to best coordinate the integrated treatment. If more than one child had been abused, as is often the case when a community leader is the offender, multiple family groups can be utilized. The treatment of the extrafamilial offender follows the same format as for the incest offender. The offender receives individual, marital (if applicable), family-of-origin, and group therapy.

One of the unique components of this therapy program is the Apology Session the offender is sometimes required to have with the family of the child he has abused. Both he and that family will have been prepared for months by the therapist, and the session will not occur unless the therapist is convinced that it will take place without unpleasant incident. This session is important for a number of reasons. First, it permits the child to hear directly from the offender that she was not in any way responsible for the abuse. Second, it allows the offender to make a "public apology," which has a confessional quality and can be quite therapeutic. Third, it permits the family members to confront the offender, to make real the pain and suffering they have experienced as a result of his actions. This is particularly important, since many offenders have the cognitive distortion that having sex with the child was not really harmful to anyone. Finally, the Apology Session permits the child's family to set the guidelines for reestablishing a relationship with the offender, should they want this. This happens most often when the offender is a relative or "functional relative" (such as a minister or close friend of the family) who will probably maintain some contact with the family.

In the following example, the offender was a boy scout leader who molested several boys in his troop. He was also a youth leader at his church. The boys and their families were in therapy at the same clinic the offender was attending. After four months of therapy the offender, who had a very close relationship with the boys and their families prior to the sexual abuse, apologized to each boy.

Therapist: It's pretty clear to everyone why we are here. Thank you for coming. I really do believe that this will be helpful to all of you. Bill?

Bill (the offender): I want to tell you, Joey, and your whole family how sorry I am for all the pain and shame I have caused you. I know "sorry" does not take away anything that I have done. I do not want to take it away. It is something that I have to live with; unfortunately, I have made it something that you have to live with, too. I know your therapist has explained a lot of things to you about why men abuse little boys and girls. I will be more than happy to answer any questions that you or your parents have about my problems. But there are a few things I want to say first.

Joey, under no circumstances do I want you to blame yourself for what happened. There was absolutely nothing that you did that caused me to abuse you. I don't want you to think that you look like you are gay, or act any different than any kid. It had nothing to do with how you dressed, looked, talked, acted, or anything else. I knew you, I knew your family, but in some ways that had little to do with anything either. It just wasn't you. It is my fault, my responsibility, my blame, my problem.

We are going to be seeing each other at church from time to time. My therapist says it is too much to expect to be able to be friendly with your family, but I at least want you to not be afraid of me. Now I am getting the help I need, and you know what? You may have protected a lot of other boys from getting hurt. My therapist says that you really are a hero for being brave enough to tell your parents that I abused you. And now I understand why she says that, you *are* a hero and that is how I hope you look at yourself . . . a hero.

Appendix: Purdue Sex History Form

KAREN LEE FONTAINE

Date ________________

Personal Data
Name: ________________________________
Address: ________________________________
Telephone: home ________________ work ________________
Education: ________________ employment ________________
Job satisfaction: ________________________________

Current Family Structure

	Name	Age	Education	Occupation	Religion
Partner					
Child					
Child					
Child					
Child					

Others living in the home ________________________________

Medical History
Describe present state of health ________________________________
Last physical exam ________________________________
Medications: prescribed ________________ over the counter ________________
Significant past illnesses/surgery ________________________________
Miscarriages/abortions ________________ Birth control ________________
Alcohol/drug use ________________________________
Emotional/psychiatric illness (family/self) ________________________________

Family of Origin History
Siblngs:

Age	Name	General adjustment in life

____
____
____

Mother: age ______ Cultural background ________________
Educational background ____________ Occupation ____________
Relationship with you growing up ____________________
Relationship with you now ________________________
Attitude toward sex ____________________________

Father: age ______ Cultural background ________________
Educational background ____________ Occupation ____________
Relationship with you growing up ____________________
Relationship with you now ________________________
Attitude toward sex ____________________________

Parents' sex life ______________________________
Family sex education: By whom ________________________
Topics discussed: anatomy ____ menstruation ____ wet dreams ____ reproduction ____ masturbation ____ sexual activity ____ sexual values ____ contraception ____
Use of touch in family (hugging, holding, etc.) ________________
Verbal expression of affection ________________________
Discipline in family: By whom ____________ Type ____________

Significant Past Relationships
Significant partners/lovers ________________________
Type of relationship ____________________________
Length of relationship __________________________
Quality of sexual activity in relationship __________________
Cause for ending relationship ________________________
Impact on current life __________________________

Current Relationship
How did you meet your partner ______________________
What attracted you to her/him ________________________
____
What did she/he find attractive about you __________________
____
Length of relationship ____________ Marriage ____________
Sexual activity: in beginning of relationship/prior to marriage ____________
____
as relationship continued/after marriage __________________
____
What are the best aspects of this relationship ________________
What are the most painful aspects of this relationship ____________
____
How long have problems existed ______________________
Previous help ________________________________
What are your goals in treatment ______________________

Family Assessment

Communication patterns ____

Gender roles in family ____

Discipline of children: By whom ____ Type ____

Agreements/disagreements of discipline ____

Sex education of children: By whom ____ Type ____

Quality/quantity of time spent with children: Self ____
partner ____ Satisfaction ____

How do you manage privacy away from children ____
satisfaction with this ____

Social/sport activities ____

How are disagreements handled ____

Use of touch in family ____

Verbal expression of affection ____

Demands from other relatives ____

Significant losses/deaths ____

Emotional Assessment

On a continuum, describe yourself:
sad(1)/happy(10) ____ insecure(1)/secure(10) ____
out of control of self(1)/ in control of self(10) ____

How do others value you ____
____

What qualities do you like about yourself ____

What would you like to change about yourself ____

Anxiety producing situations ____

Appetite ____ Weight loss/gain ____ Sleeping difficulties ____

What qualities do you like in your partner ____

What would you like to change in your partner ____

Love/commitment: Self ____ Partner ____

SEXUAL HISTORY

Describe the positive and negative aspects of your own sexual functioning ____
____

Describe the positive and negative aspects of partner's sexual functioning ____
____

Expression of affection: verbal ____ frequency ____
nonverbal ____ frequency ____

Frequency of sexual activity: past week ____ past month ____ past 6 months ____

How often would you like to have sexual activity ____

How often would your partner like to have sexual activity ____

Do you or your partner have any difficulties in the following areas: interest in sex ____
lubrication ____ erection ____ orgasm ____ pain ____ satisfaction ____

How have the two of you tried to manage the problem so far ____

What areas of sex are most difficult to talk about with your partner ____
____

How is self-stimulation for you ______ For your partner ______
Are you able to fantasize by yourself ______ When with partner ______
Who initiates sexual activity ______ How is sexual activity initiated ______
______
Who controls the frequency of sexual activity ______
What time(s) of day do you engage in sexual activity ______
Locations of sexual activity ______
Who decides on type of sexual activities ______ How is this decided
______
Length of foreplay ______ Who decides on length ______
Length of intercourse ______ Satifactory? ______
Variety of positions ______ Who decides on variety ______
Verbal expressions of affection: prior to activity ______
during sexual activity ______ following sexual activity ______
How do you request specific activities during sex ______
How do you know what your partner wants ______
How do you refuse requests ______
How does your partner refuse requests ______
While in this relationship: have you had other partners ______
Is your partner aware of this ______
Has your partner had other partners ______
How did you arrive at this knowledge ______

Past sexual history
Memories of childhood sex play ______
Were you sexually abused as a child ______
______
Have you been a victim of physical abuse: as a child ______
as an adult ______
Have you been a victim of emotional abuse: as a child ______
as an adult ______
Have you ever been the victim of rape ______
In what way have you been a sexual victim as an adult ______

Discuss the following activities according to the categories.

Activity	*Do & like*	*Do & don't like*	*Don't do/ would like to try*	*Don't do/do not wish to try*
Kissing				
Nudity				
Total body touching apart from genitals				
Caressing breasts				
Touching partner's genitals				
Touching own genitals				
Partner touching your genitals				

Manual stimulation to orgasm: ______________________
done to you
done by you ______________________
Oral sex: ______________________
done to you
done by you ______________________
Vibrator ______________________
Variety in positions ______________________
Share fantasies ______________________

What sexual activities would you like to occur more often ______________________
____

Sources of anxiety about sex ______________________
Sources of guilt about sex ______________________
Sources of shame about sex ______________________

Potential sofa session topics:

Bibliography

Abel, G. G., Becker, J. V., Murphy, W. D., & Flannagan, B. (1981). Identifying dangerous child molesters. In R. B. Stuart (Ed.), *Violent behavior: Social learning approaches to prediction, management, and treatment*. New York: Brunner/Mazel.

Abel, G. G., Blanchard, E. B., & Becker, J. V. (1976). Psychological treatment for rapists. In M. Walker & S. Brodsky (Eds.), *Sexual assault*. Lexington, MA: Lexington Books.

Alexander, J., & Parsons, B. V. (1982). *Functional family therapy*. Monterey, CA: Brooks/Cole.

Alexander, P. C. (1985). A systems theory conceptualization of incest. *Family Process, 24*, 79–88.

Allgeier, A. R., & Allgeier, E. R. (1988). *Sexual interactions* (2nd Ed.). Lexington, MA: D. C. Heath.

American Psychiatric Association (1987). *Diagnostic and statistical manual of mental disorders, third edition, revised*. Washington, DC: American Psychiatric Association.

Anderson, C. M., & Stewart, S. (1983). *Mastering resistance: A practical guide to family therapy*. New York: Guilford Press.

Anderson, L. M., & Shafer, G. (1979). The character-disordered family: A community treatment model for family sexual abuse. *American Journal of Orthopsychiatry, 49*, 436–445.

Araji, S., & Finkelhor, D. (1985). Explanations of pedophilia: Review of empirical research. *Bulletin of the American Academy of Psychiatry and the Law, 13*, 17–37.

Armstrong, L. (1987). *Kiss daddy goodnight: Ten years later*. New York: Pocket Books.

Avery-Clark, C. A., & Laws, D. R. (1984). Differential erection response patterns of sexual child abusers to stimuli describing activities with children. *Behavior Therapy, 15*, 71–83.

Bagley, C. (1969). Incest behavior and the incest taboo. *Social Problems, 16*, 505–519.

Bandura, A. (1977). *Social learning theory*. Englewood Cliffs, NJ: Prentice-Hall.

Barbach, L. G. (1975). *For yourself: The fulfillment of female sexuality*. New York: Free Press.

Barnard, C. P., & Hirsch, C. (1985). Borderline personality and victims of incest. *Psychological Reports, 57*, 715–718.

Barrett, M. J., Sykes, C., & Byrnes, W. (1986). A systemic model for the treatment of intrafamily child sexual abuse. In T. S. Trepper & M. J. Barrett (Eds.), *Treating incest: A multiple systems perspective*. New York: Haworth Press.

Batten, D. A. (1983). Incest: A review of the literature. *Medical and Scientific Law, 23*, 245–253.

Becker, J. V., Skinner, L. J., Abel, G. G., Axelrod, R., & Cichon, J. (1984). Sexual problems of sexual assault survivors. *Women and Health, 9*, 5–20.

Bender, M. J., & Blau, A. (1937). The reaction of children to sexual relations with adults. *American Journal of Orthopsychiatry, 7*, 500–518.

Bepko, C., & Krestan, J. (1985). *The responsibility trap*. New York: Guilford Press.

Boatman, B. (1981). Treatment of child victims of incest. *American Journal of Family Therapy, 9*, 43–51.

Bograd, M. (1984). Family systems approaches to wife battering: A feminist critique. *American Journal of Orthopsychiatry, 54*, 558–568.

Breines, W., & Gordon, L. (1983). The new scholarship on family violence. *Signs, 8*, 490–531.

Brickman, J. (1984). Feminist, nonsexist, and traditional models of therapy: Implications for working with incest. *Women and Therapy, 3,* 49–67.

Browning, D. H., & Boatman, B. (1977). Incest: Children at risk. *American Journal of Psychiatry, 134,* 69–72.

Bullough, V. L. (1985). Child abuse: Myth or reality? *Council for Democratic and Secular Humanism, 5,* 51–52.

Burgess, A. W., Holmstrom, L. L., & Mocausland, M. P. (1977). Child sexual assault by a family member: Decisions following disclosure. *Victimology 2,* 236–250.

Busch, R. C., & Gundlach, J. (1977). Excess access and incest: A new look at the demographic explanation of the incest taboo. *American Anthropologist, 79,* 912–914.

Carnes, P. (1985). *Out of the shadows: Understanding sexual addictions.* Minneapolis, MN: CompCare Publications.

Cavallin, H. (1966). Incestuous fathers: A clinical report. *American Journal of Psychiatry, 122,* 1132.

Chasnoff, I. J., Burns, W. J., Schnoll, S. H., Burns, K., Chisum, G., & Kyle-Spore, L. (1986). Maternal-neonatal incest. *American Journal of Orthopsychiatry, 56,* 577–580.

Child Sexual Abuse Project (1983). Child sexual abuse: Description of nine program approaches to treatment. Social Planning and Research: United Way of the Lower Mainland.

Cohen, T. (1983). The incestuous family revisited. *Social Casework, 64,* 154–161.

Constantine, L. (1981). Child-adult sexual experiences: New studies report some positive outcomes. *Sexuality Today, 4*(50), 1–2.

Conte, J. R. (1982). Sexual abuse of children: Enduring questions for social work. In J. R. Conte & D. A. Shore (Eds.), *Social work and child sexual abuse.* New York: Haworth Press.

Conte, J. R. (1985). The effects of sexual abuse of children: Preliminary findings. Unpublished research report.

Conte, J. R. (1986). Sexual abuse and the family: A critical analysis. In T. S. Trepper & M. J. Barrett (Eds.), *Treating incest: A multiple systems perspective.* New York: Haworth Press.

De Jung, A. R., Hervada, A. R., & Emmett, G. A. (1983). Epidemiologic variations in childhood sexual abuse. *Child Abuse and Neglect, 7,* 155–162.

de Shazer, S. (1985). *Keys to solutions in brief therapy.* New York: W. W. Norton.

deChesnay, M. (1985). Father-daughter incest: An overview. *Behavioral Sciences and the Law, 3,* 391–402.

Denney, N. W., & Quadagno, D. (1988). *Human sexuality.* St. Louis: Mosby Books.

Derogatis, L. R., & Melisaratos, N. (1979). The DSFI: A multidimensional measure of sexual functioning. *Journal of Sex and Marital Therapy, 5,* 244–281.

deYoung, M. (1982). *The sexual victimization of children.* Jefferson, N.C.: McFarland & Company.

Dietz, C. A., & Craft, J. L. (1980). Family dynamics of incest: A new perspective. *Social Casework, 61,* 602–609.

Dixon, J., & Jenkins, J. O. (1981). Incestuous child sexual abuse: A review of treatment strategies. *Clinical Psychology Review, 1,* 211–222.

Dixon, K. N., Arnold, L. E., & Calestro, K. (1978). Father-son incest: Underreported psychiatric problem? *American Journal of Psychiatry, 135* (7), 835–838.

Dobash, R. E., & Dobash, R. (1979). *Violence against wives: The case against the patriarchy.* New York: Free Press.

Ellerstein, N. S., & Canavan, W. (1980). Sexual abuse of boys. *American Journal of Diseases of Children, 134,* 255–257.

Figley, C. R. (1983). Catastrophes: An overview to family reactions. In C. R. Figley & H. I. McCubbin (Eds.), *Stress and the family: Coping with catastrophe* (Vol. II). New York: Brunner/Mazel.

Finkelhor, D. (1978). Psychological, cultural, and structural factors in incest and family sexual abuse. *Journal of Marriage and Family Counseling, 4,* 45–50.

Finkelhor, D. (1979). What's wrong with sex between adults and children? *American Journal of Orthopsychiatry, 49,* 692–697.

Finkelhor, D. (1980a). Risk factors in the sexual victimization of children. *Child Abuse and Neglect, 4,* 265–273.

Finkelhor, D. (1980b). Sex among siblings: A survey report on its prevalence, variety, and effects. *Archives of Sexual Behavior, 9,* 171–194.

Finkelhor, D. (1984). *Child sexual abuse: New theory and research.* New York: The Free Press.

Fowler, C., Burns, S. R., & Roehl, J. E. (1983). Counseling the incest offender. *International Journal of Family Therapy, 5,* 92–97.

Fowler, C., Burns, S. R., & Roehl, J. E. (1983). The role of group therapy in incest counseling. *International Journal of Family Therapy, 5,* 127–135.

Fromuth, M. E. (1986). The relationship of childhood sexual abuse with later psychological and sexual adjustment in a sample of college women. *Child Abuse and Neglect, 10,* 5–15.

Frude, N. (1982). The sexual nature of sexual abuse: A review of the literature. *Child Sexual Abuse and Neglect, 6,* 211–223.

Gagnon, J. H. (1965). Female child victims of sex offenses. *Social Problems, 13,* 176–192.

Garbirano, J. (1977). The human ecology of child maltreatment. *Journal of Marriage and the Family, 39,* 721–735.

Gaudin, J., & Pollane, L. (1983). Social networks, stress, and child abuse. *Children and Youth Services Review, 5,* 91–102.

Gebhard, P. H., Gagnon, J., Pomeroy, W., & Christenson, C. (1965). *Sex offenders: An analysis of types.* New York: Harper & Row.

Gelles, R. C. (1980). Violence in the family: A review of research in the seventies. *Journal of Marriage and the Family, 42,* 873–885.

Giaretto, H. (1978). Humanistic treatment of father-daughter incest. *Journal of Humanistic Psychology, 18,* 17–21.

Giaretto, H. (1981). A comprehensive child sexual abuse treatment program. In P. B. Mrazek & C. H. Kempe (Eds.), *Sexually abused children and their families.* London: Pergamon Press.

Giaretto, H. (1982). *Integrated treatment of child sexual abuse: A treatment and training manual.* Palo Alto, CA: Human Sciences and Behavior Books.

Gordon, L., & O'Keefe, P. (1984). Incest as a form of family violence: Evidence from historical case records. *Journal of Marriage and the Family,* February, 27–34.

Gottschalk, L. A. (1983). Vulnerability to "stress." *American Journal of Psychotherapy, 37,* 5–23.

Groff, M. G., & Hubble, L. M. (1984). A comparison of father-daughter and stepfather-stepdaughter incest. *Criminal Justice and Behavior, 11,* 461–475.

Groth, A. N. (1982). The incest offender. In S. M. Sgroi (Ed.), *Handbook of clinical interventions in child sexual abuse.* Lexington, MA: Lexington Books.

Haley, J. (1980). *Leaving home.* New York: McGraw-Hill.

Hartman, C. R., & Burgess, A. W. (1986). Child sexual abuse: Generic roots of the victim experience. In T. S. Trepper & M. J. Barrett (Eds.), *Treating incest: A multiple systems perspective.* New York: Haworth Press.

Henderson, J. (1983). Is incest harmful? *Canadian Journal of Psychiatry, 28,* 34–40.

Herman, J., & Hirschman, L. (1977). Father-daughter incest. *Signs, 4,* 735–756.

Herman, J., & Hirschman, L. (1981). Families at risk for father-daughter incest. *American Journal of Psychiatry, 138,* 967–970.

Herman, J., Russell, D., & Trocki, K. (1986). Long-term effects of incestuous abuse in childhood. *American Journal of Psychiatry, 143,* 1293–1296.

Hoke, S., Sykes, C., & Winn, M. (in press). Systemic-strategic interventions targeting denial in the incestuous family. *Journal of Strategic and Systemic Therapy.*

Hoorwitz, A. H. (1983). Guidelines for treating father-daughter incest. *Journal of Contemporary Social Work,* November, 515–524.

Jackson, T. L., & Ferguson, W. P. (1983). Attribution of blame in incest. *American Journal of Community Psychology, 11,* 313–322.

Jacobson, N. S., Follette, W. C., & Revenstorf, D. (1984). Psychotherapy outcome research: Methods for reporting variability and evaluating clinical significance. *Behavior Therapy, 15,* 336–352.

James, B. J., & Nasjileti, M. (1983). *Treating sexually abused children and their families.* Palto Alto, CA: Consulting Psychologists Press.

James, J., Womack, W. M., & Stauss, F. Physician reporting of sexual abuse of children. *JAMA, 240,* 1145–1146.

Julian, V., & Mohr, C. (1979). Father-daughter incest: Profile of the offender. *Victimology, 4, 348–360.*

Justice, B., & Justice, R. (1979). *The broken taboo: Sex in the Family.* New York: Human Sciences Press.

Kaplan, H. S. (1974). *The new sex therapy.* New York: Brunner/Mazel.

Kaplan, H. S. (1979). *Disorders of sexual desire.* New York: Brunner/Mazel.

Kaplan, H. S. (1983). *The evaluation of sexual disorders: Psychological and medical aspects.* New York: Brunner/Mazel.

Kaufman, J., & Zigler, E. (1987). Do abused children become abusive parents? *American Journal of Orthopsychiatry, 57,* 186–191.

Kempe, R. S., & Kempe, C. H. (1984). *The common secret: Sexual abuse of children and adolescents.* New York: W. H. Freeman & Company.

Kennedy, M., & Cormier, B. M. (1969). Father-daughter incest: Treament of the family. *Laval Medical, 40,* 946–950.

Kercher, G., & McShane, M. (1984). Characterizing child sexual abuse on the basis of a multi-agency sample. *Victimology, 9,* 364–382.

LaBarbara, J. D. (1984). Seductive father-daughter relationships and sex roles in women. *Sex Roles, 11,* 941–951.

Laing, R. D. (1965). Mystification, confusion, and conflict. In I. Boszormenyi-Nagy & J. L. Framo (Eds.), *Intensive family therapy: Theoretical and practical aspects.* New York: Harper & Row.

Langevin, R., & Lang, R. A. (1985). Psychological treatment of pedophiles. *Behavioral Sciences and the Law, 3,* 403–419.

Larson, N. R., & Maddock, J. W. (1984). Incest management and treatment: Family systems vs. victim advocacy. Paper presented at the Annual Meeting of the American Association for Marriage and Family Therapy, San Francisco.

Larson, N. R., & Maddock, J. W. (1986). Structural and functional variables in incest family systems: Implications for assessment and treatment. In T. S. Trepper & M. J. Barrett (Eds.), *Treating incest: A multiple systems perspective.* New York: Haworth Press.

Leiblum, S. R., & Pervin, L. A. (Eds.). (1980). *Principles and practice of sex therapy.* New York: Guilford Press.

LoPiccolo, J. (1979). Direct treatment of sexual dysfunction. In J. LoPiccolo & L. LoPiccolo (Eds.), *The handbook of sex therapy.* New York: Guilford Press.

LoPiccolo, J. (1985). Guidelines for assessment and treatment of sexual deviance. Unpublished paper, available from the author, Department of Psychology, University of Missouri.

LoPiccolo, J., & LoPiccolo, L. (Eds.). (1979). *The handbook of sex therapy.* New York: Guilford Press.

MacFarlane, K., & Waterman, J. (Eds.) (1986). *Sexual abuse of young children.* New York: Guilford Press.

Machotka, P., Pittman, F. S., & Flomenhaft, K. (1967). Incest as a family affair. *Family Process, 6,* 98–116.

Magal, V., & Winnik, H. Z. (1968). Role of incest in family structure. *Israel Annals of Psychiatry and Related Disciplines, 6,* 173–189.

Maisch, H. (1973). *Incest.* London: Andre Deutsch.

Marcuse, M. (1923). Incest. *American Journal of Urology and Sexology, 16,* 273–281.

Marshall, W. L., & Barbaree, H. E. (1978). The reduction of deviant arousal: Satiation treatment for sexual aggressors. *Criminal Justice and Behavior, 5*, 294–303.
Marshall, W. L., Earls, C. M., Segal, Z., & Darke, J. (1983). A behavioral program for the assessment and treatment of sexual aggressors. In K. D. Craig & R. J. MacMahon (Eds.), *Advances in clinical behavior therapy*. New York: Brunner/Mazel.
Martin, M. J., & Walters, M. (1982). Familial correlates of selected types of child abuse and neglect. *Journal of Marriage and the Family, 42*, 267–276.
Masters, W. H., & Johnson, V. E. (1970). *Human sexual inadequacy*. Boston: Little, Brown.
Mayer, A. (1983). *Incest: A treatment manual for therapy with victims, spouses, and offenders*. Holmes Beach, FL: Learning Publications.
McCarthy, B. W. (1986). A cognitive-behavioral approach to understanding and treating sexual trauma. *Journal of Sex and Marital Therapy, 12*, 322–329.
McGoldrick, M., & Gerson, R. (1985). *Genograms in family assessment*. New York: W. W. Norton.
Meiselman, K. (1978). *Incest: A psychological study of causes and effects with treatment recommendations*. San Francisco: Jossey-Bass.
Minuchin, S. (1974). *Families and family therapy*. Cambridge, MA: Harvard University Press.
Minuchin, S. (1981). Constructing a therapeutic reality. In G. Berenson & H. White (Eds.), *Annual review of family therapy, Vol. 1*. New York: Human Sciences Press.
Minuchin, S., & Fishman, H. C. (1981). *Family therapy techniques*. Cambridge, MA: Harvard University Press.
Minuchin, S., Montalvo, B., Guerney, B. G. Jr., Rosman, B. L., & Schumer, F. (1967). *Families of the slums: An exploration of their structure and treatment*. New York: Basic Books.
Morgan, P. (1982). Alcohol and family violence: A review of the literature. *Alcohol and Health Monograph 1*. National Institute of Alcoholism and Alcohol Abuse, Washington, D.C.
Nichols, M. P. (1987). *The self in the system*. New York: Brunner/Mazel.
Olson, D. H., & Killorin, E. (1985). *Clinical rating scale for the circumplex model of marital and family systems*. St. Paul, MN: Family Social Science, University of Minnesota.
Olson, D. H., McCubbin, H. I., Barnes, H., Larsen, A., Muxen, M., & Wilson, M. (1982). *Family inventories*. St. Paul, MN: Family Social Science, University of Minnesota.
Olson, D. H., Portner, J., & Lavee, Y. (1985). *FACES-III*. St. Paul, MN: Family Social Science, University of Minnesota.
Olson, D. H., Russell, C. S., & Sprenkle, D. H. (1983). Circumplex model of marital and family systems: VI. Theoretical update. *Family Process, 22*, 69–83.
Owens, L. H. (1984). Personality traits of female psychotherapy patients with a history of incest: A research note. *Journal of Personality Assessment, 48*, 606–608.
Pagelow, M. D. (1984). *Family violence*. New York: Praeger.
Panton, J. H. (1979). MMPI profile configurations associated with incestuous and non-incestuous child molesting. *Psychological Reports, 45*, 335–338.
Parker, H., & Parker, S. (1986). Father-daughter sexual abuse: An emerging perspective. *American Journal of Orthopsychiatry, 56*, 531–549.
Perlmutter, L. H., Engel, L., & Sagar, C. J. (1982). The incest taboo: Loosened sexual boundaries in remarried families. *Journal of Sex and Marital Therapy, 8*, 83–96.
Piccolo Publications. (1987). *Family letters*. Distributed by Curtis Circulation Company, 21 Henderson Drive, West Caldwell, New Jersey, 07006.
Piercy, F. P., & Frankel, B. (1987). Training manual: Purdue Brief Family Therapy. West Lafayette: Center for Instructional Services, Purdue University.
Quinsey, V. L., Chaplin, T. C., & Carrigan, W. F. (1979). Sexual preference among incestuous and nonincestuous child molestors. *Behavior Therapy, 10*, 562–565.
Reimer, S. A. (1940). A research note on incest. *American Journal of Sociology, 45*, 566–575.
Renshaw, D. (1982). *Incest: Understanding and treatment*. Boston: Little, Brown.
Renvoize, J. (1982). *Incest: A family pattern*. London: Routledge and Kegan Paul.

Rist, K. (1979). Incest: Theoretical and clinical views. *American Journal of Orthopsychiatry, 49*, 630–691.
Rosenberg, J. B. (1983). Structural family therapy. In B. B. Wolman & G. Stricker (Eds.), *Handbook of family and marital therapy*. New York: Plenum.
Rosenfeld, A. A. (1979). Endogamic incest and the victim-perpetrator model. *Journal of Diseases of Children, 133*, 406–410.
Rosenthal, D. (1971). *Genetics of psychopathology*. New York: McGraw-Hill.
Russell, D. E. H. (1983). The incidence and prevalence of intrafamilial and extrafamilial sexual abuse of female children. *Child Abuse and Neglect, 7*, 133–146.
Russell, D. E. H. (1984). The prevalence and seriousness of incestuous abuse: Stepfathers vs. biological fathers. *Child Abuse and Neglect, 8*, 15–22.
Russell, D. E. H. (1986). *The secret trauma: Incest in the lives of girls and women*. New York: Basic Books.
Sagatun, I. J. (1982). Attributional effects of therapy with incestuous families. *Journal of Marital and Family Therapy, 8*, 99–104.
Schwartz, R. (1987). Our multiple selves. *Family Therapy Networker, 11*, 25–31, 80–83.
Scott, R. L., & Stone, D. A. (1986). MMPI measures of psychological disturbance in adolescent and adult victims of father-daughter incest. *Journal of Clinical Psychology, 42*, 251–259.
Sgroi, S. M. (1975). Molestation of children: The last frontier in child abuse. *Children Today*, May-June, 19–21, 44.
Sgroi, S. M. (1982). *Handbook of clinical intervention in child sexual abuse*. Lexington, MA: Lexington Books.
Solin, C. A. (1986). Displacement of affect in families following incest disclosure. *American Journal of Orthopsychiatry, 56*, 570–576.
Straus, M. A. (1973). A general systems theory approach to a theory of violence between family members. *Social Science Information, 12*, 105–125.
Straus, M. A. (1980). Stress and child abuse. In C. H. Kempe & R. E. Helfer (Eds.), *The battered child* (3rd Ed.). Chicago: University of Chicago Press.
Stuart, R. B. (1980). *Helping couples change*. New York: Guilford Press.
Summit, R., & Kryso, J. (1978). Sexual abuse of children: A clinical spectrum. *American Journal of Orthopsychiatry, 48*, 237–251.
Tierney, K. J., & Corwin, D. L. (1983). Exploring intrafamily child sexual abuse: A systems approach. In D. Finkelhor et al. (Eds.), *The dark side of families*. Beverly Hills, CA: Sage.
Toobert, S., Bartelme, K. F., & Jones, E. S. (1959). Some factors related to pedophilia. *International Journal of Psychiatry, 4*, 272–279.
Trepper, T. S. (1986). The apology session. *Journal of Psychotherapy and the Family, 2*, 93–101.
Trepper, T. S. (1989). Intrafamily child sexual abuse. In C. R. Figley (Ed.), *Stress and the family*. New York: Brunner/Mazel.
Trepper, T. S., & Barrett, M. J. (1986). Vulnerability to incest: A framework for assessment. In T. S. Trepper & M. J. Barrett (Eds.), *Treating incest: A multiple systems perspective*. New York: Haworth Press.
Trepper, T. S., & Sprenkle, D. H. (1988). The clinical use of the Circumplex model in the clinical assessment of intrafamily child sexual abuse. *Journal of Psychotherapy and the Family 4*, 93–111.
Trepper, T. S., & Traicoff, E. M. (1983). Treatment of intrafamily sexuality: Issues in therapy and research. *Journal of Sex Education and Therapy, 9*, 14–18.
Trepper, T. S., & Traicoff, E. M. (1985). Treatment of incest: Conceptual rationale and model for family therapy. *Journal of Sex Education and Therapy, 11*, 18–23.
Tsai, M., Summers, S. F., & Edgar, M. (1979). Childhood molestation: Variables related to differential impact of psychosexual functioning in adult women. *Journal of Abnormal Psychology, 88*, 407–417.
Tucker, N. (1985). A panic over child abuse. *New Society, 74*, 96–98.

Turbett, J. P. (1979). Intervention strategies and conceptions of child abuse. *Children and Youth Services Review, 1,* 205–213.

Tyler, A. H., & Brassard, M. R. (1984). Abuse in the investigation and treatment of intrafamilial child sexual abuse. *Child Abuse and Neglect, 8,* 47–53.

Vander Mey, B. J., & Neff, R. L. (1982). Adult-child incest: A review of research and treatment. *Adolescence, 17,* 717–735.

Vander Mey, B. J., & Neff, R. L. (1984). Adult-child incest: A sample of substantiated cases. *Family Relations, 33,* 549–557.

Verleur, D., Hughes, R. E., & de Rios, M. D. (1986). Enhancement of self-esteem among female adolescent incest victims: A controlled comparison. *Adolescence, 21,* 843–854.

Virkkunen, M. (1974). Incest offenses and alcoholism. *Medical and Scientific Law, 14,* 124.

Watzlawick, P., Weakland, J. H., & Fisch, R. (1974). *Change: Principles of problem formation and problem resolution.* New York: Norton.

Weinburg, S. K. (1955). *Incest behavior.* New York: Citadel.

Weiss, E. H. (1984). Incest accusation: Assessing credibility. *Journal of Psychiatry and Law,* Fall, 305–317.

Wheeler, D. (1989). Faulty fathering: Working ideas on the treatment of male incest perpetrators. *Journal of Feminist Family Therapy, 1*(2), 27–48.

Will, D. (1983). Approaching the incestuous and sexually abusive family. *Journal of Adolescence, 6,* 229–246.

Williams, G., & Money, J. (Eds.). (1980). *Abuse and neglect of children at home.* Baltimore: Johns Hopkins Press.

Wolfe, D. A. (1985). Child abusive parents: An empirical review and analysis. *Psychological Bulletin, 97,* 462–482.

Wooley, M. W. (1982). Incest victim symptomatology: Product of double bind situation. *Sexuality Today, 5*(17), 1–2.

Yates, A., Hill, J. W., & Huebner, P. B. (1983). Predicting the abusive parent's response to intervention. *Child Abuse and Neglect, 7,* 37–44.

Zimrin, H. (1984). Child abuse: A dynamic process of encounter between needs and personality traits within the family. *American Journal of Family Therapy, 12,* 37–47.

Zubin, J., & Spring, B. (1977). Vulnerability: A new view of schizophrenia. *Journal of Abnormal Psychology, 86,* 103–126.

Zuelzer, M. B., & Reposa, R. E. (1983). Mothers in incestuous families. *International Journal of Family Therapy, 5,* 98–109.

Name Index

Subject Index

For Product Safety Concerns and Information please contact our EU representative GPSR@taylorandfrancis.com
Taylor & Francis Verlag GmbH, Kaufingerstraße 24, 80331 München, Germany

www.ingramcontent.com/pod-product-compliance
Ingram Content Group UK Ltd.
Pitfield, Milton Keynes, MK11 3LW, UK
UKHW022014180926
475701UK00003B/364

* 9 7 8 1 1 3 8 0 0 4 6 8 9 *